THE NINE

THE NINE

The True Story of a Band of Women
Who Survived the Worst of Nazi Germany

GWEN STRAUSS

ST. MARTIN'S PRESS
NEW YORK

First published in the United States by St. Martin's Press,
an imprint of St. Martin's Publishing Group

www.stmartins.com

Designed by Devan Norman

Jacket photographs of the women, from left to right: Madelon Verstijnen
(Lon) courtesy of Patricia Elisabeth Frédérique Wensink and Wladimir
Schreiber; Hélène Podliasky Bénédite courtesy of Martine Fourcaut; Guille-
mette Daendels (Guigui) courtesy of Olivier Clémentin; Yvonne Le Guillou
(Mena) courtesy of Jean-Louis Leplâtre; Jacqueline Aubéry (Jacky) courtesy
of Michel Lévy; Joséphine Bordanava (Josée) courtesy of her family and les
Amis de la Fondation pour la Memoire de la Deportation de l'Allier; Nicole
Clarence (*Droits réservés*); Suzanne Maudet (Zaza) courtesy of the family;
Renée Lebon (Zinka) courtesy of France Lebon Châtenay Dubroeucq.

Library of Congress Cataloging-in-Publication Data

Names: Strauss, Gwen, author.
Title: The nine : the true story of a band of women who survived the
worst of Nazi Germany / Gwen Strauss.
Other titles: True story of a band of women who survived the worst of
Nazi Germany
Description: First edition. | New York : St. Martin's Press, 2021. |
Includes bibliographical references.
Identifiers: LCCN 2020053539 | ISBN 9781250239297 (hardcover) |
ISBN 9781250279248 (Canadian) | ISBN 9781250239303 (ebook)
Subjects: LCSH: Podliasky, Hélène, 1920–2012. | World War, 1939–1945—
Prisoners and prisons, German. | Women political prisoners—
France—Biography. | Women concentration camp inmates—France—
Biography. | Prisoner-of-war escapes—Germany. | Prisoners of war—
Germany—Biography. | Guerrillas—France—Biography. | Guerrillas—
Netherlands—Biography. | World War, 1939–1945—Underground
movements—France. | Ravensbrück (Concentration camp)
Classification: LCC D805.G3 S79644 2021 | DDC 940.53/174309252—dc23
LC record available at https://lccn.loc.gov/2020053539

Our books may be purchased in bulk for promotional, educational, or
business use. Please contact your local bookseller or the Macmillan
Corporate and Premium Sales Department at 1-800-221-7945, extension
5442, or by email at MacmillanSpecialMarkets@macmillan.com.

First Edition: 2021
First International Edition: 2021

10 9 8 7 6 5 4 3 2 1

For Eliza, Noah, and Sophie

Ce que nous avons partagé
Dans la peur, le froid, la faim, l'espoir.
L'épreuve, tant physique que psychique
Ne se répète pas, même pour nous.
Elle se limite au monde de jamais plus.
Ce que nous avons enduré ensemble
Est à nous, à cette vie, de ces instants,
Comme une transmutation de l'une, à l'autre,
dans une autre vie.

What we shared
In fear, cold, hunger, hope.
The ordeal, both physical and mental.
Can't be repeated, even for us.
It is limited to the world of never again.
What we have endured together
Is ours, that life, those moments,
Like a transmutation from one to the other,
in another life.

—NICOLE CLARENCE, ONE OF THE NINE

CONTENTS

THE NINE

Hélène Podliasky, my great-aunt, known by the eight others as "Christine." Twenty-four years old when arrested while working in the Résistance in northeastern France. A brilliant engineer, she spoke five languages. Considered the leader during the escape.

Suzanne Maudet (Zaza), Hélène's friend from high school. Twenty-two when arrested while working with the Auberge de Jeunesse in Paris. Recently married to René Maudet, she considered herself the scribe of the group. Wrote an optimistic book about the escape immediately after the war; it was finally published in 2004.

Nicole Clarence held a position of importance in the Résistance. Twenty-two when arrested in Paris a day after her birthday. She was one of the "57,000," the name given to the famous last transport of prisoners deported from Paris in August 1944, days before the city was liberated.

Madelon Verstijnen (Lon), one of two Dutch women in the group. Twenty-seven when arrested after she came to Paris to join her brother in the Dutch resistance network. She and Hélène spoke the best German in the group and were the advance scouts. Stubborn and brave, she wrote her account of the escape in 1991.

Guillemette Daendels (Guigui), Lon's friend from Holland. Twenty-three when arrested with Lon the day after their arrival together in Paris. She was serene, the group's diplomat. She became close friends with Mena.

Renée Lebon Châtenay (Zinka), the bravest of the group. Twenty-nine when arrested after she went to a prison in search of her husband. Gave birth in a French prison. Part of the Comète network, she helped downed and stranded Allied soldiers escape to Spain.

Joséphine Bordanava (Josée), Spanish and the youngest of the nine. Twenty when arrested in Marseille. She was raised in foster care in the south of France. Worked with the Marcel network, providing care parcels to hidden Jewish children and Résistance families. She was known for her beautiful singing voice.

Jacqueline Aubéry du Boulley (Jacky), a war widow; suffered from diphtheria during the escape. Twenty-nine when arrested in Paris. She worked in the Brutus network. She was tough, spoke her mind, and was prone to colorful curses. With Nicole, one of the "57,000" on the last transport out of Paris in August 1944.

Yvonne Le Guillou (Mena) worked with Dutch resistance networks in Paris. Twenty-two when arrested. She was flirtatious, charming, and whimsical, always falling in love. A working-class girl from Paris, but her family came from Brittany.

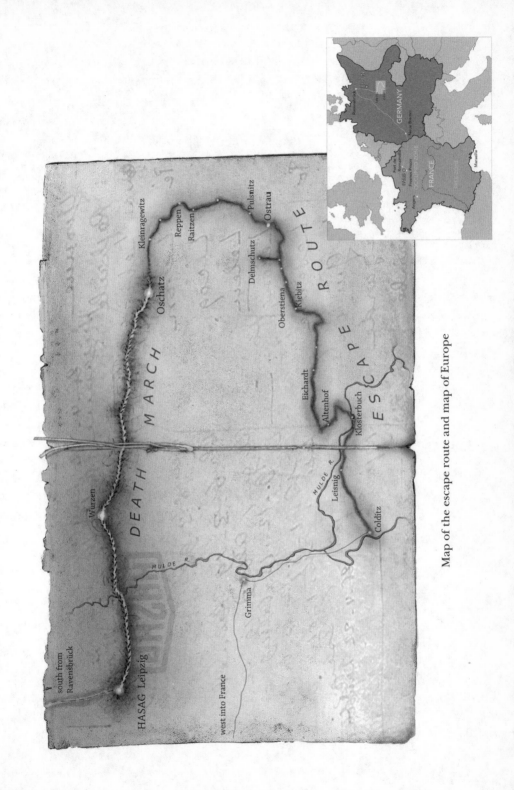

Map of the escape route and map of Europe

THE NINE

CHAPTER ONE

— HÉLÈNE —

Hélène Podliasky

A WOMAN BROKE FROM THE line and ran into the field of undulating bright yellow rape flowers. She ripped the blossoms from the stems with both hands, stuffing them into her mouth. Though exhausted and dazed, everyone noticed, and her action sent an electric panic through the rows of women. Stunned, Hélène waited for the sound of the gunshot that would surely follow. It could be machine-gun fire that would take out a whole section—any section, maybe theirs. The guards could do this: shoot indiscriminately into the rows to teach them a lesson. But nothing happened. All she heard was the continuous drumming of wooden clogs from thousands of marching feet.

When the woman ran back to the column, Hélène saw that her face was speckled with bits of yellow; she was smiling.

Then another woman ran into the field and gathered as many flowers as she could, using the rags of her tattered coat to hold them. When she got back into line, women jostled one another to reach her, grabbing at the flowers in a frenzy and eating them.

Why were they getting away with this?

Yesterday, a woman only a few rows ahead of Hélène had been shot in the head when she tried to pick up a half-rotted apple.

Hélène looked around. Their column was overextended. There were gaps between the rows and the sections. There were no guards in sight.

"Now!" she whispered urgently to Jacky, elbowing her.

"But we agreed to wait for dark," Jacky whispered back, her voice raspy and terrified.

Hélène tapped Zinka's shoulder. "Look!" she said. "No guards!"

"*Oui*, I see." Zinka nodded and grabbed Zaza's hand, saying, "It's our best chance."

They came to a curve in the road. A dirt road intersected their route, and parallel to that was a deep ditch. Hélène knew this was the moment. They had to go as two rows, all together, so they wouldn't be noticed. Zinka, Zaza, Lon, Mena, and Guigui, who were in the row in front of her, slid out, and then Hélène led Jacky, Nicole, and Josée. A fifth woman who had fallen into their row balked, saying she was too tired.

"Forget her, then!" Hélène hissed, and pulled her friends along. "Quick!"

They were nine women in all. Holding hands, they slipped sideways out of the column and jumped into the trench, one after the other. They lay flat on the ground in the deepest part of the ditch, where the earth was damp. Hélène felt her heart beating against her ribs. She was so thirsty she tried licking the mud. She couldn't bring herself to look up to see if they were about to be discovered, to see if she would die shot in a ditch as she licked the earth. Instead she looked over to Lon, who was staring up at the road.

"What do you see?" Hélène whispered. "Are we visible?"

"Just feet." Lon watched the endless rows of women trudging by, half of them barefoot, half of them in wooden clogs. All of the muddied, bare feet were red and bleeding.

Lon reassured her that they were hidden from view. In any case, the marchers had passed so many corpses along the way that this heap of women at the bottom of a ditch probably looked just like another pile of dead bodies.

With their arms draped around one another and their hearts pounding, they waited for the beat of the clogs dragging on the ground to fade. When the column was no longer in sight and they could no longer hear the rhythmic pounding of feet, Lon said, "It's clear."

"Now! We need to move." Hélène stood and led them along the ditch in the opposite direction. But they were soon out of breath and overcome with sheer euphoria. They climbed out of the ditch and collapsed in the field. They lay there looking up at the sky, clasping hands, and laughing hysterically.

They had done it! They had escaped!

But now they were in the middle of Saxony, facing frightened and hostile German villagers, angry fleeing officers of Germany's Schutzstaffel (SS), the Russian army, and Allied bombers overhead. The Americans were somewhere nearby, they hoped. They had to find the Americans or die trying.

My aunt, Tante Hélène, was a beautiful young woman. She had a high forehead and a wide smile. She had raven-black hair and dark eyes with thick, sensuous eyebrows. She appeared small and delicate, but you sensed an underlying strength. Even in old age, when I knew her, she had a regal demeanor; she was always elegantly dressed and impeccably manicured, and she radiated intelligence. In the photos of her in her twenties, she looked poised and clever. She was a natural leader.

In May 1943, she joined the Résistance, working for the Bureau des opérations aériennes (BOA) for the M region. The BOA had been created that April to act as a liaison between the Forces françaises de l'intérieur (FFI, the name used by Charles de Gaulle for the Résistance) and England. The BOA's role was to ensure the transport of agents and messages and to receive parachute drops of arms. The M region, which was the largest in the FFI, covered Normandy, Brittany, and Anjou. Right before the Normandy landing, managing this territory was crucial and dangerous. The Gestapo was successfully capturing or killing an alarming number of leaders and network members. In the frenetic months surrounding D-Day, Hélène's region was a hotbed of activity both for the Résistance and for the Gestapo's increasingly vicious and desperate attempts to break the underground networks.

Hélène was twenty-three years old when she joined. On a break from her physics and mathematics studies at the Sorbonne, she had taken a significant job as a chemist in a lamp company. But as her Résistance activities grew in importance, she left that job to work full-time in the struggle against the fascists. She lied to her parents about what she was doing. Her nom de guerre was "Christine," and in the Nazi records she is recorded with that name.[1] She would always be known by the group of women who escaped together as Christine.

Her commander, code-named "Kim," was Paul Schmidt. At the start of the war, Schmidt was the leader of an elite troop of French mountain infantry. In 1940, he fought in Norway; his battalion was evacuated to England, where he was treated for severe frostbite. After his recovery he joined the Forces françaises de l'intérieur and returned to France clandestinely. In March 1943, he was put in charge of the BOA and set up a series of "reception committees" in the northern region. Hélène was one of the fourteen agents he recruited. She was responsible for finding terrain suitable for parachute drops. For each drop she had to gather a team of Résistance workers to be ready at the landing sites. Eventually her work evolved to include establishing liaisons between the different Résistance networks in the M region. To communicate information to London about the reality on the ground she coded and decoded messages that were broadcast over the radio.

She waited with anticipation for the full moon, when the planes could find the drop site at night. Three days before, she'd listened to the radio. The secret codes were broadcast on the BBC, during a special fifteen-minute portion called "Les Français Parlent aux Français" (the French speak to the French). Hélène often wondered what ordinary listeners thought when they heard phrases like "les souliers de cuir d'Irène sont trop grands" (Irene's leather slippers are too big).

She and her team were waiting in the shadow of the woods that skirted the small field of her favorite reception site in Semblançay, outside Tours. They heard the engine of the plane approaching. She turned her flashlight on and off in Morse code, beaming the agreed-upon letter as a signal. To her great relief, after a moment the little airplane blinked on its lights.

"Now," she whispered to her team, and one by one, like dominoes, they lit their flashlights, outlining the perimeter of the reception area. The little plane circled a few times. Hélène's heart raced as she thought of people in the village hearing the loud engine or seeing the white silk of the parachutes glowing in the moonlight as they descended to earth. As soon as the containers hit the ground her team ran into the field to gather them. They were filled with small arms, explosives, a new transmitter, and new code sheets. And for the morale of her group, the British had included chocolates and cigarettes.

As they filled their pockets with cigarettes and their backpacks with small arms, her team heard the plane returning to circle again, and they paused. Something else dropped into the night sky. Hélène saw the dark outline of a man floating down beneath a glowing white silk parachute. She quickly distributed the contents of the remaining packages to her team, ordering them to disperse in different directions. It was better if they left before the parachutist landed; the less anyone knew, the better. Only two men remained behind to get rid of the empty containers and to bury the parachutes. Not for the first time, she wished she could keep the lovely silk to make a dress. But there were orders.

The mysterious man unhooked himself from the harness and lit a cigarette. He stood off to the side and watched Hélène directing the two remaining men. She did not approach him either. Before they spoke, she wanted to gather her thoughts. Besides, this part of the operation had to go fast. They had to be dispersed from the site within fifteen minutes, so that if anyone had seen the parachutes or heard the plane, they would find no one around when they got here.

Finally Hélène approached the new arrival. He was tall and thin. When he pulled on his cigarette, the ember glowed, and she could see his sharp, angular face. He seemed amused. "I wasn't told there would be living cargo," she said, barely hiding her anger.

"Fantassin," he replied, putting out his hand for her to shake.

Reluctantly she took it. "And you must be Christine? I was told about you."

"Why wasn't I told about you? I don't have anything prepared." When she was scared, Hélène tended to sound angry. *Fantassin* meant "foot soldier" in French, and the code name had been whispered about. He was someone important. She was glad it was dark so he couldn't see her blush.

"We didn't want to risk it being known that I'm back in France. The *boches* have breached our networks. We have to be very careful."

He handed Hélène a cigarette and lit it for her. This gave her some time to think.

"But I don't know where to take you," she said, dropping her tough demeanor.

"We trust you. I will stay in your apartment until I can make contact." He didn't ask her. He ordered her. And he seemed amused that it made her uncomfortable. If my mother knew . . . , she thought. Her mother had gone to a school where boys and girls were strictly separated, and the nuns who taught them would tell the girls to avert their gaze as they passed the boys' building, to avoid the temptation of sin.

Her apartment was a long bike ride away in another town far from the landing site. Fantassin had a black leather briefcase that had been tied to his wrist during the jump so that it wouldn't be lost. Now he handed it to her and said that they would ride her bicycle together. She could sit on the back. With one hand she clutched the briefcase and with the other she held on to this strange man as he pedaled them through the night. She tried not to grip him too tightly, but she felt the heat from his back. They did not speak except for when she told him to turn here or there. A few times she made him pull the bike over and hide behind a wall or bush while she checked to see if they were being followed. It was a routine she had worked out over time, but this night she was especially careful.

The long ride in the damp early morning helped calm her nerves. They arrived just before sunrise. She was exhausted. Her place was small, one main room with a kitchenette and a tiny bedroom. She had decided she would give him the bed and sleep in the living room. But once inside the small apartment she felt suddenly shy. She told herself that this was her job. She stiffened her back and stood up straight.

Fantassin placed the briefcase on the kitchen table and opened it. It was full of money, more money than she had ever seen in her life. He reached in and handed her some bills.

"No," she said, feeling her face flush red, "I don't do this for money. I do it for France, for my honor." She might have appeared indignant, but she was scared. She did not want him to think she was that sort of woman.

"It's not for you, it's for your team. For the men who were there last night."

"They do it for France too." She spoke almost without thinking, something she rarely did.

"For the families then, the ones who have already sacrificed," he said.

She nodded, because he was right. Her pride and discomfort had gotten in the way of her thinking. Many people were in hiding and did not have access to ration cards; they were hungry. This money would help them. She needed to pull herself together. She took a deep breath.

"You must be tired." His voice softened. "How old are you?"

She told him she had just turned twenty-four a few weeks earlier.

He sat down in the chair by the sofa and lit a cigarette. There was a long silence.

"You can take the bedroom," she said after a moment.

"No, please, I will be fine here." He indicated the couch.

When Hélène protested that he was her superior officer, he said, "Yes, we are soldiers, but please, let me also be a gentleman."

Fantassin's real name was Valentin Abeille. He was the head of the entire M region.[2] The Germans had put a large bounty on his head. At this stage in the war, the Gestapo was relentless. It had been able to plant a few double agents in Résistance cells. These groups consisted mostly of idealistic young people who received little or no training and were unable to keep a tight grip on security. Some of the younger men would boast about what they were doing to get *les boches*, told too many people, allowed themselves to be followed, or didn't observe the proper safety rules. The average time a person lasted in the Résistance before being caught was three to six months.

In the end Fantassin was most likely betrayed by his secretary for the bounty. He was arrested by the Gestapo, and on the way to the infamous Gestapo torture site on the rue des Saussaies, in Paris, he jumped from the car. He was shot multiple times not far from the Arc de Triomphe and died soon after in the hospital. He had told Hélène during the brief few days they spent together that he could not allow himself to be taken alive. He showed her the cyanide tablets he carried. The less she knew, the better, he said.

While she worked in the Résistance, Hélène had more liberty than a young woman in France at that time would normally have. At the start of the war her parents and sisters had moved to Grenoble, where her father was now running a factory. Her parents thought she had stayed behind to pursue her studies. They would only find out the truth about her activities later, when someone from the network contacted them.

Hélène remembered those months as exhilarating. She was a young, independent woman entrusted with an important role and in charge of older men. Lives depended on her. There were moments of high adrenaline like nothing she had ever experienced before. One such shock came when she arrived at the assigned drop site one early evening and was greeted by a group of French gendarmes. Sure they had been sent to arrest her, she felt ice-cold panic wash down her spine. She had already turned to cycle away when one called out the password. She froze, trying to make the calculations. If they knew the code, then they must know everything. She felt a wave of nausea mixed with a resigned feeling of relief. The game was up. There was no point in running away. But she mechanically answered their code with her own, and then the men walked up to her, asking for their orders.

It took her a moment to realize they weren't there to arrest her. This was her reception team. What she had assumed was the end of the line for her was only another strange twist. An entire barracks of uniformed gendarmes had joined the Résistance together. This incident bolstered Hélène and gave her a sense of invincibility.

On February 4, 1944, she was supposed to deliver a message to

General Marcel Allard, who commanded a part of the M region. When she arrived at the small hotel in Brittany where they were meeting, she saw him running out one door just as a group of five German soldiers entered by another. She was trapped in the middle. They arrested her simply because she was there and they were rounding up everyone in the hotel lobby. The message she was carrying was sewn into the lining of her purse, and miraculously the Gestapo did not find it. She was able to maintain that she did not know this Allard fellow they were after. They had nothing on her and her papers were in order, so she played the docile, empty-headed girl—a role she had played before.

They held her in the prison in Vannes for a few days, but one guard reassured her that it was only a matter of paperwork. Not to worry—she would soon be allowed to go home to her mother and father. But then instead of releasing her, they transferred her to a prison in Rennes, where she was held for two weeks. Still there was no formal interrogation. They asked nothing besides why she had happened to be at that hotel at that particular moment.

Then one day two guards came into the cell where she was being held with twenty other women and called her name. The men handcuffed her and led her to a waiting black car. The men bristled with a violent anger, and refused to answer her questions or to speak to her. They transported her to the prison in Angers, in the Loire Valley, where she spent two months.

Fifty-eight years later, during our interview in her apartment, where Hélène had allowed me to record her story, she said, "Angers stays in my memory as the symbol of suffering itself."

That was the place she was interrogated and tortured, sometimes to the point of being returned to her cell on a stretcher. The worst was *le supplice de la baignoire*, or waterboarding. They would take her into an ordinary bathroom where the tub had been filled with cold water. Her arms were handcuffed behind her. She was forced to kneel on the tile floor next to the tub. Then two men, one on each shoulder, would push her head into the water. They would hold her head submerged as she struggled for air. She felt their hands on her, one gripping her neck and the other pushing the back of her head. She tried to stay calm, but as her lungs begged for air, panic rose in her.

She felt a terrible pain in her chest, her neck and her head throbbed, and the longing for air grew. She struggled, but it was hopeless. Water flooded her mouth and choked her.

When they felt the fight leave her, they would pull her back out of the water by her hair and recommence the interrogation. She would retch over and over. It was in these moments of extreme pain that she felt most acutely the presence of her body, of her corporal existence. It was almost as if her body was her enemy, making her suffer.

They had discovered who she was, what network she worked for, and some of the people she worked with. They knew Fantassin had stayed with her. Each day they interrogated her, asking for the names of other agents, the code words, the message centers, drop-off points, dates, times. She tried not to reveal any useful information. For several nights, wet and cold with her hands bound behind her back and tied to a radiator, she tried to work out plausible stories, pure inventions that would fit with what they already knew but would not betray anyone.

She was hung by her arms. She was taken to the same tiled bathroom and almost drowned over and over again. Her fingernails were pulled out with pliers. Other terrible things were done to her. In our interview, Hélène stopped there, and I did not push for more details. There was a pause as she lit another cigarette, and I noticed her carefully polished manicure.

When she started to talk again, she told me about a Jesuit priest. "Père Alcantara," she said, remembering his name. "He had permission to visit certain prisons. One day he handed me a small package. I saw the label with my name written on it. It was my mother's handwriting. That's when I cried."

When she saw the package, her knees buckled and she began to sob. It was the first time she had cried since being arrested. In order to keep her courage, in order to not break under torture, she had avoided thinking about anyone she loved, about her family. The package meant that they now knew what she had been doing behind their backs. She felt a stab of guilt for causing them pain, and a terrible longing to hear her mother's voice.

The German guard in charge of her cell was an Alsatian about the same age as Hélène. She spoke perfect German, so they talked occasionally. He was disturbed by what he saw the Gestapo doing to her. He hated them, and his eyes filled with tears when she was returned bloodied and battered on a stretcher. He whispered encouragements through her cell window, which she only half heard in her semiconscious state. He told her that she should just tell them what they wanted to know and then she would be left alone. He told her that he wished she wasn't so brave. One time he brought her a kilo of butter. She was grateful, but it was a strange thing to have to hide in her cell. She had no idea what to do with the butter, where to put it. She had nothing to eat it with. Later he brought her sugar, a much more practical gift.

He took a short letter she had written to her family and mailed it to her godfather. Hélène knew that way it wouldn't be traced to her. The young Alsatian soldier must have kept the address because later, after the war, he looked for her by contacting her godfather. He wanted to know if she had survived and how she was. But by then, so many worse things had happened to her, and she was no longer the relatively innocent young girl whom he had guarded in the prison cell in Angers. She wrote back to him to say that yes, she had survived, but that was all. She asked him not to contact her again.

In the prison in Angers she wasn't permitted to have anything in her cell, and all alone, with no books, no paper, no magazines, she felt herself slipping over the edge. She begged the guard for a pencil. On the white walls of her cell, she worked on mathematical problems. When I asked what sort of problems, Hélène scribbled down an equation on a scrap of paper.

$$\int_{-\infty}^{\infty} dx\, e^{-ax^2} = \sqrt{\frac{\pi}{a}}$$

I showed my sister Annie, a mathematician, this equation, and asked what Hélène had been doing. Annie said, "She was computing the Gaussian integral," which involves e and pi. Annie explained that e and pi are called "transcendental numbers." Transcendental numbers, like imaginary numbers, exist outside of ordinary math. In the history of math, the concept of imaginary numbers was the cause of great anxiety and drama through the ages as different mathematicians gradually discovered their necessity. In the early nineteenth century, a hotheaded young French mathematician named Évariste Galois was expelled from the École Normale for political activity. Though he was recognized as having promise, his mathematical ideas were too radical to be accepted by the establishment. He wrote feverish letters the night before he died in a duel, making some notes in the margins of his proofs that involved transcendental and imaginary numbers. Galois recognized there were some problems that cannot be solved with only the concrete numbers of our daily existence. His final words to his brother were, "Don't cry, Alfred! I need all my strength to die at twenty."

In her cell, at twenty-four, Hélène was gathering her strength to die. She worked on a number of classic mathematical problems, showing that you cannot trisect an angle or square a circle using just a straightedge and compass. There exist numbers that cannot be constructed.

Later, when Hélène landed in the Ravensbrück concentration camp, she would recognize her friend Zaza from the lycée they had attended together. They would cling to each other in the shower, fearing that the rumors were true and that the tiny holes in the ceiling would soon release a gas that would kill them. But instead they were drenched in freezing water. They were assigned numbers: Hélène became prisoner number 43209, Zaza number 43203. The prisoners endured endless roll calls, the *Appells*, when they were counted again and again. People became numbers and then nothing.

Not only are real numbers infinite, my sister says, but there must be an infinite amount of transcendental numbers as well. But we know of only a few. Annie thinks that this could be because of our human obsession with our tools: the straightedge and the compass have limited our imagination. Our thinking limits our understanding.

As I write this story, I wonder whether language also limits our thinking. The families I interviewed, the descendants of the nine women who escaped that day in Germany, would say the same thing: that their mothers or grandmothers or aunts felt unable to fully describe what they had experienced. There was a limit to what they could say; their stories, if told at all, were only half told.

At the prison in Angers in June 1944, they could hear the sound of bombardment in the distance. The Allies were storming the beaches in Normandy. Hélène's young Alsatian guard told her, "Tomorrow you will be free, and I will be the prisoner."

She allowed herself to hope. But then she sat all day in her cell, with her arms hugging her calves and her chin on her knees, looking at the complex spread of equations, her attempt at transcendence. Outside in the prison courtyard, at regular intervals, jarring rounds of gunfire tore away at her focus as the German guards systematically executed all the male prisoners. Prepare for the worst, she told herself.

Late that night, perhaps exhausted by the killing, the same German guards loaded the few remaining women onto trains headed for Romainville, the transit camp outside Paris.

Some of the women had prepared tiny scraps of stolen paper, called *papillons* (butterflies), with short notes to their families and marked with their addresses. As they were driven through Paris, they tossed their bits of paper out of the cracks in the sides of the wagons. These last notes were sometimes picked up by brave people and sent on to the women's families. Often these were the last traces of their daughters, sisters, and mothers.

In the camp at Romainville, Hélène remembers watching a woman dying as she lay in the dirt. Supposedly she had syphilis and had infected some German soldiers, and so she was left to die all alone in front of them.

Hélène had no recollection of what she did during those days sitting on the ground surrounded by barbed wire—nothing but a vague memory of endless waiting. She had retreated into herself. She would allow no feeling to weaken her resolve to survive. A kind of numb blankness took over as she tried to adjust to her new reality. It was hot and dusty. They were held in large pens with no shade or shelter. People sat in silent misery, staring at nothing. There was the hum of flies and low moaning, but nothing that resembled language. There were the smells of rotting flesh, death, human excrement, filth, sweat, and fear.

After several days—Hélène did not know how many—she was

loaded onto a crowded train car meant to transport livestock. She began the journey east into Germany, toward Ravensbrück, ninety kilometers north of Berlin.

In my family, we knew that Tante Hélène had been highly decorated. She was an Officier de la Légion d'honneur, which is considered one of the most prestigious French honors, especially since the *officier* grade was rarely given to a woman in her generation. She received the Croix de Guerre, given for acts of special bravery during the war; and she had both the Médaille de la Résistance française and the Médaille de la France libre for her work in the Résistance. The family was proud of her, but we rarely talked about her past. As happened in many families after the war, people wanted to leave those dark days behind. It was thought best for everyone to just forget about the past. Not to talk about it. Not to dwell in darkness. There was survivor's guilt as well, along with the memory lapses caused by trauma, by the unspeakable ways some people had behaved. Hélène wanted to spare her family the grim details. And if you hadn't experienced it, you couldn't really imagine it. It took time; it took the generation who had not been through the war to start asking questions. In 2002, during a lunch with my grandmother, Hélène told me how she had escaped the Nazis with eight other women. Astounded, I asked her if I could record an interview with her to get the full story.

My aunt Eva and I traveled to Hélène's apartment in a very nice neighborhood near Neuilly on the edge of Paris. The small rooms were filled with photographs and books. Hélène was beautifully coiffed and dressed in a Chanel skirt and jacket. We were served tea. But after I thanked her for allowing us to record her, the first thing Hélène said to me was: "What's the point?"

"It's important," I offered, suddenly embarrassed by my youth, my easygoing American enthusiasm, and my relatively comfortable life.

"This story can only tell about the fate of a few human beings among many others who strive to live with dignity, despite the possible degradation, despite the efforts of the Nazis working to destroy them," she said. It was as if she had practiced this phrase, prepared it in advance.

I asked her why she had joined the Résistance. "Because of the horror of Nazism and all totalitarian regimes," she replied.

I asked her if she had been scared, and she said no. She had been happy, even knowing the risks, because she was helping fight for her country.

She wondered out loud if it was meaningless to dig up all these old memories. I wondered to myself if I was being rude to probe and push her to remember things she may have wanted to forget. She said she preferred not to discuss the past, even though, as she admitted, she thought about the war all the time, every single day. You could say she was haunted by it and that her life afterward had been profoundly informed by what had happened to her then.

As the hours passed, she warmed up to the telling. I vaguely assumed that we would have many more conversations and that over time she would fill in the details. I left thinking that she had been happy to talk, and maybe felt only a bit of regret at having opened up to me. But whether because of her reticence or my hesitancy, we never did speak of the past again.

Later, when I began to write her story and delve into our family history, I felt I was breaking a taboo. The voices in my head told me it was not my business; I should be ashamed of myself for exploiting her story. Let the past rest in peace. But the past is restless. History, like individual memory, is not fixed. It is constantly revived.

Two years after my interview with Hélène, I stumbled upon Suzanne Maudet's book *Neuf filles jeunes qui ne voulaient pas mourir* (Nine young girls who didn't want to die). Zaza was Hélène's friend. She recorded her memories immediately, in the months after their escape, but her manuscript was not published until 2004, ten years after her death.[3] The details in Zaza's book led me to find another account, written by Nicole Clarence for *Elle* magazine in 1964, on the twentieth anniversary of her deportation. From this article, I discovered a few radio interviews Nicole had given.[4] And right before Hélène passed away in 2012, two Dutch filmmakers, Ange Wieberdink and Jetske Spanjer, made a documentary called *Ontsnapt* (Escaped), in which Hélène was reunited with Lon Verstijnen, another member of their group.[5] The film was largely based on Lon's book, *Mijn Oorlogskroniek* (My war chronicle). Some years later, Guigui's son Marc Spijker sent me Lon's own English translation of her book, which she had shared with his mother.

Collectively, Hélène, Zaza, Nicole, and Lon tell a story of friendship, incredible bravery, and survival. Their accounts differ in some details but converge at key points. There are large missing pieces; I will never know if they are willful omissions or lapses in memory. At the start, I knew eight of the nine women only by their nicknames: besides Christine (my great-aunt Hélène), they were Zaza, Lon, Guigui, Zinka, Josée, Mena, Nicole, and Jacky. They were all political prisoners. I would later learn that Hélène's father was Jewish and that Nicole came from a Jewish family, though neither woman talked about being Jewish nor, probably, identified as such. And if they did, they kept it hidden from the Germans. As bad as it was to be a prisoner in the concentration camps, it was much worse to be a Jewish prisoner.

Women in rows of five

As a young man, Hélène's father was a Russian professor of math in Lithuania before he went to Heidelberg to continue his studies. He then went to France to the Sorbonne. Hélène's mother was one of only two women enrolled in the Sorbonne at the time. Martine was a farm girl from the Lot region; her father was a great winemaker. A point of pride for the family was that the priest used their wine for the Sunday Mass. Martine had been raised in a devout Catholic family and educated by nuns. She could never be naked, not even to bathe. But

she must have been unusually brilliant, because after she passed her high school exams, the nuns suggested that she continue her studies—something virtually unheard of at the time, when it was thought too much education would ruin a proper girl's chances for marriage. Astoundingly, her parents agreed to allow her to go to Paris to study chemistry. Hélène's father, a talented musician who had given up a career in the symphony, was working in atomic physics. They met at the university, and six months after their quick marriage, Hélène was born.

The brilliant Martine was forced to give up her studies. Maybe this frustrated intelligence made for a complicated mother-daughter relationship. In any case, Hélène identified with her father. Two more daughters were born, seven and eight years later. There was a long-lasting resentment between Hélène and her much younger sisters. She was forced to babysit, and her father clearly adored her above the others. When the family learned that Hélène had been deported to Germany, her father was distraught. One night at dinner one of the younger daughters was asking him a question, and when he didn't respond, Martine said to him, "Won't you answer your daughter?"

He replied, "I have only one daughter and she's in Germany."[6]

Hélène was the intellectual among the sisters. She had an impressive list of diplomas in engineering and mathematics. She had a gift for languages and spoke several fluently, including Polish, German, English, and Russian. It was her facility with languages, her clear thinking in moments of danger, and her sense of cool diplomacy that made her a natural leader in Ravensbrück. Nicole later remembered her as the "pillar" of their group.

———

For five days Hélène traveled in an overcrowded cattle car, with little or no water, food, light, air, or a place to relieve herself. She was in a transport with 200 mostly French female political prisoners—les résistantes. They survived the inhuman transport by organizing themselves, taking turns standing and lying down. The sickest were moved closest to the small window, where there was fresh air. They kept up their morale by singing "La Marseillaise" and other songs.

Hélène had no idea where they were when the train made its final stop at the station of Fürstenberg, the town closest to the Ravensbrück

concentration camp. The town and the camp were on opposite sides of a lake. The area, close to the Baltic, is subject to freezing winds and was known locally as "Little Siberia."

They arrived at night; the platform was violently lit with spotlights and guarded by SS and by female guards known as *Aufseherinnen*, their leashed German shepherds barking and lunging furiously. The prisoners had to jump from the wagon to the platform, and some of the older women fell badly, twisting an ankle or a knee. The guards pushed them. In the chaos, they stumbled over one another. The *Aufseherinnen* beat them with whips and shouted in German. If someone still had luggage, it was taken and thrown into the back of a truck.

Those who had died along the way had to be lifted into another truck, while the German guards shouted, "Schnell! Raus!"

Two columns were formed: those women who were still strong enough to march and those who could barely stand. The feeble were invited to ride in the truck with the baggage. Some daughters encouraged their tired and weary mothers to get on. They had no way of knowing that they were participating in the first selection for the crematorium and that they would never see their mothers again.

"Zu fünft!" the guards screamed, kicking them as they struggled to understand what was being demanded of them.

"They want us in rows of five," Hélène whispered urgently.

"Rows of five," she heard repeated in French, echoing through the crowd.

They marched from the train station to the camp, roughly four kilometers away. On June 14, 1944, when Hélène arrived, the camp was covered in mud and reeked of rotting flesh, human excrement, and dense, ashy smoke from the crematorium.

———✦———

Hélène had "a face you never forget, and in all that crowd I recognized her at once," Zaza wrote, recalling their arrival and how she had spotted her friend from the lycée in the throng of women.[7] In many ways Hélène's opposite, Zaza was the poet who noticed the color of the sky, while the rest were thinking only of their hunger. Where Hélène could be cool and calculating, Zaza was warm and open. Twenty-two year old when arrested, she was an optimist, with a sense of humor and

immense love of life. Always patient, she was everyone's friend, but she was closest to Hélène, the one person Hélène allowed past her reserve. From the moment of their arrival in Ravensbrück, they stuck together. While Hélène was relentlessly plotting escape, Zaza was more passive. Trusting in nature, she waited to see what would happen.

Ravensbrück, open from 1939 to 1945, was the only German concentration camp built exclusively for women. Most female prisoners, like the nine, passed through Ravensbrück on their way to one of hundreds of slave labor camps or extermination camps. But many were murdered there. A majority of the records at Ravensbrück were burned by the Nazis in the final weeks of the war. But thanks to historians and to former prisoners such as Germaine Tillion, a trained ethnologist who was able to keep detailed notes in the final months, much evidence about the camp has been gathered.

Roughly 123,000 women and children passed through the camp, along with 20,000 men. Ravensbrück had forty satellite camps, a smaller men's camp, the Siemens factory camp, and what was called the Youth Camp of Ückermark but was in fact an extermination camp. Estimates of the death toll at Ravensbrück range from 30,000 to 90,000. The Fondation pour la mémoire de la déportation estimates that approximately 40,000 died there, but it is difficult to know for sure. Most of the women who arrived in the last chaotic months of the war were never registered. And there has been no accounting for the number of women who were "sent away" to be gassed in mobile trucks; one estimate reported that 5,000 to 6,000 women were killed in provisional gas chambers.[8] Nor were the deaths in all the subcamps counted. And then there were the babies, murdered at birth or starved to death following their birth, who were not included in this official count. The women who died on the death marches were not counted either.

In the end, survivors feel that names are more important than numbers.[9] But the numbers give an idea of the enormity of the suffering. By June 1944, when seven out of the nine women in Hélène's group were in Ravensbrück, the camp, which was built to house 3,000 prisoners, held 30,849.[10] The morning roll calls lasted three or more hours, during which prisoners were forced to stand in place to be counted. The situation in the camp had reached hellish proportions with the overcrowding and lack of basic resources.

As the women marched into the camp, they were led first to the *Effektenkammer*, or storage room, where they were told to strip completely. They were ordered to put their clothes in large brown paper bags. When they handed the bags to the guards, their number was noted and the bag thrown into a pile. Their smaller personal effects such as jewelry and money, if they had any, were handed over as well. With the Nazi flourish for recordkeeping, these items were carefully noted. After making a request for Hélène's Nazi records in 2018, I received from the International Tracing Service in Bad Arolsen many documents, including a few pages of these personal-possession records. I read that Zaza handed over her wedding ring and five francs. Hélène handed over a bracelet, a watch, and seventy centimes.

Their heads were shaved. They had to stand spread-eagled while someone shaved their pubic hair in a brutal manner that left slashes and bleeding wounds that would easily get infected.

They were pushed to the showers. Once in the room with holes on the ceiling, Zaza grabbed hold of Hélène's hand. Looking up, she asked, "What do you think will come out of those: gas or water?"

After the violence of the drenching showers they were moved along to the next room, where clothes were redistributed. By this time the camp authorities had run out of striped prisoner outfits. So instead, new arrivals were given dead women's clothes. Each week trucks arrived from Auschwitz with clothes from the Jews who had been exterminated there.[11] The clothes were distributed haphazardly—a woman might have gotten an evening gown from a nightclub dancer or a schoolgirl's pajamas—so when the women emerged from this gauntlet, they looked grotesque. But in that moment meant to humiliate them and reduce them, the women were able to laugh at themselves and at one another. Lise London, one of the *résistantes* in the same transport, remembered the moment in her memoir and, quoting Rabelais, she wrote, "Le rire est bien le propre de l'homme" (Laughter is a human trait).[12] With laughter and song they would hold on to their humanity and fight back.

The French group was sent to a quarantine block where there were already about 400 prisoners. German officials, terrified of the spread of illness and germs, were strict about putting the newly arrived prisoners in quarantine for the first few weeks. Their block also housed those whom the Germans called *asozial*, or asocial: prostitutes, homosexuals, Sinti and Roma (called *Zigeuner* or "Gypsies"), and common criminals.

One half of the massive hall was an open area with tables, and the other half contained wooden bunks, four levels high. Hélène and Zaza were able to find a place together on a top bunk. From there, Hélène hoped, they could keep a vigilant watch over everything.

While they were in quarantine, Hélène remembered, they spent their days taking apart piles of German uniforms. They had to remove the buttons, take apart the seams, and sort the fabric. The uniforms all had bloodstains, and most featured bullet holes. These were the uniforms of German soldiers who had died on the Eastern Front. The women would sometimes find in a pocket a letter that had not yet been posted. Reading the soldiers' letters, Hélène detected the low morale of the troops in the east.

A week later, on June 23, another transport arrived that included two friends from Holland: Lon, age twenty-eight, and Guigui, age twenty-five. Together they had left their studies in Leiden in 1944 to join the Résistance in Paris.

Athletic and graceful, Guigui had straight brown hair cut in a pageboy just below her chin, with bangs across her forehead. Serene gray eyes graced her long oval face. She had the demure, peaceful look of a Madonna. In the chaotic block, she was nonchalant and reassuringly calm.

Lon was the opposite. Words flew out of her mouth in combinations of the six languages she spoke. Lon was brave and thought fast on her feet, jumping where the more cautious might hesitate. Vibrant and extroverted, with a stout, compact body and a large laugh, she made friends across different nationalities. Lon could be bossy and domineering, but her courage would save the nine on more than one occasion.

One day, standing at one of the interminable roll calls, Hélène whispered to Lon, "What are you thinking?"

And Lon replied, "I'm thinking that six months ago my fiancé wanted me to make love and I refused. I regret it."[13]

Lon recalled being visited in quarantine by another Dutch prisoner: "The only cheery note came from Sabine, a Dutch girl who had lived near my parents' home in The Hague. Regularly, and unshaken, she came along tapping on our window to have a chat. Of course, just as regularly she was chased away, but she remained unperturbed, and came back time and again. These hurried little chats, however, were precious to both of us, and with some sadness we remembered our neighborhood."[14]

Sabine filled Lon in about who was in the camp. There was a group of French political prisoners who were already out of quarantine, and Zaza heard that her friend Zinka from Fresnes was there.

In the group of nine, Zaza and Zinka were the only ones who had husbands. Zaza had been married only a month before her arrest, and Zinka only nine months before her husband had been arrested. Both men had been deported to unknown destinations. This was a source of great anxiety for the young brides.

At twenty-nine, Zinka was the oldest of the nine, but her natural jubilance made her appear much younger. She had a beautiful mass of tight blond ringlets, large blue eyes, a charming gap between her front teeth, and a delicate upturned nose, which made her appear slightly defiant. She was impervious to fear. She stuck her chin out and laughed off the threats from some of the most violent factions in the camp. When others would repeat dire rumors, she shrugged and admonished them, "Stop your pessimistic *bobards*." She was tiny. Her feet were so small, the wooden clogs she was given to wear were like large boats; they gave her blisters and bleeding sores. But she inspired others with her iron willpower. Little Zinka was the one who always tried to take the heaviest load, the worst job, so much so that her friends invented elaborate strategies to thwart her.

———◈———

Hélène heard from Lon's Dutch friend that her friend Geneviève de Gaulle was in the camp. Geneviève was the niece of Charles de Gaulle. By 1943 many people had heard this little-known *général de brigade*'s voice on the radio telling them to resist, but they weren't sure who he was. Geneviève had written two articles about her uncle, under the pseudonym "Gallia," for the clandestine Résistance newspaper *Défense*. Her writing had helped reassure people in the Résistance about this apparently self-appointed leader in London.[15]

Hélène wanted to see Geneviève to find out if there was an organized Résistance group in the camp. But she needed to get out of
quarantine to do it. The women were lucky to have a friendly *blockova*.
Blockovas, the prisoners (mostly Polish) who headed each block, were
there to police the prisoners. Some *blockovas* used their privilege to
help and resist. Others used it to enrich themselves. Some were worse
than the Germans. But their *blockova*, Hilda Synkova, a Czech communist, taught the French prisoners the ropes. One Sunday Hélène
asked her if she could slip out in search of her friend Geneviève, and
Hilda said yes.

The camp was immense, with long alleyways bordered by wooden
blocks in a brutally geometric grid. Hélène miscounted, made a
wrong turn, and was lost in the maze. Everything looked the same,
all of it gray and muddy. On Sunday afternoons the prisoners stayed
inside if they could. It was their one break of the week. Only the Jews,
the Jehovah's Witnesses, and women who had been given an extra
punishment were forced to work. In the heat and putrid odors, the
camp felt empty of life. Suddenly disoriented, Hélène panicked and
turned too quickly around a corner. There she ran straight into two
SS guards. They smiled when they saw her. One was a large man, a bit
fatter than most people during that time when food was so hard to
find. His sidekick was skinny and scrappy, with cruel eyes. The large
one spoke and the small one giggled.

Hélène was rattled. She wouldn't be this unprepared again, but
at that moment she was unable to come up with a reason for being
where she was, or any way to defend herself. The men grabbed her,
each taking an arm.

"We will have to help you find your way, won't we?" the fat one said.
The small one laughed as they dragged her into a small guardroom.

They pushed her up against a wall. She felt the rough wood planks
against her back. She tried to go into that place in her head where
she had found a kind of refuge in Angers during the torture sessions.
But she could smell their acrid sweat as they joked about what they
might do to "help her."

She wanted to close her eyes, but she had learned that doing so
showed weakness, and weakness emboldened the bullies. She forced
herself to stare right into the big one's eyes. He took out a pair of

pliers and waved them in front of her face. "Let's make her pretty," he said. He bent down close so he could whisper into her ear, "You will be prettier this way."[16]

He barked, "Open it!" With his thick sausage fingers, he pried open her mouth.

She tasted the oily metal of the pliers against her tongue as he rooted in her mouth and then chose one of her molars. She felt the pincers of the tool grip. "Hold her still!" he ordered the other man. She felt the sweaty arms of the smaller soldier as he grabbed her and pushed her down as her tooth was ripped out of her mouth, the sharp pain of the tearing of roots like sparks, followed by the warm gush as her mouth filled with blood. She felt cold sweat and nausea overcome her. But she swallowed.

"*Ja*, it's good! Much better." The guard held the tooth with its bloodied roots up to her face. Hélène could tell he wasn't satisfied; his kind never were. But, mercifully, they were interrupted by the sound of bells announcing the next round of their hourly regimented schedule. She saw the soldiers register that they had things to do, the routine that must be followed. Reluctantly they shoved her out the door. She stumbled, spitting blood on the ground, and miraculously found her way back to the relative safety of her friends in the quarantine block.

CHAPTER TWO

— ZAZA —

Suzanne Maudet (Zaza)

THE SS ADMINISTERED THE CONCENTRATION camp sys-
tem with a strategy of divide and conquer. Prisoners were entrusted
with the internal running of the camp, giving some relative power
and a stake in keeping the status quo. For the most part, women were
separated by nationalities in an effort to weaken their ability to form
alliances across groups. New arrivals had to learn the hierarchies and
unwritten codes of the camp to survive.

In the early years of Ravensbrück, the prisoners with the green
and black triangles—the criminals and so-called *asozial* prisoners,
respectively—were in charge of discipline. But in the summer of
1941, fearing a polio epidemic, the SS temporarily left the camp completely in the prisoners' hands. As the largest group, the Poles were
able to use this opportunity to take over most positions of authority

in the camp's internal administration. The Poles were said to be anti-Semitic, anti-Soviet, and cooperating with the German authorities. But there were also Poles who came from the upper classes—the "Krakow intelligentsia"—who had been active in resisting the Germans. Many of them too harbored anti-Semitic sentiments with deep historical origins. This was a delicate subject that Lon struggled over with her close friend, a Polish prisoner named Alina. As Lon put it, "As a neutral observer, she also told me about the hatred between Jewish and non-Jewish Poles. That hatred is rooted very deeply but I never found out exactly why."[1]

There were complex hierarchies within nationalities. Some Russian prisoners had actually been handed over to the German authorities by Stalin before Hitler broke the alliance between the two countries. These women had fought on the losing side of the Russian Revolution, and the communists hated them. There were many Russian civilians who had been swept up during Hitler's invasion of their country, and there was also a group of Red Army soldiers, most of them doctors and medics captured at the Battle of Stalingrad. The Nazis called them the *Flintenweiber*, or gunwomen, and they had a heroic aura from their well-known story of protest in the camp. Under the clandestine leadership of Yevgenia Lazarevna Klemm, a large group of Russian army women, learning that they were meant to work in a munitions factory, refused as a group to make bullets that would kill their brothers and sons. They took the stance that as prisoners of war, under the Geneva Conventions they could not be forced to make armaments. As a punishment, the camp authorities made them stand outside for days with no food or water, but the Russians did not break, which first angered the Germans and then amazed them. In the end, astonishingly, the authorities buckled and assigned the women kitchen duties.

A Bolshevik soldier and a fervent communist, Klemm was able to organize and motivate the group of roughly 500 Red Army women. They trusted her and followed her orders with unerring discipline. But the Germans could not figure out who the Russians' leader was. On one famous occasion, a Sunday afternoon in Ravensbrück when it was announced that all the prisoners would be required to march around the *Appellplatz*, the area where they daily stood for the long roll call, the Red Army women, even though starving and sick with typhus or TB, carefully washed themselves with what little water they had, "ironed" their uniforms by placing them under their mattresses the night before, and dressed themselves as immaculately as possible. Dagmar Hajkova, a Czech communist, later described the scene. Everyone was limping along, giving an insipid, exhausted rendition of a march or a military song, just longing for the stupid exercise to end, when a roar broke out across the camp and everyone turned to see the Soviet women march out and line up perfectly:

> When they arrived in the centre of the square, they all began to sing a Red Army fighting song. They sang in loud clear voices, one song after another. They walked into the centre of the square, young faces, shaven heads as a sign of shame, but with their heads up high: and everyone froze on the spot. They walked as if they were parading on Red Square.[2]

Their heroism and discipline were greatly admired by all the other women except the non-Jewish Poles. Among the Poles there were arguments about who was worse for Poland, Stalin or Hitler.

The French prisoners admired the Soviet army women, even though they feared and disdained the "common" Russians for what the French called their "brutish nature." Many of the French prisoners were also communists and admirers of the Russian Revolution.

But the French had a bad reputation among the prisoners of other nationalities. It dated back to February 1944, when the first large group of French political prisoners arrived in Ravensbrück. Known as *les vingt-sept mille* (the 27,000) because the registration numbers they were given upon arrival started with 27, the newly arrived prisoners were completely unprepared for survival in a concentration camp; they were sure there had been some sort of administrative mistake and they would soon be transferred to a better place. Upon arrival, the French prisoners were placed in the "slums"—blocks 27 to 32, which were occupied by the *asozial* prisoners. These blocks were woefully overcrowded, having been built for 200 and now housing 600, with more arriving every day. These first French arrivals were shocked to find themselves mixed in with this population.

They brought with them the racism and social mores of their times and class. Instead of finding allies, the French were frightened by the Roma and Sinti, repelled by the prostitutes, and shocked by the lesbians. These blocks were overseen by Polish *blockovas* and *stubovas* (room chiefs), who harbored a deep-seated animosity toward the French for not coming to their aid against Hitler in 1939. The French were generally held in contempt by other nationalities as well: by the Czechs because of the Munich Agreement allowing Hitler to annex the Sudetenland, by the Spanish because of France's ambivalence toward Franco during the Spanish Civil War, and by the German prisoners because of the Vichy government's collaboration with the Nazis.

Soon the French of the *vingt-sept mille* began to die. They had arrived looking proud and chic, wearing makeup and dressed beautifully with Hermès scarves and fancy handbags. But within weeks they were covered in boils and lice, dying of TB and typhus. Stunned by the predicament they found themselves in, they seemed to lose their will to live. The other prisoners could see that the French were failing, but it was said it was their own fault: they didn't know how to wash themselves properly; they weren't tough enough; they tried too hard to look good instead of focusing on saving themselves; they didn't fight for their food and so they starved.

But when they arrived, the French prisoners of the *vingt-sept mille* had no allies within the camp hierarchy who could help them. It would take time for them to learn the ways of the camp. Later groups fared better. And a large convoy of prisoners who came in April from Paris brought hopeful news: the war was going badly for the Germans.

———— ❧ ————

By June 1944, when seven of the nine women were at Ravensbrück, Germany had suffered catastrophic losses on the Russian front. Hitler's war was basically lost. But, delusional with pride, the German high command decided on a final push to build more weaponry, especially the V-2 rockets, which were the first long-range guided ballistic missiles. On the night of August 17–18, 1943, the Allies had carried out a successful bombardment of Peenemünde, where the rockets were being produced. Wernher von Braun, the scientist in charge, rescued the plans from the flames, and ten days later the Nazis requisitioned underground tunnels in central Germany to restart the secret production of the V-2. This would become the camp known as Mittelbau-Dora. They believed that these magical weapons would turn the war around. All of Germany's able-bodied men were fighting on various fronts, so the Nazis expanded their network of concentration camps with *Kommandos*, satellite forced-labor camps. By the middle of the war there were as many as 15,000 *Kommandos* with 100,000 prisoners linked to the main concentration camps. The Germans would use this vast network to build weapons.

Heinrich Himmler oversaw this system of concentration camps, or *Konzentrationslager*. As a young man Himmler was an unlikely soldier; weak, with poor eyesight, he had been excluded from the officer class in the German military. But he found a home in the far-right paramilitary units in Munich, which soon morphed into the National Socialist Party. Himmler would become Hitler's chief henchman. By 1933, Himmler had transformed the SS into an elite squad.[3] The SS would run the concentration camp system.[4]

The forced labor camps generated enormous profits for the Nazi war machine. German industries paid for the prisoners' labor, and that money went directly into the Nazi Party coffers. The SS rented female prisoners at four reichsmarks per woman per day to nineteen German companies, including Krupp, BMW, IG Farben, and Siemens. As camp secretary, Germaine Tillion was able to see that Himmler and other Nazis amassed a considerable profit from renting out prisoners at rates far above the pittance it cost to keep the prisoners minimally alive (as well as from the fortunes they stole from the prisoners, including the gold extracted from their teeth).[5] In September 1943, Siemens boss Rudolf Bingel was so pleased with the profits from the female laborers that he donated 100,000 reichsmarks to Himmler's "circle of supporters."[6] German banks along with German industries benefited, and went largely unpunished in the aftermath of Germany's defeat.

In July 1944, soon after Zaza and the others emerged from quarantine, the head guard at Ravensbrück announced that there was going to be a large selection for the *Kommandos*. Zaza was terrified. She and Hélène had found solace in friendships with Zinka, Lon, and Guigui. Where would they be sent? Would the conditions be worse? And, most important, would they be separated? They had established a tenuous routine in Ravensbrück. Though life there was hellish, it had at least become a familiar hell.

If on selection day a prisoner was deemed no longer useful, she would be chosen for extermination. Other selections led to forced prostitution in Himmler's brothels, serving the SS guards or as part of a bonus system for male prisoners. Originally Himmler had staffed his brothels with prostitutes picked up off the streets in Berlin and then from other invaded countries. But by the summer of 1944, he needed new recruits. More than 200 women were sent to the so-called *Sonderblocks*, or "special blocks."[7] Some women volunteered because of the promise that they would be given extra rations and would be released after their "service." Many women selected for sexual slavery died from disease and the abuse they suffered. A woman who returned to Ravensbrück from one of these brothels in 1944 after just six weeks reported the horror: "Every morning the prostitutes had to get up and let themselves be cleaned by female guards. After coffee the SS men would come and start to rape and abuse the women. It would go on for sixteen hours a day, and only two and a half hours for lunch and dinner."[8]

Zaza worried that her new friend Josée might be selected for the *Sonderblocks*. A child of Spanish immigrants, Josée was just eighteen when she joined the Résistance; a year and a half later, she was arrested by the Gestapo. Even in that bleak landscape of shaved heads and starved, asexual bodies, Josée's beauty could not be stamped out. Miraculously, she had kept her mass of rich black hair, and the others prayed it would not be shaved by one of the blond German guards. She had movie-star looks; with her high cheekbones, long oval face, and graceful lips, she was a more elegant version of Anna Magnani. She was more overtly emotional, perhaps because she was so young. The others tried to protect her. But Josée wasn't as vulnerable as they thought; she'd spent her adolescence in a foster home in the south of France.

Josée was beloved for her singing voice. At night in their crowded bunks, as they whispered the latest terrifying rumors, preparing one another for the selection, the women begged Josée to serenade them. If she could overcome her fear, Josée sang Schubert, exquisitely, with all her heart.

On July 18, the morning of the selection, they were told to strip at roll call. Zaza noticed some of the younger girls shivering with fear and humiliation, trying to cover their breasts and private parts. Zaza felt herself floating away, until Hélène elbowed her. She had to be present. It was too dangerous in these moments to forget where they were. Zaza looked at Hélène briefly, wanting to give her privacy. Hélène gave a slight smile, and Zaza could see that her missing tooth was bothering her. She had confessed to Zaza that when she felt with her tongue the place of her missing tooth, it gave her the strength of rage. It reminded her of what she would do when this whole thing was over. Hélène lifted her chin defiantly, not bothering to mask her anger.

They were marched in front of a commission of SS officers and civilian businessmen, the owners of the various factories. The men pointed out the women they wanted and jeered at the bodies of those they rejected: "Look at that thing, is it a woman even?" They made faces of disgust: "She's been used up!" Another laughed and with his hands indicated he was making fun of an older woman for her sagging breasts. With a simple nod of the SS commander's head, the ridiculed woman was taken out of the lineup and led away to be executed.

Some of the younger women were trembling with fear, but Zaza followed the example of Hélène and Zinka. She refused to give those men the satisfaction. Instead she felt the flood of rage as the older women whose bodies bore the evidence of childbirth were pulled from this parade and sent directly to the crematorium. The healthy and strong were then inspected for scabies, rashes, and infections. They were given a vaginal examination for venereal disease by an SS guard who never changed his rubber glove.

One young girl, Rosie, fell apart after this humiliating procedure and started to cry. She was on the verge of breaking ranks, but two of the other women grabbed her and held her in place. Rosie, like Josée, was very young; she had never had a man kiss her or see her

naked, much less touch her. Hélène watched out of the corner of her
eye as the older women tried to calm her, whispering to her to stay
strong. It would take several months of love and attention to bring
Rosie back to herself.[9]

Zaza felt a wave of relief when they were then given gray-and-blue-
striped pajama outfits. She thought, They wouldn't give us these
clothes if they were going to kill us. Instead, they would be sent to a
Kommando. They were also given a red triangle, which indicated that
they were political prisoners, a number stamped on a strip of cloth,
and needle and thread to sew the badges onto their jackets (the tat-
tooing of numbers on the arms was a particularity of Auschwitz, and
almost exclusively for Jewish prisoners). Later, Zaza proudly showed
Hélène that she had been able to steal the needle and thread, highly
useful items.

From July 18 to 21, they were held in a large pen awaiting transport, and during that time the other prisoners snuck over to give
them farewell gifts: a sweater, a piece of soap, a poem on a scrap of
paper, a pair of socks. This solidarity kept the women going. But it
made the impending separation especially heartbreaking.

During their transport by train from Ravensbrück to the new labor camp, the cars were shunted off for a time onto a side spur outside of Berlin, and one of the prisoners who spoke German overheard
a couple of railway workers talking. There had been an attempt on
Hitler's life by high-ranking officers within the upper echelon of the
Nazi Party. The news spread rapidly from car to car. Though Zaza
and the others hated the fact that Hitler had survived, they found it
promising that even high up in his inner circle, people were turning
against him.

The Nazi army had once seemed so unassailable. Zaza had been nineteen when she watched from her apartment balcony as German soldiers paraded into Paris. She watched the crowds fleeing Paris with
their suitcases, baby carriages, and handcarts, gas masks slung over
their shoulders with string, heading south, ahead of the invading
army. She may have wondered where the Résistance was.

Zaza would have experienced the repressive regime slowly taking hold: rules forbidding any gathering of more than three people, curfews, rations, censorship. Then posters appeared around the city about the hostages killed in retaliation for some kind of act of resistance against the Germans. The lists of the executed were meant to discourage the Résistance but only fed the flames of bitterness and revolt. Maybe Zaza's first acts of opposition were simple: quickly writing "ASSASSIN" on those German posters, or drawing the Croix de Lorraine, the symbol of the Résistance, on walls. She may have passed out clandestine flyers, illegal newspapers at the entrances to the metro, but after the first mass arrests of Jews she, like many others, would have wanted to do more. By 1943, Zaza had become an *ajiste*—one of those working for the Auberge de la Jeunesse (AJ).

Founded between the wars, the AJ was inspired by German youth hostels. The idea was that young people would travel, hike, and share experiences across borders, creating an atmosphere of peace and understanding. It was part of a general utopian fervor among the younger generation after the debacle of World War I. Zaza met her future husband, René, while working for the AJ.

With the German occupation of France, apolitical organizations were allowed to continue to operate, and this was initially the case for the AJ. But the founder, Marc Sagnier, refused to bar Jews from membership.[10] When the AJ was outlawed in 1943, many of its leaders slipped into the Résistance, and the organization shifted into clandestine work. Though Sagnier remained president, he along with the national secretary fled into France's free zone, in the south. René Maudet and Rolland Beauramier were appointed to run the AJ in the northern zone. René also gathered military intelligence about the location of German troops and fortifications and transmitted it to the Allies.

The Germans had started a system of voluntary labor in France—at age twenty, French men were to volunteer to work in Germany in exchange for the release of French prisoners of war. The Germans did not get a sufficient number of volunteers, and by 1943 the labor system became obligatory, with young men conscripted into the Service du travail obligatoire (STO). But the AJ developed a plan to help young men escape this forced labor by providing false papers and orienting them toward various clandestine networks.

Zaza's cousin recalled going to the AJ headquarters in Paris to type letters to former AJ members who were about to be conscripted into the STO. The letters proposed a camping trip at one of the AJ's hostels in the Jura before the former members headed east to labor for the German war machine. Once the young men had arrived at the hostel, René's job was to delicately determine whom he could safely talk to about the options he could offer if they didn't want to go to Germany. There would be a moment, perhaps at night after a long day of hiking as they sat in front of an open fire singing songs, talking about France before the humiliating defeat, when René would broach the subject.

I can imagine how twenty-two-year-old Zaza and twenty-three-year-old René became a couple. Together they offered young men who faced deportation and forced labor one or two weeks in the Jura with plenty of fresh air and exercise. René would have been the leader of these trips, and blue-eyed Zaza one of the volunteer helpers. She didn't complain about the cold or the rain. She was the kind who would eagerly gather firewood, help peel potatoes, and after dinner lead the group in song. While René was the one who had to put out feelers, it was Zaza who created the atmosphere of trust and openness. Thin and lanky, René was an ardent socialist with no time for small talk. He wasn't good at opening up to people, at lighthearted banter. But with Zaza helping him, he could talk to the boys. She made him feel strong, capable. René would have felt grateful to have her by his side and would have admired her kindness and generosity. They developed a sense of complicity and understanding, a few inside jokes, nicknames. These were intense times. In the early morning Zaza would bring René his cup of hot tea just the way he liked it. In the evenings René could look across the glow of the campfire and see Zaza smiling at him, hanging on his every word. René, who hadn't thought much about marriage, suddenly saw Zaza as someone he would want to share his life with. I imagine that on one of those trips he would have taken her hand and they would have exchanged their first kisses.

In February 1944 they were married. They moved into an apartment at 12, rue d'Hauteville, in the Tenth Arrondissement; it was tiny and dark but full of joy. This was the happiest time in Zaza's young life. Though the world around them had gone crazy and there were dangers everywhere, she and René felt so lucky to have found each other. She couldn't believe that every morning she got to wake up by his side. They celebrated the smallest of victories: so-and-so had made it safely to the southern zone and joined one of the bands of guerrilla fighters, the Maquis; she had found almost-real-tasting ersatz coffee on the black market; he had gotten a letter through with a new list of recruits. She believed their love was a magic shield.

One month after their marriage, on March 22, 1944, during a clandestine meeting at their apartment, Zaza, along with René and the other gathered AJ members, was arrested in a devastating sweep of the whole operation. Someone had informed on them.

Juliette Bes was arrested in the same large round-up of *ajists*. The interrogation she describes in her memoir is most likely similar to what Zaza experienced. Bes was stripped naked in a room with four men, two in front and two behind her. From time to time, when she refused to answer their questions, the men behind her would beat her with a whip. Or the men in front would slap her across the face. She writes that besides the utter humiliation of being a young woman naked in front of strange men, the worst part was anticipating the beatings.[11]

After her interrogation, Zaza was sent to Fresnes prison. She saw René one more time during those three months. One day, as he was marched past the prison yard where she was standing with a group of women, they called out to each other. He told her to be strong, that they would find each other again. And then she heard that he had been deported to Germany.

René was sent to the Neuengamme concentration camp, outside Hamburg. From there he was sent to one of the eighty subcamps and placed on a bomb disposal squad. Concentration camp prisoners were used to dig up and transport the thousands of unexploded bombs buried meters deep in the earth and rubble. Many bombs had delayed action fuses that were particularly dangerous to disarm. SS guards and technicians stayed at a safe distance while the prisoners worked, digging out the bombs often using their bare hands. The prisoners took turns, two at a time, because that way only two people would die if a bomb exploded. The estimated survival rate in these units was bleak: only one out of ten would live to the end of the war. One such survivor remembered bringing his comrades back to the camp at night in buckets, their bodies having been blown apart.

Zaza would not know what happened to René until after her own ordeal was over. But she held on to the hope that he would survive and that after the war they could resume their lives together. She was deported to Germany a few weeks after him, on June 14, 1944.

The train from Ravensbrück took the selected women prisoners to a *Kommando* in Leipzig. In January 2017, I asked my twenty-year-old daughter Sophie if she would come to Germany to help me retrace Hélène and Zaza's steps.

Before this trip, I had spent a total of eight days in Germany. I had never been to Berlin. I didn't speak German. But Sophie and I are both naturalized Germans; we hold German passports. One of my grandfathers, her great-grandfather, was a German Jew who fled in 1934 and was made stateless by Hitler. Because of that history we were able to reclaim our German identity and be citizens of Europe.

We began our trip in Leipzig. At the small museum for the Nazi Forced Labor Memorial, we met the archivist Anne Friebel. Soft-spoken, welcoming, and curious, she offered to search the archives for me. I wrote down Hélène's full name and birthdate, and I told Anne that she may have been known by her nom de guerre, "Christine." I also gave her the real names of the two other women I knew were in the group, Zaza and Lon. The next day Friebel emailed me two documents.

One document was the transport list from the selection in Ravensbrück on July 21, 1944, the largest transport of enslaved labor to Leipzig—more than 2,000 women from France, Poland, the Soviet Union, Greece, the Netherlands, Hungary, and other countries.

On page three of the scan, I found Hélène, listed as "Jeannine Podliasky." Her Leipzig camp number was 4063. It was noted that she was an unmarried engineer. The second document was a list of all the prisoners at the HASAG Leipzig camp on August 22, 1944. There she appears under the name Christine Podliasky, with her old number from Ravensbrück and the new one from Leipzig. Right below

Hélène's name on the list was Zaza (she was listed under the misspelling "Susanne Mandet"), and up a few names was Lon (listed as "Magdalena"). There was no alphabetical order to the list; prisoners' names never mattered. They were made to line up according to their Ravensbrück numbers, and those numbers reflected only who had been standing near them when the numbers were assigned. Not far from Zaza and Hélène on the list there was a "Jose," and I wondered if this was their Josée; higher up was Guigui's name.

Seeing Hélène's name on the Nazi list had an overwhelming effect on me. Here was the formal bureaucracy of unthinkable crimes. I imagined the women's arrival at the HASAG Leipzig camp after their transport by train from Ravensbrück: the scramble to line up, the fear and uncertainty as they waited to give their details, the shuffling sound as they made their way forward in line.

———⚬———

The HASAG munitions factory in the Schönefeld suburb of Leipzig was a series of large red brick buildings encircled by electrified fences, barbed wire, and guard towers. The *Kommando*, a subcamp of Buchenwald, used 5,067 female forced laborers to produce ammunition and the *Panzerfaust*, a shoulder-fired rocket-propelled grenade launcher similar to the bazooka. HASAG (Hugo-Schneider-Aktiengesellschaft) was Germany's largest arms manufacturer, with factories in Poland and Germany drawing on the labor from subcamps there. From 1936 to the end of the war, Paul Budin was the general manager of the entire HASAG complex. In contrast to Nazis such as Himmler, who felt women's functions should remain *Kinder, Kirche, Küche* (children, church, and kitchen), Budin was modern in his approach to female labor, being the first industrialist in occupied Poland to assign women to operate machinery. He was given special recognition by Hitler for his "model factories." Furthermore, the SS charged less for women, and they had a lower mortality rate.

Earlier in the war the directors of HASAG had asked the commandant of Buchenwald to improve the workers' conditions. The brutal work environments and the twelve-hour shifts meant HASAG was losing too many workers too fast. The average life expectancy of a male worker in one of the HASAG plants was three and a half months.[12]

Most of the women arriving in July 1944 would spend nine months at the armament factory.

When they arrived at the HASAG camp, Zaza and the others were gathered in a large roll-call area as the women wardens, the *Aufseherinnen*, ordered the prisoners by their numbers into rows of five. The camp commandant, SS-Obersturmführer Wolfgang Plaul, a tall, thin man in an impeccably clean uniform, looked on, tapping his riding crop impatiently against his shiny black boots. Plaul had come from Buchenwald, where he was remembered for his role as the hangman and for how he enjoyed forcing Jews to sing anti-Semitic songs as they labored. Later, near the end of the war, he would appear to have a change of heart, becoming "nicer" toward his female prisoners. When the end of the war was imminent he got orders from Buchenwald's commandant, Hermann Pister, to ease his harsh management.[13]

Next to Plaul stood a beautiful young woman with ice-blue eyes and a crown of golden braids. She was Joanna Szumańska, the camp *Lagerälteste*, the prisoner who oversaw the internal conduct of the camp.

Plaul gave a short "welcome" speech, which was translated into French, Polish, and Russian by a few of the polyglot prisoners. The women were told that here the motto was "Whoever doesn't work doesn't eat." They would be treated well or harshly according to their behavior. The first rule was absolute obedience.

"You are murderers!" a young woman screamed, interrupting Plaul's speech. Exhausted and at the edge of her sanity from having watched her mother being led away to execution in Ravensbrück, she had snapped. Everyone felt the shock when her rage erupted. A guard slapped her, and the girl slapped back.

The guards rushed to surround her. They beat and kicked her, including Commandant Plaul, who whipped her with his riding crop. Her limp body was carried into the camp offices by two SS men. When she reappeared ten days later, she was barely alive, a zombie. She had been put in a black box that was too small to sit up in, with barely any air, no light, and no food. The women carefully pooled their resources to nurse her back to life.[14]

Despite this horrific incident, the women were relieved to find the conditions considerably better than where they had come from. Their greatest joy was the washroom in the block, which contained a long stainless-steel sink with twenty faucets and actual running water. In Ravensbrück there had been one meager faucet of polluted water for every 1,000 women. Here, even though they were without soap, they could actually clean themselves for the first time in months.

※

The day began at 4:00 AM with the cries of "Aufstehen, schnell!" and a quick turn at the washroom. There was a frantic rush of women trying to get to the toilets—it would be their one chance to go to the bathroom all day. There was a scramble to find shoes and clothes. Guigui couldn't find her left clog and was in a panic. As usual, her friend Mena searched and found it on the other side of the block.

Mena came from a Breton family, but at age twenty-two, she felt herself to be very Parisian. She was a working-class girl with big dreams of being an artist. She had an impish, playful nature, loved to be in love, told a good story, and laughed easily. She admitted she hadn't joined the Résistance to save the world; she'd joined "for love of a boy," she said, shrugging.

Hélène calmly wrapped her head in a rag turban and checked on Zaza, who was still lying in the bed they shared. She had been feverish all night, and Hélène was worried. She gently nudged her. "Sorry. Moving slowly this morning," Zaza said, struggling to sit up.

Zaza was burning up with fever. "You should go to the *Revier*," Hélène said.

Revier was short for *Krankenrevier*, or sick bay, the German military term for an infirmary. But the French prisoners refused to use the full term since the *Reviers* dispensed no medicine. In most camps they were where prisoners went to die. But in Leipzig, a sick prisoner might actually get to rest, which was often what the ill person needed most.

"I'm fine," Zaza insisted. "I can work."

Hélène took a long look at her friend. They both knew that for them to be down one member of their team was a real hardship. They were already struggling to keep up with the daily quota. In twelve hours, their team of seven was supposed to load fifty tons of iron shells—seven tons per person. Jacky was unable to meet her quota due to her poor health. At twenty-seven, she was already a war widow and hardened by life. She was suffering from diphtheria. Today, because there is a vaccine and an antitoxin, diphtheria is no longer a real threat, but in the 1940s it was often deadly. The invading German army had brought the disease with them, and the "strangling angel" had turned into a pandemic across Europe. It was deadly in the camps. A thick gray coating builds up in the throat, causing the person to struggle for breath.

Jacky tried to keep pace with the others, but sometimes she had to stop to catch her breath. All she wanted was to be back in her beloved Paris, in her neighborhood café, smoking a cigarette and drinking a glass of wine. "Make it enough to get a sailor and his whore drunk," she added in her deep, raspy voice.

The women did not know that it was diphtheria that was making it extremely difficult for her to breathe, but they covered for her. She had stayed too long and too often at the *Revier*. They had been warned not to let her go there again. If Commandant Plaul found out about her "weak heart," she would be selected for the infamous transports to the camp where prisoners were exterminated in gas chambers upon arrival.

The women needed the labor of everyone in their group, but if Zaza was in such bad shape, if she couldn't do the work anyway, she might as well rest in the *Revier*. They would take the consequences. And yet, Hélène knew, those consequences could be lethal.

"Really, I'm stronger today," insisted Zaza.

Hélène nodded. She knew Zaza was lying. She felt a pang of guilt. The other women in the bathroom gave Zaza space to splash her face and pull herself together.

There was a quick line-up for the "coffee" that was brought into the block by two Soviet prisoners. A putrid black liquid that had nothing to do with coffee, its one good quality was that it was hot. The women had saved a piece of bread from the night before and carefully divided it up into small crumbs, so each could get an equal part.

Then there was a rush to line up outside for roll call in rows of five. Hélène helped Zaza walk and stand tall so the commandant or his guards wouldn't notice—the camp administrators too had a sinister quota to fill, culling the herd. Two *Aufseherinnen* watched as the *blockova* ran the roll call. Then there was the counting and recounting. One of the overseers held a menacing dog on a leash; it snapped and lunged at the women's feet. The guard laughed when the dog was able to grab a foot or ankle and draw a little blood before she pulled it back. Hélène was number 4063, Zaza was 4062, Josée was 4065, and Lon was 4059, which means they stood close together through many long roll calls.

The *blockova* for each section presented her report: the number present, the number who were at the infirmary, the number of deaths. The overseers recounted, and if the number came out correctly, the register was signed and the women began their march to the nearby factory.

Hélène's team was in charge of forging and tempering the shells for the *Panzerfaust* in the electric forges. After a turn in the ovens, the shells had to be loaded into wagons and transported to the acid baths. Hélène's group was given this task because it was the most backbreaking and they were the youngest and strongest. Each woman had to load the ovens and then unload them after the heating process: seven tons of shells in twelve hours. They worked without a break. The shells had to cook for three hours at 600 degrees Celsius. Once all the forges were loaded and running, they had a few moments to rest.

The work was dangerous. If they loaded the wagons too fast, they could tip over. Feet were often crushed in such accidents. In other parts of the factory, women produced highly toxic explosives that were sifted into the *Panzerfaust* shells. No one wore protective clothing. At least 5,000 forced laborers died in the HASAG plants.

That day Zaza had almost finished loading one of the wagons with the red-hot shells from the oven when, feeling dizzy, she put her hand on the wagon rim to steady herself. The wobbly wagon tipped just enough to roll some glowing red shells to the side, crushing Zaza's fingers. Guigui and the others hurriedly tried to remove the shells pinning Zaza's hand. There was the smell of flesh searing on the hot steel.

"Oh, how silly of me," Zaza repeated to her friends, tears pouring from her eyes. "I'm so foolish. I'm so sorry."

Hélène knew she should have tried harder to stop Zaza from

coming to work; she was too sick to work properly, and that was how the accident had happened. Hélène used the rag she'd put on her head to wrap up Zaza's mangled fingers. The German foreman in charge of their area of the factory, Fritz Stupitz, gave Zaza permission to go to the *Revier*. Hélène thanked him under her breath and then told Zaza, "I'll come see you when we get off."

For the rest of the shift, Hélène made frantic calculations of the number of wagons and the tonnage. She pushed the other women and hated herself for it, but already they were behind the necessary count and she didn't know how they would make up the tonnage in time. Certain foremen took the quota seriously and meted out punishments accordingly: sometimes reducing the women's already impossibly meager food rations, sometimes shaving their heads, sometimes beating them. And sometimes the worst happened: the whole group would be selected for transport.

Soon after arriving in Leipzig the women learned about the constant danger of Commandant Plaul's selections. Anyone not producing their quota could be selected and sent on a transport to one of the camps where, it was rumored, they would be executed upon arrival. The first selections were of children and pregnant women. Plaul said that they were going to be given extra rations and lighter workloads. For a few weeks this appeared to be true. He wanted to register every child under sixteen. But then they were given old, tattered clothes and told they were going to be sent to another camp. The Nazi records show that seventy-five people—young orphans, the sick, and pregnant women (with the number of months of pregnancy carefully noted for each)—were sent from Leipzig to Auschwitz, and most were killed in the gas chambers upon their arrival on August 29, 1944.[15] A French prisoner, Simone Jean, would be the lone survivor of this transport.

Some of the adolescent girls had been smart enough to misstate their age, saying they were older, and so they survived this first selection. A few women were able to hide their pregnancies up to a certain point, but when their bellies began to show they were sent away immediately. There were transports loaded with the weak and dying sent out every few weeks, and the process of selection seemed to be linked to productivity. If a woman looked exhausted or too pale, Commandant Plaul would select her. The local civilians who worked at the plant ran a high-priced black market in lipstick and rouge— worth up to three or four days of bread rations. But if a prisoner put on too much makeup, Plaul would catch them. One time he pulled a woman for selection, saying, "You come too, you floozy." And one woman caught putting on makeup was shot dead on the spot.[16]

At the end of their shift, the foreman in charge of their section had to verify that they had met their quota. On the day of Zaza's accident, Hélène knew they had failed. But then something strange happened. The foreman, Fritz, looked at Hélène and said simply, "You've met the quota. Line up." And there it was, fluttering inside her: a wild hope that here was a good person, a person with humanity. Someone who might help her escape.

———❧———

That evening Hélène negotiated with the *blockova* in charge to slip out and visit Zaza. Luckily, the *blockova* was known to have a sweet tooth. A few of the women in their block donated their carefully hoarded sugar for the bribe.

At the *Revier*, Hélène found Zaza surrounded by Polish prisoners. They were all speaking French and talking about Proust. Zaza saw Hélène's dumbfounded expression. "It seems that I resemble someone they all loved dearly," she said, explaining about her sudden popularity.

"Yes, yes, poor Ianka," one of the Poles said.

"She died in Majdanek," another offered, stroking Zaza's curls. "She has the same blue eyes, the same blond curls . . ."

Zaza passed a few days at the *Revier* being coddled by the Polish prisoners, who held most of the positions of power in the camp. Though they too were brutalized by the SS, they had access to better food and a few small luxuries such as soap and warmer clothes. They knew Zaza wasn't Ianka, but they were happy to take care of someone who looked just like her. Zaza was given extra food and even a wonderful pair of felt slippers that fit inside her wooden clogs. Those slippers would make a difference later during the escape. Zaza, ever the cheerful optimist, later confided to Hélène, "You see, it was all for the best: if I hadn't crushed my fingers, you never would have talked with Stupitz and I wouldn't have gotten my warm slippers."

———◆———

During the desperate final year of the war, all able-bodied German men were being sent to the front, and civilians were being hired to supervise the factories. These Germans were older, less influenced by the Nazi propaganda, and worn down by the personal losses of sons and family members. The war was not going well, and perhaps these Germans were thinking about their future after the war. In any case, there are several accounts of German civilian supervisors at HASAG being "kind" to the prisoners.

Survivor Felicja Karay writes about several such incidents. One Jewish prisoner recounted that a German civilian hid a newspaper in the lavatory for her that described the establishment of a Jewish state in Palestine. Despite his loyalty to the Führer, an old foreman named Wilhelm brought "his girls" a pot of food from home each day. Then one day in the spring of 1944 the women arrived at the plant to find him hanging by a rope. He had left them another pot of food, this time with a note stating he could not bear the shame of defeat, that the Nazis were wrong, and that he hoped they would remember "old Wilhelm who loved you like daughters."[17]

A Polish foreman at the factory fell in love with Mena and would hide little gifts by her machine. One time he left her a beautiful comb decorated with scrap metal and wires scavenged from the factory floor. Another time he brought her a potato, which she cooked patiently in the glowing red shells coming from the ovens.[18]

The Leipzig factory ran night and day. The women worked twelve-hour shifts six days a week and a half day on Sunday. One week they had the day shift and the next week the night shift. Production never ceased except during Allied bombardments, when the women were ordered down to the basement shelters. Cheered by the break in the grueling work, the women smiled and laughed as they left the factory and rushed to the shelter. Hélène loved the bombardments even if they were potentially deadly, because they held the promise of liberation. The Allies were winning—and soon the Nazis would be defeated.

In the shelter, they sat on the ground, leaning against the stone wall, illuminated by a single bulb. Most took the opportunity to sleep. Josée lay with her head on Zaza's lap. In the stillness they could hear the rumble of exploding bombs and feel the ground shudder.

Hélène sat next to Zaza, peering into the dim light of the cool basement, watching as the last people filed in. Among them was Fritz Stupitz. He stood at the entrance looking through the crowd of exhausted women, and she knew he was looking for her. As Zaza said, "Hélène had a face you could not forget." When his eyes found hers, she acknowledged him with a nod. Stepping carefully around the seated women, he made his way over to sit next to her.

For a long time neither of them spoke. Eventually, at the urging of the others, Josée began to sing a melody from Schubert. The air was dank with the smell of the earth and their bodies. But everyone enjoyed the soft melody moving through the dark basement. Hélène did not look at Fritz, but she could feel him next to her listening.

Abruptly a large explosion interrupted Josée's crystal-clear voice. Several women screamed. Then there was silence. Hélène had not flinched. She exhaled and whispered to Fritz, "That sounded like a direct hit."

"I think they are targeting the rail yard."

"Yes," Hélène agreed. "That's what I would do."

"So, you've thought about it?"

Hélène frowned at his question, but then she saw that he was smiling. She smiled too.

"You've thought about how you would beat the great German army?" he continued.

She was sure it was there, a tiny hint of sarcasm. "Every day," she whispered emphatically. "Wouldn't you? In my position?"

He might have been surprised that she would risk speaking so openly, but he probably appreciated it as well. As they talked, Fritz found out that Hélène was far more educated than he was.

"An engineer?" He did not hide his surprise.

"I was studying in Paris before the war."

"You're not—?" He stopped abruptly. The Germans working in the factory had been told that all the female forced laborers there were criminals and prostitutes. But hearing Hélène talk about her studies, he realized that was not why she had been arrested.

He had gray hair and deep grooves in his forehead from worry. He was a handsome man, Hélène thought, kinder than these times allowed him to be. His sensitive face betrayed his thoughts. He was not one of the foremen who seemed to revel in their newfound power. There were foremen who yelled and pushed the women, who took perverse pleasure in making their already hard lot harder. They might tip over the wagon of loaded shells to make them load the tons of hot steel all over again. Hélène was grateful that Fritz was often their overseer on the day shifts. Later, she realized that Fritz *chose* her group. She knew other women, other teams, had to manage much more difficult men, in awful and terrifying ways.

Fritz was courteous and respectful. And for this Hélène had already noticed him. Her work scouting for people to join her teams in the Résistance networks had honed her skills at reading people. But his act of kindness when Zaza was injured—one that could be dangerous for him—made her curious and even hopeful.

"What were you going to say?" she challenged him. She knew what he was insinuating.

"Nothing." He shook his head and looked down at his hands. "It's just what we were told about you. All of you women. About why you are here."

"We are all soldiers, prisoners of war," Hélène answered proudly. "We are here because we are patriots who fought the fascist occupation of our country."

Fritz whispered, "I didn't like this war from the beginning. I don't like that man." Hélène knew he meant Hitler. "It's not my war." They looked at each other for a long moment of acknowledgment. Then the all-clear siren sounded, and they were ordered back to their stations.

——◈——

Hélène now looked forward to the bombardments, when she and Fritz would find each other and resume their conversation. Hélène learned that Fritz had been the head of his union and a labor organizer. He was married and had lost his only son on the Eastern Front. She wondered if one of those bullet-ridden and bloodstained uniforms she had carefully taken apart in Ravensbrück could have been his son's. His wife was not in Leipzig; with the constant bombardments, the city was too dangerous. And since their son's death her nerves were shattered. He had sent her to live in his small village with his parents. Her grief had been too much for him to handle, he admitted, and he added, "I didn't know what else to do for her."

Hélène remembered once hearing her mother soothing a war widow from the Great War. She had said something like "Time will help."

"I think it takes time," she offered. She wasn't good at comforting others, even when she wanted to be.

"Can I show you something?" Fritz asked.

In the dark of the shelter he took out a picture of his son. His grief was palpable; the sadness made this wisp of a photograph feel as weighty as one of the panzer shells that passed through Hélène's hands. She realized in a visceral way that many Germans were as sickened by this war as the prisoners were.

She told him about her family and her sisters. They talked about music and food they liked. Fritz loved to read, and they talked about their favorite writers and poets. One of them was Rilke—"a strange poet," he said, who had helped him so much with the loss of his son. And he recited a fragment of a poem to her.

Fritz and Hélène talked about what they would like to do when the war was over. He would go back to farm in his village. And if it wasn't too late for his wife, he would like to have more children. "Maybe this is too much to ask for," he said quietly.

"I want to go back to my studies. I want to keep studying math."

"And children?" he asked her.

"I don't know." She shook her head. "It's hard for me to imagine bringing a child into this world now."

Because Hélène was an engineer, Fritz put her in charge of supervising the thermostats of the six factory forges. He knew that this would enable her to sabotage the weapons fabrication, which she did. She tweaked the thermostat gauges to show a high temperature even as she actually turned the ovens off during the middle part of the process, then she raised the temperature again at the end so that the shells and tubes coming out of the forges would be red-hot and no one would suspect a thing. The shells made this way shattered either in the acid baths or the first time they were used, killing the German soldier pulling the trigger.

Reports of the defective shells exploding at the wrong time and wounding German soldiers reached the high command. A group of officials was dispatched to the factory to inspect the machinery. They were shown around by a very nervous German engineer, the chief foreman of the factory, an idiot whom Hélène avoided whenever possible. He led them to the bridge where Hélène watched over the thermostats. Here they could observe the women working in several areas of the factory. Many of the women had their heads wrapped with rags and their sleeves rolled up. They were covered in sweat and filth. They did not look at the inspectors, even as they were all acutely aware that they were being watched. The racket of the machinery was deafening.

"The problem is not the machines," the foreman shouted over the din. "It's the poor quality of the primary materials we've been given."

"That's not good enough!" the German official snapped back at him. "I don't want to hear your excuses."

Hélène hoped they would not look too closely at what was going on below. Zaza and Jacky were emptying a load of shells, stacking them onto the wagon to transport them to the acid baths. The shells weren't as hot as they should be. Ever since Zaza's accident, Hélène had tried to make sure her loads wouldn't be too hot, since Zaza was basically working one-handed. She hadn't been prepared for this surprise inspection.

Soon another oven would be ready for unloading. Hélène was turning up the heat to be sure the shells looked red-hot when the oven door opened. She didn't want to call any attention to her team. Across the way she saw Fritz watching her, looking scared. She wished he could hide his emotions better.

"What is your job?" the high commander screamed at her. He leaned down close to her to be heard above the noise, and she was startled by his sudden proximity.

"I oversee the ovens," she shouted back.

"Why are you in charge of this?"

"I'm an engineer."

He burst out laughing. "She says she's an engineer," he repeated to the others in the group and they all laughed along obligingly.

"Then explain as an engineer what you are doing." He leaned back in, as if speaking to a small child.

"I have no idea," she said, shrugging. "I just do as I am told. I am supposed to keep this needle pointing to this number."

He patted her on the shoulder, "Good girl. You must work hard for the Fatherland and you shall be redeemed."

Sometimes, Hélène thought, it was so easy to use men's low expectations for women to her advantage. They couldn't conceive for one moment that the factory was being sabotaged. These starved, stupid women would not be capable of that. Hélène felt a moment of happiness; she was still able to resist. These acts of sabotage made them all feel still useful and alive.

The next day, Fritz brought Hélène's group some potatoes, which they cooked in the incandescent shells coming out of the ovens. It was a feast. Normally they had only one meal a day, and that was often a watery soup. He was congratulating Hélène, in his own clandestine way, for getting away with sabotage.

Eventually Hélène asked Fritz to help her escape. What had been unspoken but understood became overt. They talked in that dark cellar about how she might do it. He kept her current with news from the front. He told her that soon he was planning to abandon his post at the factory. He wanted to get back to his wife and village. He did not want to be here when everything crumbled. "Who knows how they will behave when their great Führer topples?"

Fritz drew a map in the dirt of the shelter with his finger. He showed her where Leipzig was located in relation to the French border so that she would know in what direction to go when she escaped. And then, before anyone could see it, they swept the floor with their hands.

Hélène told me that there was nothing between her and Fritz, nothing "like that." She went on, "One couldn't feel anything like that at that time. It wasn't possible. Still, I felt grateful to him. He was a good man in a bad position."[19]

———— ❦ ————

On August 4, 1944, 1,200 Polish Jewish women arrived in Leipzig. These prisoners were selected for forced labor instead of outright extermination because the Nazis were desperately in need of workers. The women were not a homogeneous group; some came from the Warsaw ghetto, some were from the Majdanek camp, and another

large group came from small shtetls in the countryside. Later a small
group arrived from Auschwitz, and that December they were joined
by a group of Hungarian Jews. The Jewish prisoners were given the
worst rations, worst living conditions, and the hardest jobs. They were
already the most traumatized group, having suffered pogroms, witnessed mass murders, and narrowly escaped the gas chambers. All
of them had probably seen their loved ones die, and they may or may
not have counted themselves lucky to be alive.

The French prisoners reached out to the Jewish prisoners, especially since several of them arrived in Leipzig with daughters between
the ages of six and thirteen. The French invited the young girls to their
block, where they fed them from their hidden stores of food, including
some prized chocolate. They played with them and pampered them.
The mothers were moved by this kindness. Some of the French women,
like Josée, had been arrested for hiding Jewish children. Others had
gotten involved in the Résistance to help Jewish families escape. Some
of the French prisoners were Jewish and had managed to keep this
hidden from the Nazis. There were good relations between these two
groups, even though it was difficult for them to communicate. Hélène,
who spoke English, German, Russian, and Polish as well as French,
often acted as go-between and information gatherer.

Commandant Plaul worked to maintain the national, racial, and
cultural divisions in Leipzig, but at times the women were able to
transcend them. The prisoners organized small acts of resistance.
On November 11, 1944, they had a complete work stoppage for a few
minutes—a moment of silence in remembrance of the fallen from
the Great War. Besides Hélène's sabotage of the thermostats, different parts of the factory organized other forms of sabotage. They
would not leave the shells in the acid baths long enough; they sent
letters through the local civilians; they sang "La Marseillaise" and
other militant songs. There was a quota system in Leipzig. If the prisoners surpassed their quota, they were rewarded with coupons. The
coupons could be exchanged for items in the canteen, such as a can
of sardines, bread, cigarettes, toothbrushes, or combs. But the French
prisoners refused to participate in this system of rewards, saying they
would do only the minimum required and even less when possible.

Many of the women remembered with pride the folk celebration

they organized for St. Catherine's Day on November 25, when unmarried girls would traditionally wear fancy hats and dance through
the streets of their villages. In the years before the war, St. Catherine's Day was celebrated less and less except in the fashion world of
Paris, where hat makers and haute couture dressmakers used the
tradition to show off their prowess. Some women in the barracks
who had been seamstresses in haute couture in Paris before the war
took charge. For many weeks leading up to the day, the French were
busy in their spare hours creating hats. The married women helped
the unmarried, and the hats they were able to make out of nothing
were astonishing. Lon wrote, "It is unbelievable how inventive the
French girls were to create without any means—a bit of straw from a
mattress, some rags and bits of paper, a toothbrush or an accidentally
found piece of wire or wood, in short anything they could lay hands
on—the most beautiful hats, bonnets, and intricate hairdos."[20] There
were hats of every shape and color, featuring feathers, flowers made
of paper, ribbons, bits of chain, broken glass, paper birds. It was a
glorious moment. Mena would remember with amazement the mag-
nificent things they were able to make out of scavenged scraps, and
how this act of solidarity, among others, kept her going.[21]

Mena had a romantic turban with paper grapes on the side. Josée
had a tall Spanish comb adorned with black lace. There was a hat that
held a cage with a white bird inside. Another woman had a cardboard
Eiffel Tower on her head. The celebrations began in the French block
but spilled into the other barracks. The women in the hats sang songs
and danced the farandole as they snaked through the blocks, singing
and dancing. They visited the Ukrainians, the Russians, the Poles,
the Jews, and even the sick in the *Revier*. Everyone wanted to see what
the French had made. Even the guards and *blockovas* were impressed
by the creations; they clapped along and allowed the celebration to
last through the night. The next day the women were exhausted, but
it didn't matter, because they had remembered that they were still
alive and capable of more than just drudgery.

The political prisoners used the camp's different national and
ethnic holidays to strengthen and create bonds. Together they celebrated the birthdays of their missing children. The French prisoners each "adopted" an orphaned Jewish child—a child under sixteen

(some as young as nine) who was trying to pass as older. The women
would save food for their adopted child and make them gifts. They
helped the Jewish women when they were fasting for Yom Kippur.

——◆——

Throughout the fall of 1944 the Leipzig factory was shelled by the
Allies. By September the radio that the Germans had installed in the
factory to broadcast at noon each day on loudspeakers the glorious
victories of the Wehrmacht suddenly went silent. The women knew
this was because Germany was now losing the war.

The last two members of their group of nine arrived on a late
transport in September. Nicole, with her freckles and striking green
eyes, had turned twenty-two the day before she was arrested by the
Gestapo. Nicole's intelligence and resolve made her an excellent agent
in the Résistance, and she had risen to a level of leadership that was
unusual for a woman her age at that time. When she was put onto the
very last transport of prisoners from Paris to Germany, Nicole, along
with Jacky, could hear the Allied bombing at the outskirts of the city.
Paris was only few days away from being liberated. She believed that
they'd be home by Christmas, and she convinced the others at the
camp of this. In the meantime, though, food grew scarcer, and the
brutality and pace of their work grew more vicious.

By the end of November, the field visible through the barbed-wire
fence on the other side of the road was covered in a blanket of snow.
On Sundays, German families from Leipzig would stroll by. With tod-
dlers holding their hands or pushing baby carriages, they would look
at the strange creatures on the other side of the fence: starved women
with zebra-striped rags on display inside their cage.

The wind bit with an arctic cold and the punishments increased in
cruelty. The daily roll call seemed endless. But the women felt an inner
force because they had decided they would be home for Christmas.
They counted the weeks and the days as if this were a fact, not a hope.

By mid-December, the days were short and dark. Roll calls happened
in darkness. December 1944 was viciously cold, one of the worst European winters on record. The wind was unyielding. It got through every
seam in their worn-out rags; it got through the cracks in the windows
and the cracks in the boards of the blocks. They tried to ignore their

frozen bodies and sleep, but the bitterly cold wind blew through their hearts. They heard that the German troops had rallied and taken the offensive; they were back in Alsace and back in the Ardennes. It was clear now that the women would not be home for Christmas.

Lise London, a fellow prisoner in their block, wrote that at this point many gave up and turned away from the others. This was deadly. The first sign was usually that a woman no longer washed herself or her clothes. The prisoners had formed a team of "social workers" who would intervene when this happened. They would remind the woman of her children or the other family members waiting for her back home. They said they understood she was too tired to wash her clothes, so they would do it for her. Sometimes a woman had grown mute and refused any help, and then the "social workers" would actually undress her by force and wash her clothes and bathe her. Lise writes that this act of solidarity and care almost always brought the despairing woman back to herself.[22]

When Lise and her group of "social workers" brought up the idea of a Christmas celebration, there was a near riot. They were shouted down.

"Don't talk to us about Christmas anymore!"

"We want the day to just pass by without thinking of it!"

"We're never getting out of here!"

"How could we celebrate when our brothers and husbands and fathers are dying in the Ardennes?"

But the young ones in the block, including the nine friends, agreed: "We will celebrate Christmas because it will be our last Christmas here, and in the spring we shall be free."

Each night after their twelve hours of work and their long, freezing roll calls, even though their bodies ached and their stomachs cried for food, they would wait for the guards to head back to their sleeping quarters, and then the women would tiptoe to different parts of the building to rehearse. One group was preparing a choral piece, another a play, and another a dance recital.

The talk now was about their Christmas party and their preparations. The block was animated despite the cold, the hunger, and the snow that would cover them during every roll call. They worked on creating gifts out of the scraps they could scavenge. They wanted to bring something back to their families when, finally, they were free of this place. Lon made a booklet, *Gems of Wisdom and Beauty*, for her brother, Eric. Mena sewed a small stuffed teddy bear for Zinka's child. Zinka and Zaza, using small pieces of sacking torn from their thin mattresses, some thread, and paper, wove cigarette cases for their husbands. Nicole and Guigui wrote poetry. They made belts and little pouches or booklets of poems so that on Christmas Day they had something to give each other.

In the brutal cold of January 1945, a group of women on a death march from Auschwitz staggered into the camp. In the confusion and chaos of their arrival, the French prisoners from Hélène's block managed to save a few by ripping off their yellow stars and hiding them in the French block. Each gave a portion of her already small rations to feed these hidden women. The arrivals confirmed the rumors they had heard about the gas chambers. The French women learned from them about the frantic German evacuation of Auschwitz and the harrowing death march that followed. This knowledge helped them prepare for their own death march a few months later.

Clandestine photograph of prisoners
marching to Dachau

In early April, as Hélène and Fritz were sitting in the basement shelter during another bombardment, pretending not to speak to each other, Fritz whispered, "Here, take this." From beneath his coat he pulled out a bundle wrapped in cloth. Without looking at it, Hélène slipped it into the large pocket she'd made inside her uniform. Whatever it was felt heavy and important.

"I couldn't get the documents," he said softly. Fritz had said he would try to get her false papers. She had asked for papers for Zaza too. But they both knew it was a long shot. "It was impossible."

"We'll just have to do without," she replied.

She felt him turning to face her, and he said, "I am leaving tomorrow."

"To join your wife?" she asked. She felt a lump in her throat. He was saying goodbye.

He nodded and, drawing a map in the dirt, showed her the location of his village and repeated the name to her. Then, brushing away the outlines, he whispered urgently, "You must get away from here. Soon. It's going to get worse."

At last they were looking directly at each other. She wanted to say something to him, but she was never good at openly showing her feelings.

"After this is all over," he said slowly, the words catching in his throat, "please let me know that you are safe."

"I will," she promised.

Later, unwrapping the bundle, Hélène discovered that Fritz's final gift to her was a pair of wire cutters.

Nearing the end of the war, between January and May 1945, as the German army was collapsing, the SS used their diminishing resources to empty the camps ahead of the oncoming armies. They burned documents to destroy paper evidence of their crimes. Hitler ordered that no prisoner should fall into enemy hands alive; they should be "liquidated" or evacuated. The SS executed as many prisoners as possible, leaving piles of corpses as brutal evidence. And they forced the remaining prisoners on death marches, at first often to other death camps farther into the interior of Germany, and then by the end with no clear destination.

Himmler, recognizing defeat was near, tried to negotiate a way out.

He had begun to take stock of valuable hostages—people of importance, like Geneviève de Gaulle, who was still in Ravensbrück. For a period in February 1945 she was held in isolation in a cell bunker, in what might be called protective custody. Himmler claimed they could use the remaining labor force to rebuild the great Nazi army, but he probably hoped that the prisoners would be useful as currency or collateral. In any case, it is hard to make sense of the shuttling of prisoners from one camp to another. Why force-march thousands of prisoners from Auschwitz to Ravensbrück just to exterminate them upon arrival?

The routes of the various death marches crisscrossed Germany in final, hysterical death throes. Records were carefully collated after the war, based on eyewitness testimony, in an attempt to document each march with a map, a list of towns passed, and the number of kilometers traveled each day, along with the number of dead and living at each step; they come with margin notes such as "Burned alive in a barn in Gardelegen," "10 executed in field by machine gun," and "Mass grave said to be near here." An estimated 250,000 of the 714,000 survivors in the camps at the beginning of 1945 would die during the forced evacuations, between January and May, in the snow, in the cold, in the rain, without food, without shelter, without shoes or proper clothes.[23] After years of imprisonment on starvation rations, suffering from illness, they died of pure exhaustion.[24] If they fell or were no longer able to walk, they were shot.

———————

On April 10 and 11, the HASAG Leipzig factory was critically damaged in an Allied bombardment. Some prisoners died, and their bodies remained under the rubble. The camp was chaotic, with virtually no food distribution. The women saw the growing alarm in their SS guards as the Allies advanced on all sides. It was rumored that the entire camp and factory complex was ringed with explosives. The plan was to blow it up with all the evidence and bodies that remained there.

Administratively, since June 1944 the Leipzig *Kommando* had been a subcamp of Buchenwald, roughly 120 kilometers to the southwest. On April 11, the prisoners in Buchenwald turned against the heavily armed SS in the guard towers, and at 3:15 PM they liberated themselves. Soon after, two French soldiers working with the US 4th Armored Division, Lieutenant Emmanuel Desard and Sergeant Paul Bodot, entered the Buchenwald camp. They reported back to the US Army about the exact location of the camp.

Some of the newly freed prisoners armed themselves and marched out of the gates, where they ran into two Jewish American soldiers, Egon W. Fleck and Edward A. Tenenbaum, in an army jeep. The two later wrote: "We turned a corner onto a main highway and saw thousands of ragged, hungry-looking men, marching in orderly formation, marching East . . . They laughed and waved."[25]

News of the liberation at Buchenwald reached Plaul at Leipzig. He along with the other SS commanders scrambled to hide any evidence of war crimes. They attempted to burn critical documents, though one brave prisoner, Odette Pilpoul, was able to save incriminating evidence from the fires.

On the night of April 13, the camp's 5,000 women were ordered to assemble outside. It was cold, with a slight drizzle of freezing rain. The atmosphere was charged with anxiety and confusion. The women clung to small bundles of their few cherished possessions. There was a frenzied distribution of food: a few slices of bread, a tablespoon of margarine, and four tablespoons of rancid meat paste. This was more than their normal starvation rations, but they did not know this would be the last food they would receive. The women were also given pamphlets about the *Panzerfaust* to use as toilet paper.[26] The nine tried to huddle together. "We mustn't be separated," Lon said to the others.

At two in the morning on April 14, 1945, the women were marched out of the camp gates heading east, though the actual destination was vague. As Zaza described it, the women were "like ants surprised by the destruction of their nest."[27] Five thousand women were divided into groups of 1,000, and then into blocks of 100 in rows of five across. They moved in starts and stops as the columns were being formed; sometimes they were forced to walk backward, sometimes they had to jog, and occasionally they were abruptly ordered to halt. As their eyes adjusted to the dark, they saw stars shining above. They passed a sign for Dresden.

That first night under the stars, Zaza felt a certain sense of release.

They had successfully stayed together as a group. The end of the war had to be near. The Germans would soon be defeated. They just had to hold on a little longer.

At first their muscles were stiff. They had waited in the cold for so long to get started. Some of them, like Josée, had been working the night shift. Forced to carry wheelbarrows of documents to a bonfire, she had not slept for almost two days. But gradually the march found a good pace. There was a gentle breeze and the air was fresh.

Trying to relieve themselves was almost impossible, however, because any prisoner who stepped out of line would be shot. They bided their time, waiting for a moment when the column halted, hoping that the guard might be distracted. That would be their chance. Then they would quickly undo the belt holding up their work pants and crouch where they stood as their friends kept a lookout.

At dawn the wind picked up. It was cold, and the women marched with thin blankets hooded over their heads. Zaza didn't see the shadow of the guards' uniforms as they herded and shoved the women, nor did she hear their hostile cries or the sound of the machine gun firing in the distance. She walked as if in a dream, leading the group in singing at the top of their lungs the old songs from her youth hostel camping days, when she would hike with René, her husband, by her side. She was happy that the nine of them had managed to keep their little group together.[28]

Walking next to Zaza were brave Zinka; the two Dutch friends, bossy Lon and serene Guigui; and whimsical Mena. Behind Zaza, Hélène walked in a line with the beautiful Josée, with Jacky, who was struggling to breathe, and with Nicole, who had arrived with Jacky in September. Nicole could barely walk; she was suffering from pneumonia. Even so, her friends had pushed her to leave the *Revier*. If the whole camp was set to explode, anyone left behind would be killed.

Their section of a hundred women was guarded by two SS guards with guns and one female guard who carried a whip. The male guard, known to all as "the little bastard," had slapped Nicole several times in the face at the start of the march because in her feverish daze she had stumbled out of line. The other male guard was seen as "kind" because he tried to give them information about what was happening, as much as he knew, and he encouraged the women to continue.

On that first day, the female guard tucked her whip into her belt and picked a flowering branch. The women saw this as a hopeful sign. It was springtime and the sun was warm. They passed the occasional tree in bloom and smelled the green grass pushing out of the recently thawed fields of the flat countryside.

As the sun rose higher, they saw Germans on the road as well. They were in crowded trucks; or pushing overloaded bicycles, wagons loaded with barrels, or handcarts piled with their belongings; or carrying bundles. Women pulled along children; old men's faces showed tired and anxious expressions. Having lived through the 1940 German invasion of Paris and the spectacle of the roads of France as people fled, the French prisoners recognized the signs. The Germans were in flight; their war was lost.

German villagers came out to see the parade of starved, desperate women in their tattered blue-and-gray-striped prison rags and wooden clogs, feet bleeding from sores, limping, collapsing in exhaustion, holding one another up, bearing the marks of beatings and deprivation. As they marched past, Nicole saw one old lady cover her face and say, "This will be our eternal shame."[29]

They walked for close to twelve hours to the outskirts of the little village of Wurzen. There they stopped in a field already occupied by a large group of male prisoners on their own death march; they were sleeping in piled heaps of rags. The women collapsed together in a circle on the ground. They were awakened only two hours later by heavy Allied bombardment. The ground shook. Dirt and pebbles flew through the air. Their group, exhausted by the previous day and the lack of food, put their bundles on their heads and tried to rest, while others panicked and darted in all directions. The dark, cold night was filled with screams, cries, and chaos. At one point there was strafing, and bullets tore a hole in Josée's backpack, lying only a few feet away from her. Josée was shaken; those bullets had come so close to her. The others had to calm her down.

Suddenly they heard the familiar sound of orders being barked in German. The guards began swinging their whips. The women were ordered to rise and continue the march. The column of 5,000 had now doubled, joined by the male prisoners from the field.

At first they were happy to be moving again. Zaza reminded Zinka of a question she had asked a few weeks earlier back in Leipzig: "Do you remember, Zinka, when you wondered if you would be scared if you were a soldier?"

Zinka and Zaza had been washing in the block when the air-raid siren went off. The women around them rushed to get to the shelter. But Zinka was in no hurry, and Zaza stayed with her, even though she wanted to bolt. Zinka paused as they heard and felt the first concussion, a bomb landing somewhere down the road.

"Do you think you'd be scared?" Zinka had asked calmly, absolutely unafraid, "if you were a soldier being shot at?"

Zaza had laughed and said, "I know you wouldn't be!"

Now that they had been strafed like real soldiers, she asked Zinka if she was scared. Zinka smiled, showing the gap in her teeth, and shrugged. "I'm not sure if I feel anything anymore," she said. The sound of her voice was so sad, a strange juxtaposition with the smile on her face.

They had to pass through the village of Wurzen, pressed close to the walls of the buildings to avoid being shot at from the air. They passed two dead Germans in the street, red blood smeared and pooled in their blond hair.

The women walked through the day and into the night. At 3:00 AM, Hélène approached the kind guard to get more information, but he had none. He was exhausted too. The only thing to do was to keep going, he told her.

Zaza would call it "the night of the stars"; it was the worst night of the march. The weather had turned frigid. They trudged through a dusting of snow, freezing in their thin clothes and light coats, which had been painted with white X's to mark them as prisoners should they try to escape. Their bodies ached everywhere. Their feet bled. The route was littered with the corpses of prisoners who had died from exhaustion or had been shot in the head for falling out of line. They passed the bleeding, the suffering, and the dying. They passed corpses that looked like skeletons. They passed corpses whose eyes looked up at the stars with a dreadful frozen gaze. Zaza saw snow collecting on the face of a dead woman like a shroud. They continued marching, sometimes holding one another up, because to fall meant certain death.

Lon said aloud, "We are on trial," not completely understanding her own words, but sensing this was the ultimate test of her will to live.[30]

At one point, Hélène with a nod of her head indicated to Zaza that they should make a run for it now, but Zaza refused. She was too tired.

With nothing to eat or drink since leaving Leipzig more than twenty-four hours earlier, they began to hallucinate.

"Please tell me if there really is a man sitting over there on that wall reading a newspaper," Hélène asked. She did not say out loud that the man looked just like her dead grandfather.

"It's all in your head," Lon answered. "Think. His paper would be drenched in this rain and snow."

Zaza was sure she saw the spires of a cathedral, but Zinka informed her, "No, it's just tall trees."

A little while later Josée veered away from their row. She was certain she was walking home from her job in Marseille. She saw her apartment lights. Her door was right over there. She was sure of it. Mena frantically pulled her back.

"Let me go home!" Josée wailed. "Let me go, please! I just want to go home!" But she was too tired to really fight. Mena and Jacky held her in place until she recovered herself, sobbing as she came back to the dreadful reality of their situation.

They slogged on like this for twenty-eight hours until they arrived at the outskirts of Oschatz, sixty kilometers to the east of Leipzig. In the twilight, they saw a group of male prisoners being herded by the SS. They could hear screams and gunshots. Suddenly they were being forced to march over heaps of recently shot male prisoners. The dogs and SS made sure they could not avoid the corpses. Their feet stumbled over the terrain of bleeding, dying bodies.

They entered a field surrounded by barbed wire. There at last they were allowed to rest. In the distance was a smoking chimney that some of the other prisoners whispered was a crematorium, but Zinka admonished them: "Stop these rumors. It's only the chimney of a house."

CHAPTER THREE

— NICOLE —

Nicole Clarence

ON THE MORNING OF APRIL 15, 1945, 8,000 to 10,000 concentration camp prisoners, men and women from several camps, lay in heaps in the fields just outside Oschatz trying to rest. They were surrounded by armed SS guards. The townspeople had now witnessed a few days of this gruesome parade of prisoners, and they could hear the cannons of the advancing Red Army. They cut down trees to block the Russian tanks from entering their town. They were in a high state of alarm, fearing that between the hordes of starving prisoners and the frenzied Russian troops they would be attacked or murdered and their town pillaged. The German guards sensed the hostility of the villagers, and this added to their growing sense of panic. Outnumbered, the guards turned to extreme brutality to keep the situation under control.

By now it was clear to everyone that there would be no more

distributions of food or water. There was no way the German guards could feed the prisoners. They understood by the look of fear on the guards' faces that there wasn't even a plan. The women were so tired, so cold, so hungry and thirsty, they had simply collapsed on the ground, curled close together to share their warmth. They dozed and shivered like this for a few hours. But no one slept. Every muscle ached. Their feet were rubbed raw and crusted in blood. Lon and Zaza rose in the dawn to search for water, leaning on each other to stay upright. But there was no water to be found anywhere.

Hélène whispered to Zaza, "Are you ready now? Will you run with me this time?"

Zaza wanted to ask the others. She wanted the whole group to run together. But as both Zaza and Lon recalled later, this was the turning point in their ordeal. It was now or never.

Hélène was unrelenting: "We have to do something. We can't continue like this."

The others moaned. Could she please just let them rest in peace? But Hélène insisted. She wanted to know who was willing to risk escape to save their lives.

Lon was the first to join Hélène. "One thing is sure," Lon said with her singing Dutch accent, "I'd like to die by machine-gun fire if they'd just hurry up and do it. But I really don't want to die slowly over fifteen days, or however long it takes to starve to death. Not another night like the last one. I agree we have to save ourselves."

Hélène persisted. "Decide now. Are you with us? Or should we go without you?"

Slowly the women pulled themselves up to sit in a circle where they could see one another. Zaza looked at her good friend. Hélène had been trying for months to convince her to escape, but each time Zaza had hesitated. There was always some reason not to go. What about their other friends? What about the preparations for Christmas? What about the rumor that the camp was about to be liberated? But here they were, finally, at the end of the line. Hélène was right: their choice was to escape and live, or to stay and die.

Zaza said, "I want to live to see René again," the husband she had only just married. She thought of how he would rub her feet when they were sore after their long hikes; the memory caused tears to well in her eyes.

Guigui, the other Dutch girl, spoke next. She wouldn't let Lon go without her. She brushed her bangs out of her gray eyes and in her quiet voice said, "I want to live. I want to sit with my mother in a café in Leiden and have a real coffee with her. Also," she whispered, forcing a sly smile, "I've told you about that man, Timen, whom I met in Gestapo headquarters." The two of them had had only a few stolen moments in the antechamber of the torture rooms, but it had been enough. They had discovered that they were both Dutch, and in those few moments they had whispered in their own language while in the distance they could hear someone crying out in pain. They had tried to gather strength from each other. As she was being led away, she gave him her pocketful of carefully saved cigarette butts.

Zinka with her gap-toothed smile spoke up next. There was no way they would leave her behind. The only one of the nine who had a child, Zinka had been arrested while pregnant. She had given birth in Fresnes prison to a baby girl she named France. She had been allowed to keep her baby for eighteen days before the child was taken away. Zinka had vowed that one day she would return to find her daughter, and she was willing to try anything to get home. "I have to live so that my child has a mother," she said. There was a murmur of agreement; the others knew she had lost her own mother to the Spanish flu when she was just a little girl. They had celebrated baby France's one-year birthday in the camp. Mena had made a small stuffed animal for Zinka to give to her when they were reunited. And for the group of nine friends, getting back to the country France and the baby France would become symbolically one and the same. They simply had to "find our France."

Mena reached over and squeezed Zinka's hand. "You will," she whispered.

"And you?" Zinka asked, smiling brightly at Mena. "What do you want to live for?"

Mena laughed in her easy way. She always seemed to be moving through life as if it were a lark, as though her present circumstances were a strange twist of events that would somehow work out. Mena said, "Oh, it's simple, I will go visit *grand-mère* in Saint-Jacut-de-la-Mer, on the coast of Brittany, the most beautiful spot on earth. I will sit with her and look out at the ocean from her kitchen window. And you will all come and visit me there for a seaside vacation."

For a moment Zaza could almost smell the sea and hear the gulls screeching overhead. "That is going to be wonderful," she agreed.

They turned to Josée, who was leaning her head against Mena's shoulder. She was the youngest, and they felt protective of her. They thought of her as innocent; they didn't know that Josée was haunted by the memory of the little group of Jewish children she had been helping to keep hidden in France. When Josée was arrested, she had been carrying some parcels of food. They were labeled with names and addresses. . . . She shuddered; it was too much for her to dwell on. She closed her eyes and shook her head. The others thought it meant she didn't want to go with them.

"You have to come with us," Zinka insisted. "Who will sing to us along the way? Come on, Josée, tell us what you have to live for."

"Yes, come on," Zaza chimed in. "You can't give up. We won't let you."

"I'm not giving up," she said.

"So?" Zinka urged. "Tell us what you will live for."

The last year had reduced Josée's life to mere survival from one day to the next. What would it mean to live *for* something? She had been playing at living before; if she survived, she wanted to really live. She wouldn't end up like her mother, a poor housewife trapped with a violent husband. She wanted to do something with her life. Now that she knew what she was capable of, she had courage. "I want to become a pilot and fly above everything," she announced, holding her chin high.

They nodded; that sounded like Josée. "You won't drop bombs on us, will you?" Zinka asked, tongue in cheek.

"No," she said. "I will take you up with me and we can see everything from high up above."

"Ach, I don't need to fly in the clouds," Jacky said gruffly. "Before I cast my last anchor, I want to walk down my street in Paris. I want to visit the little park nearby where the old grandpa feeds his pigeons." Jacky was seriously ill, and she gasped for breath between words. "If you'll have me, I'm in."

"Of course we'll have you," Guigui said.

"I don't want to slow you down."

"We stick together," Lon agreed.

Next it was Nicole's turn. Her face was flushed with fever. She was

known in Leipzig for reciting detailed recipes as if they were poems;
she entertained them with stories of feasts in the few minutes before
sleep as they picked out the lice infesting their clothes and hair. Now
she shrugged. "Isn't it obvious?" she asked. She wanted to eat a wonderful meal, a long one, with many courses, and a good Camembert,
with a good red wine from Burgundy.

Hélène wanted to see her family. "And," she added loudly, "I will
survive just to see these Nazi scum in defeat."

Lon spoke last, as if to summarize their decision. "If I die now or
tomorrow, no one will care. Sure, my family, my mother and father, a
few friends, but soon I will be forgotten. I haven't left a trace on this
earth. What have we left behind us if we give up now?"

The nine women decided they would live, and to do that they must
escape together. It was clear that the Germans guarding them were
frightened. A few guards had fainted from exhaustion. The Polish
prisoners, who tended to have better information, told Hélène that
the plan was to march them to death, since there was no longer any
food and at Leipzig they had no gas chambers or efficient ways to
execute them en masse. Other rumors had them being marched to
a death camp or set free in the middle of the countryside to fend for
themselves. The thought of 10,000 starving, crazed people swarming
the countryside was not a good one either.

In fact, the end for many would unfold over the next few weeks in
horrific scenes along the roads in Germany. Many of the women who
remained in the columns were slaughtered in a field by machine gun on
April 17. Many, many others died from starvation or dysentery. The SS
overlords soon fled, leaving the women with the lower-ranking guards,
who behaved viciously. If German citizens left pails of water along the
road for the prisoners, the guards kicked them over. If they were given
food, the guards ate first and then threw the remains in the mud, entertaining themselves with the spectacle of women wrestling for the scraps.
They walked for weeks without food. Some escaped. The large group was
broken down into smaller groups. The locals stared at the pitiable sight
of the marching women. Children laughed at them, while the adults
shrugged and said, "They're only Jews."

The Germans kept changing directions in an effort to avoid the

Russians, who terrified them. The German farmers were also fleeing, and some had written hostile slogans on the walls of their towns: "The Jews were our misfortune." From time to time American planes flew overhead, and the guards would try to conceal themselves among the women, some even going so far as to put on striped clothes taken from the dead along the way.

In April 1945 there were thousands of prisoners from camps all over Germany being marched on the roads. This led to surreal scenes. A Polish Jew from Leipzig, Romualda Stramik, recalled, "We moved like sleepwalkers. . . . In the first light I saw a young man lying in a ditch and a woman kneeling beside him and staring at him helplessly. Suddenly she let out a shriek: 'Is that you, my son?' The man raised his head and called: 'Mama!' and fell back again. I heard two shots. I got back in line and crawled along with the rest of the women."[1]

———— ❧ ————

Because the guards were exhausted and careless, some of the nine were able to take advantage of this moment to move around to the various clusters huddled on the ground to gather information.

Lon wandered from group to group among the male prisoners looking for news of her brother, Eric, who had been arrested with her. She was happy to report back to the group that one man said he thought he might have seen him in Nuremberg. This turned out not to be true, but the tidbit buoyed Lon with hope.

Hélène made a trade for a civilian dress with a group of Polish prisoners; it would prove vital in the following days. Zaza later described the dress in her book with her usual sly humor: "A simple and practical dress, just what you all want, ladies, to do your morning shopping."[2]

While the others were away, Guigui ran into trouble standing guard over their meager possessions. She caught a woman trying to steal Zaza's blanket. She cried out and chased after the woman, who turned on her and stabbed her in the thigh with something blunt. The woman called over her friends, while Guigui's yells roused Zinka to her side. A real brawl broke out. Somehow Guigui and Zinka were able to fight off the other women. But now Guigui had a large swollen bruise on her thigh.

"I'm happy we saved your blanket," she said with a grimace when recounting the fight to Zaza, "but I don't know how I am going to walk today. Well, maybe that will change things, and I won't notice the blisters all over my feet as much."

The Polish women told Hélène and Lon that they were surrounded by the Russians on one side and the Americans on the other. The nine did not want to be captured by the Russians, who were infamous for their brutality; "they will rape even a skeleton," it was said. They had to find the Americans.

They decided that the best time for their escape would be the middle of the night. They knew from their night shifts in the factory that everyone gets tired around 2:00 AM, and the German guards, who were not used to this kind of physical exertion, would be at their most inattentive then. Lon declared, "We get shot in the back, or we make it—either way we will live or die together."

When the order was given to restart the march, they slowly pulled themselves upright, back into the ranks. Every muscle in Zaza's body ached and her feet burned, but it didn't matter, she told herself. This ordeal wouldn't last forever. Whatever happened, this would be their last night in captivity.

The row in front of Zaza had changed. Now there were five Russian women so strangely dressed that they looked like old witches out of some terrifying fairy tale. They had fabricated bizarre pointed hats and capes out of black curtains taken from the Leipzig factory. They limped and hobbled like creatures from the underworld. Zaza thought wryly that the chilling sight of those women was further motivation to escape.

The nine planned to wait until nightfall, but as the column left Oschatz, it was poorly organized. The march was slow and stopped from time to time, like a bad traffic jam. Parts of the column became more dispersed and other parts were jammed up. The guards were screaming and whipping, but with less energy, it seemed. And that's when the nine saw their chance: a moment in the early morning chaos when a few women were able to steal rape flowers to eat without being shot. As Nicole said later: "In no time we made our decision. We would take our chances. And our luck was that we were young, and there were nine of us."[3]

Female prisoners in Ravensbrück with painted
X's showing selection for transport

After they had managed to slip into the ditch, after they had collapsed in the field of yellow rape flowers, laughing and gasping in their newly found freedom, Hélène was the first to recognize they couldn't linger. "We need to get organized. And we can't stay here."

They spent a moment transforming themselves. They tore off the red triangles and numbers sewn on their coats, which marked them as political prisoners. They kept these, however, in case they needed proof of their identities later. They tried putting on their clothes inside out to hide the stripes. They opened the bundles and spread their things out, sharing with one another what they had managed to bring. "We need to take an inventory," Hélène said.

Among them, they had a box of matches; a small flask of acetone, which they hoped they could use to remove the white X's on their coats marking them as prisoners (this would prove impossible); the large wire cutters that Fritz had given Hélène months earlier; a needle and thread Zaza had stolen when they were first selected in Ravensbrück; a nail file; a small mirror; Hélène's newly procured civilian dress; a small ceramic brooch of a horse that had somehow miraculously escaped all the searches and had become the group's mascot; 110 German marks; a comb; a brush; a deck of cards; an onion; the small stuffed dog that Mena had made for France's first birthday; and a can of sardines, another gift to Zaza from the Polish prisoners in gratitude for her resemblance to their beloved Ianka.

They decided that their goal was to cross the shifting front lines of the war now raging all around them and find the American troops. But their immediate concern was food. They hadn't eaten in days. They also needed to get somewhere they could hide and rest. It wasn't safe to be out in broad daylight. From Fritz's map drawn in the dirt of the bomb shelter, Hélène had some idea of where they were and that they should head southwest. But for a moment no one wanted to budge. They were completely exhausted.

"I can't," Nicole said. Nicole, who had never lost hope, had simply come to the end of her strength. Seriously ill with pneumonia, she had been in the *Revier* a day before the start of the march along with her dearest friend, Renée Astier de Villatte, with whom she shared her slender bunk. It was Renée who insisted that Nicole get out of the *Revier*, because Renée was sure the rumors were true: the Germans had ringed the factory with explosives and the whole place would be blown up before the Allies arrived. Renée herself was much too sick to leave. Years later, Nicole remembered the note Renée wrote to her, like a mother to her child, urging her, even scolding her to get out of bed and go, to save herself. Nicole's heart ached to leave her behind, and she feared the worst for Renée. Nicole wrote years later, "Having long feared we'd be separated, luck had made it so that we were together in all the transports and selections, because one without the other we would have been lost."[4]

The last two days of almost ceaseless trudging had taken everything out of Nicole. She had managed to slip out of the ranks with the others at the initial moment of escape, but as soon as it was done, she felt her will to live simply drain out of her. Her heart was broken for Renée. Sick and delirious, she didn't care anymore what happened to her.

"But we must move," Hélène insisted. Nicole heard the words like a distant, vague humming.

"Come on," Mena said. "We'll find some lovely place to rest. Someplace we can be safe from everything." Mena was just weaving her fantasies. There would be no safe place; Nicole was sure of it.

Nicole refused. "No. Just leave me here. Please. I can't go on."

The other women were slowly getting to their feet. Zinka was already standing and helping pull Jacky up. Then Jacky turned and said to Nicole, "If you drop here, you understand you're just waiting for an Ivan to jab you with his short arm or a Fritz to put a bullet in your head."

"Leave me in peace." Nicole felt herself drifting gently to sleep. At least she had gotten this: she would die in a field of yellow rape flowers, not miserably in the muddy filth of the camps.

Josée, who had been next to Nicole in the ditch, slapped her in the face. "Come on, Nic, get up!"

The sting on her cheek shook Nicole out of her dream state. Then Mena reached down, grabbed her roughly, and pulled her to her feet, slapping her as well. "Come on! Enough of that!"

Nicole, stunned to be upright, looked around at her compatriots.

"See? I can be just as stubborn as you," Josée said. In the camp, Josée had always looked up to Nicole; she respected her willpower and stubborn hopefulness, the way Nicole told everyone over and over, "We've liberated Paris! Soon we'll have these *boches* beat!" So it had felt strange to slap Nicole, the woman Josée so admired, and immediately she wanted to apologize.

Lon laughed. "We're all stubborn. That's why we're still alive!"

"We don't leave anyone behind," Mena insisted. "We shall live and die together. That's how this story goes."

"Come on," Hélène said. "We need to find a small village, a barn, somewhere to rest. There's something that way." She pointed to a clump of trees and houses far in the distance. "Maybe there will be someone who can give us advice about where to find the Americans."

"See? Hélène thinks we'll find a barn to hide in," Josée said, to encourage Nicole. "We can rest there."

They moved slowly toward the village in the distance. They crossed open, rolling fields of yellow rape and early feed grass. There were no places to hide, and about an hour into their walk they realized they were going to cross paths with a small group of German soldiers. There was nothing to be done about it.

"Oh, Jesus, Joseph, and Maria," Josée said under her breath in Spanish, crossing herself.

"Stay calm," Hélène said evenly, but with the strength of a command. "As long as they're not SS we can pretend everything is normal."

"How many do you see?" Zaza asked. She had lost her glasses upon arrival in Ravensbrück when a SS guard had slapped her and knocked them off her face. Then he had stepped on them, grinding them with his heel into the dirt. She had been devastated by the loss.

But then only a week later a selection was made: all the women wearing glasses were sent directly to the crematorium. With no glasses, Zaza had been spared.

"Just three," Zinka said. "I could beat them up myself."

"Yes, you could," Guigui agreed, "with one of those clogs of yours."

The image of little Zinka in her big wooden clogs beating the German soldiers made the whole group chuckle.

"You laugh," Guigui continued, "but I saw her fighting those women trying to steal Zaza's blanket."

"I wouldn't ever dare to fight with you, Zinka," Mena concurred.

Despite their panic and fear, they decided to behave as if all were normal, to laugh and talk and pretend as they walked past the soldiers that nothing was amiss. Hélène and Lon called out greetings to the soldiers in passing, and the women waved as if they had nothing to hide.

It worked: the soldiers responded in kind and continued on their way.

They had discovered that if they acted like they belonged, then people might accept them as belonging. This became their central operational strategy.

On the outskirts of the little village, they found a farmhouse. In the yard in front of the house they met two French POWs. The women were excited, but they quickly realized that the POWs had very little useful information. The men appeared nervous to be talking with the women, always looking behind them. But they lingered, seeming to enjoy speaking French at last.

While they were talking, a young girl and her younger brother came out of the farmhouse. The girl was beating the boy with a stick and shouting orders: "Schnell! Rechts! Links!"

It was exactly as the SS *Aufseherinnen* had done to them in the camps. The women stood horrified at the sight. Zaza whispered to Zinka, "Even the children behave as brutes?"

In the midst of this disturbing scene, a large German man burst out of the barn next to the house. The POWs whispered, "The *Bürgermeister*," and quickly darted away, clearly terrified to be seen by this man. Barrel-chested and bald, with a large reddened nose and a double chin, he was dressed in velour, his chest covered with party badges and medals. He wore impressively large boots.

"I am the mayor here! What are you doing in my village?" he shouted at the women.

It took all of her courage for Hélène to speak up firmly while smiling and explain that they were *Gastarbeiter*, guest workers. Their factory was closed because it had been bombed, and so now they were on their way home.

"Where's home?" he shouted.

When Hélène answered, "France," he exploded into a rage, his ruddy face deepening to a dark purple.

"What? You are not Germans? Then what are you doing on my streets? Foreigners are forbidden here! You belong in a camp. There's a camp in Naundorf. You shall be sent there at once!"

The women watched in horror as he shouted, spittle flying from his mouth. Those who didn't speak German didn't understand exactly what he was saying, but being screamed at by an irate German man was so familiar. This had been their life for the past many months. By habit they froze, as if during roll call back in the camp—arms at their sides, heads down, not making eye contact. They had learned to efface themselves in front of such rage.

He told the little girl to go get her mother to call the police in Oschatz, so they would come at once and get these vagrants, "these French . . ." He paused with disdain before spitting out the last word: "Women." Hélène knew he had wanted to say "whores," but perhaps the presence of the children had moderated his speech.

This was the worst possible thing to have happened, and so soon after they had escaped. Would it all end like this, so quickly?

But then the mayor, mysteriously, seemed to think that his job was done. Perhaps the timid manner that the women adopted made him think they would remain docilely standing there like lambs waiting for the slaughter, because he turned and strode away.

At that point Nicole came back to life. Having tasted freedom, she would not die in captivity. She hissed at the others, "Now!" Without another word they turned on their heels and moved as quickly as possible. At the outskirts of the village they came to a fork in the road, with one sign pointing to Naundorf and the other to Strehla.

Strehla, though due north, at that moment seemed like a paradise on earth compared to Naundorf with its camp. There was almost no discussion. They took the road to Strehla.

———◆———

Nicole Clarence was born on August 3, 1922, in Paris.[5] She learned she was an "Israelite" in grade school, around the time her parents took in two young Austrian Jews who needed refuge from the rising anti-Semitism in their country. To Nicole, these girls were much more Jewish than she was. She had only been to synagogue twice in her life. If she had sensed any social divide up to that point, it was a class divide. Her family was wealthy, bourgeois. Her childhood up to the age of ten was happy and protected. Originally from an Alsatian family, her father was a wool trader like his father. They lived in an elegant townhouse in Paris with a garden, where her mother, Lucie Thérèse, created a perfect home. She expected her daughter, Nicole, to follow the same trajectory. Nicole was never allowed to wear makeup. She wore gloves and curtsied when shaking hands. She was not encouraged to pursue her education.

Her mother was refined and aloof. She adored her own father, who was more polished than her husband. Nicole's maternal grandfather had married the daughter of an Austrian art dealer and had become the French agent for his father-in-law. He specialized in the importation of English Christmas cards, which were in vogue at the time.

But everything came crashing down in 1929, when Nicole's father, like so many others, saw his business dwindle to nothing following the disastrous financial crisis that shook the world. The pleasant bourgeois life that her mother had so carefully constructed was upended. Nicole was still young, but old enough to remember how family heirlooms were sold in a desperate rush to somehow fill the financial gap. But it was never enough. As the debts mounted, they had to let all the family servants go. They canceled the private tutors for the children. The villa in Normandy was repossessed by the bank. Their weekly purchases were kept to the strictest minimum, and they turned down the heat to save money. Her home, which had once been so cozy and warm, was empty, in disarray, and cold. And in this moment of loss and calamity both her mother and her brother, Miki, fell seriously ill. Miki needed surgery, but there was no money. Both mother and son were treated at home because they could not afford the hospital, and the treatment was substandard.

At eleven, Nicole watched this drama unfolding, but with the resilience of a child. She wasn't burdened by the changes the way the adults in her life were. She adapted. She learned to cook, to put up preserves, to make beds and wash sheets, and to change Miki's terrible putrid bandages. She had to attend the public lycée. But this was, in fact, a wonderful liberation for her. She loved being with other children her own age who were from different social classes. She walked many kilometers a day to save on the metro tickets, but she enjoyed this as well, experiencing it as freedom. These events, as traumatic as they were for her parents, were central in the development of Nicole's strong, independent character and would help her to survive later. She learned to be flexible, to see the positive side of things, to be resourceful and unafraid of change.

Meanwhile, Lucie Thérèse fell apart. She no longer put on the fashionable gowns. The beautiful moss-green dresses and the mink coats were sold or seized. Nicole's mother became obsessed with keeping her most valuable treasures from the bailiff. It was an endless round of unpaid bills, her mother's frantic efforts to camouflage and lie, followed by tears and headaches.

The marriage deteriorated. Nicole's father, Pierre, was humiliated and retreated into silence. Lucie Thérèse was forced to find work. There was an undercurrent in every exchange between them of blame and recrimination. Sometimes it exploded into shouting and even violence. Nicole longed to leave home.

Little by little, her father rebuilt his business. They were never again as affluent as before, but he was able to get out from under the crushing debt. Nicole and Miki were young adults at this point and starting to look outward. There was a lot going on: socialism, the Spanish Civil War, the Anschluss in Austria, the gathering storm of fascism in Germany.

In high school, Nicole grew into a beauty, with sharp, dazzling blue-green eyes and thick black curls. Even with modest resources she was able to dress elegantly. She was part of a group of four girlfriends, which included her cousin Claude; Claude's best friend, Claudine;

and a first cousin of Claude's named Micheline. They would often go to the cinema on the weekends. Later, both Micheline and Nicole would be deported, but only Nicole would return.

Nicole was about to turn eighteen when the Germans entered Paris in June 1940. Almost immediately her family headed for the free zone in the south. She didn't quite understand why. She had a dentist appointment and school; why leave in such a rush? she wondered. There had been talk, what her father had called "rumors," of gassing and pogroms. They had sheltered those two Austrian girls. But people didn't really believe it was all true. Often her mother would shush her father, saying, "Stop it, Pierre! We must not talk of such unpleasantness."

Nicole soon learned that their situation was serious. In Nice in 1941, Jews were forbidden from working. Her father was arrested. One of their neighbors had denounced him. Nicole realized they were surrounded by people they couldn't trust. Her father was sent to a transit camp, but they managed to get him out, and the family left immediately for Marseille. They were living under the constant danger of the *rafles*, the roundups. Nicole burned with indignation when she saw the word *juive* stamped on her ID card. Miki was almost snared in a random *rafle*. He had been walking down a street when he saw that both ends were suddenly blocked by French police checking ID cards. There was a truck parked where they were gathering up the young men who had *juif* on their cards. He was trapped. But just then a kind woman opened her door and rushed him inside. He escaped out the back of her apartment and climbed over the wall of the courtyard. Arriving home breathless, Miki told Nicole not to tell their parents. It would only upset them. She felt helpless, and she hated that feeling. She had to fight back somehow.

———◆———

Nicole joined the Éclaireurs de France, a Protestant version of the Scouts, as a troop leader. She knew about the Éclaireurs from her friend Claudine, who had been in the group in Paris before the war. This group of Scouts was very much aligned with the early Résistance. Nicole was asked by Mic Grapin, the head of the Éclaireurs, to gather information during her excursions along the coastline with her troop.

Grapin was recruiting members through the Éclaireurs to join the Alliance network, headed by the astonishing Marie-Madeleine Fourcade, one of the greatest Résistance leaders. In an interview from 1968 Fourcade appears polite, poised, the perfect bourgeois woman with her nice pillbox hat, pearls, and demure manner. I can see how the Gestapo was fooled by her appearance several times.

From early in the war, Fourcade, the mother of two children, was the head of the largest underground network in France, with more than 3,000 agents. She worked with MI6, MI9, and later the Special Operations Executive (SOE), the British agency formed to carry out espionage, sabotage, and reconnaissance activities in Axis-controlled Europe. For a long time she kept it a secret from the British that she was a woman. The Germans called her Alliance network "Noah's Ark" because of the animal nicknames she gave to her agents. She herself was known as "Hedgehog." She recruited heavily among civil servants and women. Fourcade would later say that she trusted her female agents more: they were more discreet, less apt to boast about their roles in the Résistance, and less likely to make terrible blunders with security, and she felt they did not break as easily under torture.

Alliance gathered information about German troop and naval movements and logistics inside France, and transmitted this intelligence to Britain, using a network of clandestine radios and couriers. It was extremely dangerous work; many of Fourcade's closest associates, including Léon Faye—known as "Eagle," who was her second-in-command, her lover, and the father of her child—were captured, tortured, and killed. During the war she became pregnant and gave birth even as she guided her huge network, moving constantly to stay ahead of the Germans and keeping her "condition" hidden from the British.

Alliance played a decisive role in the Battle of the Atlantic, providing precise information about German U-boat movements. Early in the war, England risked being entirely strangled by the Germans' blockade and control of the Atlantic. Alliance intelligence broke the German U-boat control. Fourcade's agents provided information on train operations, and they procured a detailed map of the Atlantic defenses, which proved essential for the D-Day landing. Perhaps one of their most important intelligence contributions was the discovery—by Alliance agent Jeannie Rousseau—of developments in the

V-1 and V-2 rocket programs and records of launch operations in northwestern France. With this intelligence the Allies were able to destroy the Peenemünde missile-testing base.

Marie-Madeleine Fourcade was a woman who gave orders to men, some of them military men, at a time when women still didn't have the right to vote. She was arrested twice, and twice she managed to escape. Her second escape was harrowing: In the small hours of the morning, she stripped naked. With her dress in her teeth and her body covered in sweat she was able with great struggle and pain to force her petite frame between the bars of the cell window.[6]

As Nicole led her troop of Scouts on hikes on the southern coast and through the Calanques, east of Marseille, she took notes of where the Germans had installed bunkers or military guard posts. She passed this information back to Grapin, who shared it with the Alliance network. When Grapin was arrested Nicole lost her sole contact to the Résistance. That had been her first experience of fighting back against the Germans, and she wanted more.

———— ❦ ————

Nicole's next chance came when her family moved to a small village in the Savoie region that was better suited for hiding and security. There they reunited with old family friends. Among them were Nicole's friend Claudine and her new husband, Gilles Arason. Nicole had attended their wedding in Lyon. Claudine knew that Gilles had a soft spot for Nicole. She could understand why: Nicole was charming and lively.

Gilles asked Nicole if she could hide a forbidden radio in her family's barn. The radio would allow them to get coded messages from London. Nicole was tasked with receiving and decoding the messages and delivering them to a person indicated by the message at a specific time and place. She became an *agent de liaison* between Annecy, Grenoble, and the Savoie.

The principal difficulty of being an *agent de liaison*—the person who carried messages between different networks or from London to the networks in France—came from the curfews, roadblocks, and constant verification of one's papers by the German and French police. The advantage Nicole had as a young girl was that she appeared innocent. A man would be required to prove why he wasn't working in Germany as part of the STO. This is why many of the *agents de liaison* were women: Nicole, Hélène, Zinka, Josée, Mena, and Jacky were all at one time or another *agents de liaison*. But this did not mean they did not get stopped often to have their papers checked. They had a freedom of movement men did not have, but they were also vulnerable; as pretty young girls out alone, they were preyed upon by the police and the Gestapo.

During a routine check of her papers in Grenoble while she was on a mission, Nicole was stopped by a young German working in the Sicherheitsdienst (SD), the intelligence agency for the SS and a sister organization of the Gestapo.[7] She was able to drop the matchbox that contained the message she was delivering into the drain by the side of the road before he took her to the office for questioning. It quickly became clear that he did not suspect her of being in the Résistance, but he did expect her to comply with his wishes.

I do not have the exact details of how Nicole was able to avoid being raped. In a private, unpublished account shared with me by her daughter, Nicole wrote that she spent an anguished night with him during which he tried many times to rape her. In her oral history interview she talks about the incident again as multiple attempts at rape and "the worst horrors," but she explains that her single-minded focus on her mission allowed her to get through the harrowing episode.

In the 1940s many assumptions were made about women that by today's standard we would not accept. For example, it was commonly understood that a young woman out alone at night was "asking for trouble." If she suffered unwanted attention, it was her fault. That was the risk Nicole and any young female *agent de liaison* were taking. A young woman who was raped might feel ashamed and so might remain silent. She would have no legal recourse, certainly not against a German police officer. Her power had to come from how she could manipulate the situation. The women in the group often admired one another for their beauty, for their ability to use their female charm on men, and for the game of playing innocent in order to get something past those in power. Nicole would have thought that her most powerful tool was her charm. It was a dangerous game, because of course in the end the women had no power. Men, like the soldier arresting Nicole, could take what they wanted with impunity.

I imagine Nicole appealed to the young German's sense of moral-ity, such as it was. She cynically called him her "guardian angel." And, feigning extreme innocence, she may have asked him questions about his sister and mother, his life back in Germany. She may have under-stood how lonely he was. She begged him to let her go, saying her parents would be sick with worry. She may have promised to return an-other day, to be his girlfriend. He finally released her in the early hours of the morning. But he had taken all her money—a considerable sum, since it was not hers but belonged to the network. He took her to the train station, to make sure she got on the train to Aix, but instead she stayed in town. She went immediately to find the discarded message. She had to search discreetly, since now the sun was rising and people were on their way to work. But eventually, with great relief, she found the matchbox and delivered her message successfully that same day.

This encounter with the brutality of the SS only reinforced her will to fight. She wanted to become even more engaged in the struggle.

———≈———

Her chance came in June 1943, when she met Eugène Claudius-Petit at a theater camp run by the Éclaireurs. An anarchist and a strong union supporter, Eugène was using the theater camp as a cover to re-cruit young men and women to the group he had co-founded, Franc-Tireur. Eugène spotted the young, ardent Nicole, and fifteen days later she was working under the nom de guerre "Annette" as an *agent de liaison* in Lyon, the center of the Résistance movement.

Not telling her parents the true nature of her new job, she left her mother and father in the remote Savoie region, saying she wanted to work and live independently. The war and the effects of the family's flight from persecution had so changed them that what would have been socially unacceptable to them a few years earlier was now al-lowed. When her mother came to visit Nicole in Lyon as a surprise and found that her daughter was not living at the address she had given them, Nicole had to tell her the truth. Soon her mother also joined the Résistance.

Franc-Tireur was one of the first groups to emerge after the defeat of the French in 1940. In addition to a clandestine newspaper with that name, they published pamphlets and printed false papers. Nicole

was exhilarated to be working so closely with a group of like-minded souls. But soon she would move even deeper into direct action.

Her mother's first cousin was Robert Lyon, the head of Acolyte, a part of the larger "Buckmaster network"—an array of French agents and organizations recruited by Maurice Buckmaster, head of the French section of the British SOE. Many of the French agents traveled secretly to England to get training and then parachuted back into France, oftentimes working directly with British intelligence. With support from SOE, new Résistance cells, the Maquis, and the early spontaneous networks like Fourcade's Alliance were able to train personnel and coordinate multiple clandestine activities that kept Germany in perpetual insecurity up to the liberation of France.

Nicole, who spoke English, begged Robert to send her to London for training at SOE headquarters. He refused, explaining that her talents would be wasted there. Because she was a woman, they would put her behind a desk. He convinced Nicole to join his group, where she would be able to help immediately. She already knew about running a clandestine radio and transmitting and receiving messages. She was also asked to find good targets for sabotage and to locate hiding places for agents, matériel, and radios. She participated in the reception of parachuted materials and smuggled arms, sometimes in the bottom of her handbag or suitcase.

Her activities quickly became a full-time job. She was in charge of maintaining contact with a Maquis group in the southern Alps near Grenoble. Among many other things, she brought them forged ration cards.

For the first parachute drop, Nicole and the farm family she was working with lit the perimeter of a dark clearing with fires. Afterward she felt elated, "like a god." She was proud to be working with people in the countryside, "chez les paysans," who helped her even though it was extremely dangerous. This solidarity with everyday people gave her great hope. A factory worker stole ten bicycles and gave them to her. She spent weeks at a time in the mountains with the Maquis. But she could not stay in the same place too many nights and was always on the move, which made for a lonely existence.

Nicole was working as a *passeur* during this period, taking the British airmen to the next stop along the way toward their escape,

and the Lyon apartment of her childhood friend Claudine and her husband, Gilles, was a safe house. Nicole could share a rare evening together with her friends when she brought an airman to their place.

On May 10, 1944, Robert was arrested a second time by the Gestapo. While he was being transferred to Paris for questioning, he was able to jump out of the train window around Villeneuve-Saint-Georges, and he found his way to the home of some friends in Tournan-en-Brie. He got word back to Nicole, and she met him there a few days later with a new set of false papers, created by her comrades in Franc-Tireur.

Nicole had been seen too often with Robert, who was now actively being hunted by the Germans, and she needed to get away. Reassigned to Paris, she was replaced in Lyon by an old friend of hers from her Éclaireur days, Denise Vernay, or "Miarka," the sister of the famous feminist Simone Veil.[8] The train on which Nicole was heading to Paris was derailed by an act of sabotage. She was traveling disguised in a Red Cross uniform. It was a great cover, but that day she had to use what little she had learned of first aid in her Scout training to help the wounded after the derailment. Luckily, there were no serious injuries.

Once in Paris she quickly made contact with other members of the Résistance. She worked under the name "Dominique" as second-in-command to Jacques Jourda, known as "Jacquemin." He was in charge of the entire network, and Nicole oversaw the *agents de liaison* for Paris and the surrounding region.

The Allies had landed in Normandy, and there was a general feeling that the tide of the war was turning. More and more people were joining the Résistance, which made it easier for Nicole to find *agents de liaison*, but it also created greater exposure and risks. The Germans were frantic to break the Résistance. Seven of the nine were arrested during this intense period between February and July 1944 when the Germans were doing everything possible to disrupt and destroy the underground networks. There were constant raids and arrests. There were betrayals. There were people who broke under torture. But there were also spies who infiltrated a small group with lax security, which would lead to entire networks being obliterated. Having learned from her past, Nicole took every precaution, but the

stress was enormous. At one point, after they had lost a whole group, Jacquemin ordered her to take a break.

While on a trip to deliver some weapons, she rested for a few days with her old Maquis friends, camping in the mountains. She loved being in the wild among comrades. She liked the campfires and the funny stories. They sang, talked about their friends who had died or been captured, and discussed the future, when all of this would be over. She felt free and happy, with a clear sense of purpose. On a sunny day in the mountains, she celebrated her twenty-second birthday. One of the men commented that soon she needed to find herself a husband. But after all the things Nicole had seen and done, she could not imagine a life like her mother's. She would have loved to have stayed in the woods longer, but she had to return to Paris that night.

The next day, August 4, 1944, only three weeks before the liberation of the city, an agent of the Gestapo stopped her on her bicycle in the place de Breteuil. He seemed to know exactly who she was, and in any case there was enough compromising material in her bicycle bags for her to know that as soon as he looked inside them, she was done for. She had been informed on by one of her *agents de liaison*, who had been recently arrested and tortured. The Germans had been waiting for her.

———— ❦ ————

Nicole was taken to the infamous Gestapo location on the rue de la Pompe for interrogation.

In the period right before and after the Allied Normandy landing, from April 17 to August 17, 1944, the building on the rue de la Pompe became a secret torture and murder center for the Gestapo, which was operating with extralegal powers. Such "black sites" are an expression of desperation and signal the disintegration of a society whenever they occur in history. At the rue de la Pompe location, there were no trials, just summary executions; there were no legal processes of arrest, just threats and beatings. Foreign and French Résistance fighters, men and women, were subjected to brutal beatings and other forms of torture, including waterboarding. Many died. In later court testimony it was noted that women were forced to submit to "sexual humiliations."

The Gestapo operation on the rue de la Pompe was led by Friedrich

Berger, a civilian who hired forty-four criminals and thugs from the Paris underworld to do the work of extracting information through any means. Berger was one of those psychopaths who blossom in war and profit in dark times. He had made a fortune on the black market. In May 1942, he moved to Paris. He had an efficient system for earning money quickly: he simply tortured sellers to find out where they kept their black-market goods and then took them. In April 1944, he was hired by the Gestapo to decimate the Paris Résistance networks. Within a period of just four months Berger's agents arrested 300 people; 163, including Nicole, were deported, and 50 of those would not return.

On August 16, 1944, in the final days of the German occupation, forty-two young men who had been held in the rue de la Pompe were executed, shot in front of the water fountains in the Bois de Boulogne. Three days later, Paris was liberated by the Allies.

By that time Berger had fled to Italy. He was arrested by the English in 1947, but mysteriously escaped. Twenty-three people from his group were condemned to death, having been found guilty of treason, spying, murder, complicity to commit murder, and collaboration with the enemy. At his military trial in December 1952 he was condemned to death in absentia. Later documents revealed that he was hired after the war by the American secret services to work in the Cold War; apparently the ends justified the means. Friedrich Berger died peacefully in his sleep in Munich.

For three days Nicole was interrogated and tortured by the Gestapo at the rue de la Pompe. Her future husband, a friend from her Éclaireurs days whom she had met with a few times in Lyon, had told her that while no one could withstand torture indefinitely, if she could hold out for forty-eight hours it would give her network time to protect themselves. She had been warned about what to expect: the different instruments they could use for beatings (a wooden club, a leather whip), the use of electricity, the use of rubber tubes and water. She had anticipated the pain, at least intellectually. But the body is always shocked by the onslaught of pain, reduced to a moment-by-moment existence. She made up false rendezvous and false names; she was reinterrogated and tortured again. It was, she wrote, "three days of breathless pain, tension, and insanity." At last she was transferred to the relative peace of Fresnes prison.[9]

In her cell, she let herself cry for the first time. She was desolate, yet relieved to be alone to sort out the myriad thoughts in her head. Had she said anything compromising? Had she managed not to give anyone away? What would happen to the others? What would happen to Jacquemin? If only she hadn't had the papers with her. If only she'd stayed longer with the Maquis. A maddening, unceasing flow of questions and recriminations tormented her. Hearing her sobs, prisoners from other cells called out to her, "Hang in there." She heard anonymous voices assuring her that she wasn't alone. "We are with you," they told her. After the brutality of the rue de la Pompe, the human warmth of those voices held her like an embrace.

Soon she was transferred to the women's section. Entering a large, dark room, she could make out the vague outline of bodies and heard murmurs and whispers. Slowly the room came into focus, and she saw that seated all around her on benches were dozens of women.

Someone said her name and rushed toward her. It was her old friend Renée. They fell into each other's arms. Renée Astier de Villatte was forty, with gray hair, but a zestful, active spirit. She had always been attracted to Nicole's wild side. From the moment they found each other in prison, they did everything they could to stay together. They tried not to talk too much, worried that there were spies in the cell. They could hear the bombs falling on Rambouillet, just forty-five kilometers from Paris. The Allies were knocking at the door. The war would soon be over. There was an irrepressible feeling of joy among the prisoners. Often they would break into singing "La Marseillaise" together.

But on the morning of August 15, 1944, fleeing the advance of the Americans, the Germans organized the last transport of prisoners out of Paris to the camps in the east. The city's electricity had been cut off, and the Parisian train conductors were on strike. The Gare de l'Est was no longer functioning, so the Germans organized trains with German conductors to leave from the Gare de Pantin. The thirty-four-year-old American spy Virginia d'Albert-Lake was among the prisoners being hurried out of the city by the Germans.

As 1,654 men and 543 women were packed into the cattle cars, the Red Cross passed out care packages, assuring them: "The war will end before you reach Germany." During the transport, 143 people were able to escape, as their train made frequent stops because the tracks had been bombed—the Résistance was working to block the deportations. But the Germans were resolute, and the remaining prisoners were marched to another train waiting on the other side of the destruction. Villagers called out to them, "Bon courage! Vive la France!" Surely their train would be stopped before they reached Germany, they thought. But after a while, they saw through the slats of the crowded wagon that the signs were now in German. The prisoners wept.[10] Nine hundred and three people from that last transport would perish.

This transport of women arrived in Ravensbrück on August 21, 1944. The door of their train car was thrown open, and the women encountered screams, cries, the barking of dogs, and the shouts of the German guards. Nicole recounted later that part of their way of resisting, of showing their national pride, was maintaining elegance and style: "They could not reduce us to animals. So when our train arrived we had put on makeup, brushed our hair, tried to make ourselves look as good as possible. The Russian prisoners who saw us behave like this thought we were prostitutes and spat on us."[11] They were marched from the train station to the camp and then made to stand for hours in the heat. Nicole had lost Renée in the chaos before the transport, and she searched desperately to find her now. Where was her friend? Had she survived the journey?

They were pushed toward the *Effektenkammer*, where they were stripped naked and paraded like beasts in front of the sneering German SS. With no way of knowing if she would soon be murdered, Nicole felt deep shame and fear. Suddenly she glimpsed Renée in the group in front; somehow, she got to her without calling attention to herself. Nicole would be assigned the number 57443, Jacky would get number 57442, and Renée got 57441. The three were standing next to one another as they were registered.

They were placed in quarantine in block 22, which was already overcrowded with Polish prisoners. While Paris was being liberated, Warsaw was being burned to the ground. The Polish resistance had risen up, but the revolt had been crushed. Between August and October, 12,000 women and children from Warsaw would be sent to the camp.

Nicole and Renée held on to each other and shared a bed, a slender board that was their life raft. Though Renée had not recovered from the terrible torture she had suffered at the hands of the Gestapo (and, in fact, she would never fully recover), and though she was completely overwhelmed with fatigue but unable to sleep, clenched in a vise of fear, bitten by lice and fleas, Renée spoke calmly to Nicole, her words soothing them both. Pressed closely against each other on the sixty centimeters of board that had become their universe, Renée told Nicole about the delicious melons that grew along the borders of the Lot River, in the region of France that was her home. She described her family's large house, her mother and sister, her nieces and nephews. She painted a picture of carefree childhood summer days. Listening to Renée, Nicole was transported to another time and place. She learned the power and relief found in language, in storytelling.

The prisoners who had already been there for a time sought out the new arrivals for news. And the news was good: the Germans were in retreat. It was a matter of days, weeks, a month at most, they declared. The war would end soon. Even though Nicole found her hunger almost unbearable, she never lost faith that soon the Germans would be defeated.

But Ravensbrück in August 1944 was worse than anything she could have imagined. She later wrote that it took her eight days to adapt to the camp, to emerge from the numbing horror and fear that strangled her. She learned to eat the horrible soup made of potato peelings and water. She learned to shut up, to avoid the whips and clubs, to hide in order to avoid being assigned the worst jobs. She learned to fight, to trade, to make do. There was open hostility between the Polish and French prisoners, as well as between other factions, and Nicole had to quickly learn the camp hierarchy.

If she needed to go to the bathroom, she learned to do it at two or three in the morning before the four o'clock roll call, because then everyone would be trying to go to the bathroom and there were only a few toilets for 3,000 women. She learned to avoid being assigned to the job of emptying those few toilets because her hair and clothes became permeated with the stench of human excrement. She fought to get access to the rare working spigot so she could wash her one piece of clothing, and then walked around in it as it dried.

It was so hot, but drinking the little water that was available brought a risk of dysentery. If a prisoner fell ill, she was sent to the *Revier*. But Nicole learned that few ever returned from the Ravensbrück

Revier. Instead, if a prisoner took too long to die, she might be killed with an injection of gasoline into her veins.

She learned that everything was against the rules. Washing was against the rules. Scratching was against the rules; it showed you had lice, lice led to typhus, and the Germans, who were terrified of typhus, might select you for execution if they suspected you had the disease.

After quarantine, Nicole and the others who had arrived with her faced the daunting prospect of the daily selections. The huge influx of Jewish women from Warsaw had been pushed into makeshift tents built on the swampy ground near the lake, and the overpopulation problem needed to be solved.

Frantic not to be separated, Nicole, Renée, and Jacky were relieved to be selected together as part of a group of twenty-eight. But they didn't know what for. As they stood in rows, being endlessly counted, they felt hopeful, as everyone in their group was healthy and strong.

They were marched back to the train station and loaded onto the same cattle cars they had arrived in. They traveled through Berlin heading south, and noticed through the cracks in the train car that the city lay in ruins. They sang "La Marseillaise" proudly as they passed through the war-ravaged city. When they arrived in Leipzig, they felt relieved to see that they would be housed in a large brick building. It was less crowded here, only two to a bed. There was a mix of nationalities. Orders were broadcast by loudspeaker in Polish and German. They were assigned new numbers. Nicole became number 4444.

Quickly they found old friends from their days in the Résistance. They were thrilled to discover survivors, out of the many who had disappeared. Renée found Zinka; they had worked in the Comète network together in Paris, hiding downed British pilots. Nicole became friends with Zinka too. Ever attuned to style, she admired the way Zinka made a fashionable turban to encircle her golden curls from two red rags and a few knots tied just so. Nicole met and became friends with Hélène and the two Dutch women, Lon and Guigui.

Fleeing through the German countryside, Nicole and her eight friends from Leipzig hastened to put some distance between themselves and the red-faced mayor. But the road to Strehla ran parallel to railroad tracks, which were a target for bombers. Another Allied plane flew low overhead. There was the familiar shudder of the ground, followed by the staccato of machine-gun fire in the distance. The women jumped into the roadside ditch, where they rested with their backs against one side of the ditch, their feet up on the other side. Nicole looked up at the sky, noticing the soft white clouds drifting overhead. She could smell the green earth and feel the blades of grass in her hands. It was springtime. Those rough hands, battered by the work in the factory, now felt something soft and natural. It was striking how beautiful the world continued to be even as men were making war and destruction. These fragile green shoots had no idea there was a war going on. Distantly she was aware of the bombs landing, a vague danger. But as she lay there, she began to realize that they were actually free. True, they were in enemy territory, so their freedom was precarious. They had no idea what awaited them; maybe all the mayors in all the villages would be like the first one. But even though the American planes flying overhead posed a danger, they also gave her hope, because it meant the liberating soldiers were near.

Each time the women stopped it was harder to stand back up and move on, but they needed to find a place for the night, and they were starving. "We can't keep going without food," Lon said, repeating the obvious for the umpteenth time. The others moaned in agreement.

Hélène nodded. As frightened as they had been by the last encounter, they couldn't stop now. "We'll just have to try our luck again at the next village."

"Someone will help us," Zaza said hopefully.

They entered the small hamlet of Kleinragewitz with trepidation. Their memory of the ranting mayor from the last village was still ringing in their ears. In front of one of the first houses on the edge of the town they met a Yugoslav prisoner who had been working for the family who had lived there since the beginning of the war. Many POWs were sent to work for German families in rural areas. Though the work was hard, most POWs in agricultural areas were well fed and relatively well treated. The man saw how ragged and tired the women were and asked them if they needed anything.

"Yes, some water," was all Hélène could think to ask for in that instant. He sent a fellow prisoner to fetch some water, but then, seeing their hollowed cheeks and emaciated bodies, he asked gently, "Maybe you would like some food too?"

Hélène calmly explained that they were starving; in fact, for all practical purposes, they hadn't eaten in four days.

Touched by her predicament, he led them to a white house with a small porch with benches for them to sit on. The other Yugoslav returned with a pitcher of water and a large bowl covered by a towel. The two prisoners spoke together for a moment and then the first one explained in German, "It's really not much, but I hope you will like it. My friend here thought you looked hungry."

The women showered him with jubilant thanks when the POW removed the towel and revealed the pile of cooked potatoes. The nine were so astonished by this generosity that some began to feel tears welling up.

Moved by the sight of their emaciated bodies, half a dozen other Yugoslav prisoners had run off to get more food. They returned with a jug of fresh milk, a loaf of bread, two jars of jam (marmalade and blackberry), and some butter. Seeing this lavish spread, the women couldn't hold themselves back any longer. They took handfuls of boiled potatoes. They passed around the jug of milk. They tore off bits of bread, dipping it into the jam.

They kissed one another with full mouths. They sobbed and laughed and ate voraciously. They thanked the men over and over. The POWs watched them tenderly, like parents, as Zaza would later describe, "who are happy to see a child who has been ill eat at long last."[12]

They passed around the jam and butter and bread. Hélène tried to apologize for their bad manners, saying, "You see, we have had nothing." But the men just laughed.

Nicole lay back against the porch rail and turned her face up to the sun. As she chewed a piece of bread with butter and jam, tears rolled down her cheeks. Only a few hours earlier she had been ready to die. Now here she was, and she had never tasted anything so sweet.

One man came back with a large pair of men's boots for Zinka's miserable bleeding feet. The women thanked him, but when she put them on, they went past her knees. The sight made everyone laugh.

Eventually they were able to calm down and gather themselves. The food was gone. The feeling of ravenous, panicked hunger had abated.

But now the women felt a leaden exhaustion. Lon asked the POW they had met first if there was a place they might rest for a while in safety.

"Just for one night," Hélène added.

The Yugoslavs suggested they speak with the *Bürgermeister.*

Jacky groaned in disgust, and they all bristled at the idea of another encounter with German authority. Hélène said, "I'm not sure we like talking to *Bürgermeisters,*" and she told them the story of their close call in the previous village. But the prisoners assured her that this little village had a kind mayor. He would not be like the last one.

"You'll see. He is a good man. I'll take you to him," one of the Yugoslavs offered.

Hélène translated for the others, and with apprehension she went off to meet the mayor.

The other eight sat in the sun and tried to communicate with the remaining POWs. Lon and Guigui spoke German, and so they served as interpreters. They told one another their names, where they were from, and how long they had been away from their homes. They all hoped that this terrible war would be over soon.

Luckily, Hélène was not gone for long. She returned smiling with the sergeant in charge of the POWs. She cheerfully informed the others that he had requisitioned a loft in a barn for them.

The women climbed a ladder to the hayloft, where they were greeted by the smell of fresh, clean straw. It made them giddy. They each made a comfortable place to settle down to sleep, piling up straw to make mattresses. They took off their painful shoes and laid out their rags to make their beds.

Suddenly Zaza hushed the women: "Sssht!" They all froze.

Zaza had heard the heavy steps of the POWs returning to the barn. The women looked worriedly at one another, exchanging their silent shared thought: Would these men be a problem? Did they think because they had fed them, now the women owed them in return?

But then they heard the men knocking on the barn door.

Knocking! They all smiled at the sound and exhaled. This unexpected courtesy moved them. Zaza had a distant memory of such polite behavior. It had been years since she'd heard someone knock, since she had felt she had any kind of privacy at all.

"Entrez," a few of them called out.

They were even more elated when it turned out that the men just
wanted to give them quilts, blankets, and a bottle of schnapps.

There was another round of "thank you" and "goodnight" and
"sleep well, please rest" before the men retreated again. The women
distributed the blankets, and each one made a comfortable, warm
bed. Settled in a safe, dry place, they decided to feast on their can of
sardines, with the remaining scrap of bread Mena had tucked into
her coat from their earlier meal. "I was planning ahead," she said.

Nicole then revealed that she too had "stolen" a bit of bread "for
later, just in case." This was a habit they had learned in the camps,
the careful hoarding of meager food scraps. But now, why hold back
when things seemed to be going so well?

Mena and Zinka took charge of distributing the food. Each woman
got a sardine on a corner of bread. It was heavenly. As they reveled in
their meal they talked about their future. They talked about how astonishing this village was compared to the last one. They couldn't get
over the hospitality of the Yugoslavs, what good kind men they were.

"I say we settle down here," Jacky said, her words coming between
gasps for breath.

"I agree," Zaza said. "We're warm and safe and sheltered."

"The war's ending in a few days or weeks," Jacky continued.

"And the Yugoslavs were so kind," Mena agreed. Her charm had not
gone unremarked by the men, who had been especially generous to her,
passing her the jam and butter and potatoes whenever her hands were
empty. "Tomorrow we can wash our clothes and our hair and present
ourselves ready to work for the farmers for our food," Mena suggested.

But Nicole, who had a practical intelligence, threw cold water on
their plans. "Don't get your hopes up. We can't suddenly become
milkmaids in the middle of the front lines. Things change fast. There
is still a war, and these are just dreams," she said.

"Can't we dream a little?" Mena pleaded.

"It's better to keep our eyes open," Nicole said. "Who knows what's
coming next?"

"We should get some sleep," Hélène said, and that was the final
word on the matter.

CHAPTER FOUR

— LON AND GUIGUI —

Madelon Verstijnen (Lon)   Guillemette Daendels (Guigui)

EARLY THE NEXT MORNING, AT first light, the Yugoslavs woke the women by knocking politely on the barn door. The women sat up in the hay where they had slept so peacefully. Unused to real rest, they were slightly dazed. The Yugoslavs climbed up the ladder to present them with a pitcher of café au lait, a bowl of boiled potatoes, a bottle of liniment for their aching legs, butter, salt, and a handful of cigarettes, enough for each woman to have one.

The nine cleared a space on the floor for this precious breakfast. How long had it been since they had awakened to kindness? How long since they had been allowed to sleep instead of being roused by brutal shouts?

The sun filtered through the slats of the barn and lit up the dancing dust motes. Everyone was washed in a golden light and a quiet, hushed peacefulness. Outside they heard birds singing.

The men stood in a line. They had brushed their hair and shaved. They wore rags, but the rags were clean, and their garments had all their buttons.

"One of these three eggs is hard-boiled, but we don't know which one," a young man said as he gently placed three eggs in Mena's outstretched hands.

"Thank you," Mena said, taking the eggs carefully from him. She had straw in her hair and was still flushed from sleep, and when she smiled at him, he blushed.

"We are sorry to wake you so early, but there is some bad news." This was the POW they had first met on the road, who appeared to be in charge.

"Yes," Hélène responded somberly, unsurprised. "Please tell us what it is."

"There was an announcement. We got it last night. But we didn't want to disturb you." He took a deep breath, "We—all the POWs in the region—are being rounded up by the authorities and ordered to march east to the camp in Naundorf. This morning."

"Oh, Jesus and Maria!" Josée cried out. "We can't go there!" Nicole put her arm around Josée to calm her.

"It would be better if you left quickly, before the roundup," the blushing man said to Mena, as if they were alone. "They don't know about you yet."

"That's why we woke you," the man in charge said to Hélène. "We would have let you sleep."

Another POW held a pile of clothes in his arms. "Before we leave, we thought you might need these things." They were shy about their generosity. They had brought the women two sweaters and two pairs of trousers, hats and gloves. Jacky, who had left Leipzig in a dress so worn out that it was practically transparent, happily exchanged it for a pair of men's trousers. They were large and stiff, and she had to hold them up with a rope. At least once a day someone would have to say, "Jacky, your fly, it's open again!"

The Yugoslavs also gave the women a cast-iron pot on a tripod for cooking over a fire. It was heavy and awkward, but Nicole said, "I'll take that!" She dreamed of making a stew. It appealed to her, this practical cooking tool. They could use it to boil potatoes or make dandelion leaf soup. It reminded her of those happy days she had spent in the mountains with the Maquis.

The women ate quickly and without much conversation. No one brought up their disappointment. Their hopeful talk from the night before hung unspoken in the air as they gathered their belongings. Nicole and Josée inspected the barn. "One of the first rules of camping," Nicole proclaimed, "is to leave the campsite without a trace."

They felt the fear of the unknown in their aching bodies as they left the little town and found the road again. Their story would not end sweetly here. They would not become bucolic milkmaids waiting for the war to end. They headed back in a vaguely westerly direction, carefully avoiding Naundorf.

At a crossroads they almost bumped into a young German officer standing by a motorbike. He waved them over.

"Please, if you would," he called out politely, "I need some local advice. What do you know of the positions of the Americans and the Russians? Have you heard anything?"

Hélène elbowed Zaza to follow her lead. "We've heard rumors," she said, smiling sweetly, almost flirting. She clearly wanted Zaza to get a good look at the map that the man was holding halfway folded in his hands.

"What sort of rumors?"

Hélène drew out the conversation for as long as possible. But neither she nor Zaza, without her eyeglasses, managed to get a good look at the map.

"Well, it's been nice chatting, ladies, but I need to get back to work," the officer said, starting his motorbike. It coughed out a puff of dark exhaust fumes. After they anxiously watched him ride away, the women fell into a heap of nervous hugging and giggling. They found a dip in the field that was sunny and hidden from the road. They could nap here in the soft grass, like "lizards in the sun," Zaza wrote.[1] Nicole commented that they needed to improve their skin tone; they were the color of pale turnips. They ate a few of the Yugoslavs' cold boiled potatoes, drank schnapps, and smoked their cigarettes. It was a good place to rest and to talk about what had just happened. They discussed how absurd it was: a German officer asking escaped prisoners for the location of the front. The sun warmed them, and small insects buzzed in the sweet-smelling grass. The air was fresh and quiet. Without a watch, Zaza guessed that they rested there for at least five hours. They were too exhausted to keep going and were worried about whether the German officer might report them. Hélène felt he was harmless. Her German was so good she passed as a native speaker. And he had been a simple kind of soldier, just trying to do his job. She did not think he had suspected anything. She remembered Fritz's kindness and suspected that there were many soldiers who hated the SS and the Gestapo, who wanted nothing more than for this disastrous war to come to an end.

They discussed what story they should use. They could be either prisoners or *Gastarbeiter*, guest workers. The story Hélène had invented at the first village, that they were *Gastarbeiter* whose factory had closed, had not gone over too well. Up until now their true story of being escaped prisoners from a *Kommando* had gotten a better reception. The group decided that they should use the truth next time. Occasionally their conversation turned back to the kindness of the Yugoslav POWs and to teasing Mena for making them fall in love with her.

They also teased Josée, because all the walking had brought a blush of color to her cheeks. She was radiant. The day of their escape, Josée had her hair hidden, wrapped up in a turban with a rag. But in the morning, the Yugoslavs had noticed her long, beautiful black tresses, and Jacky had seen how the men looked at her. "Most of us look like Job's turkey, but not Josée, with her curls down her back."

"Soon we won't be able to beat the men off," Zaza agreed.

"Ha! Those boys don't have the faintest idea what to say to Josée," Jacky said.

"All the better." Zaza was feeling protective.

"Why is it better?" Josée asked defensively. She hated that they kept treating her like a child. Inside, she felt old beyond her years.

Jacky asked, "Josée, are you a virgin?"

"Yes. So what?" she replied, at which everyone burst out laughing.

They were a close-knit group of friends. They spoke frankly about their bodies and their sexual experiences. They shared their intimate histories. Zinka and Zaza were married, and Jacky was widowed, so it was acceptable that they had sexual experience. And it was clear that some of the others had had lovers before they were arrested. They were living in a time of moral upheaval. Everything was changing. Though some may have longed to go back to the old times, the work these women did in the Résistance had given them the thrill of autonomy, of agency. They had learned that they were capable of much more than they had first thought. They were different from their mothers and grandmothers. They wanted more than anything to feel alive in their bodies. If they survived, would they be able to go back to a circumscribed life of marriage and motherhood? Facing an unknown future, a few of them may have needed Josée to remain innocent, to stay fixed in that old safe world. But she would have none of it.

As the day grew cooler, they knew they needed to move toward yet another village, no matter how frightening the possibility of stumbling onto angry locals.

Just outside the town of Reppen, Lon and Hélène spotted a raw potato on the road. Then they saw another in the grass. A search revealed many more. The potatoes appeared to have fallen from someone's load. But they were raw, Josée pointed out; how would they cook them?

"If we can make a fire, we could use this," Nicole offered, indicating the heavy iron tripod and pot she had been carrying.

But Lon looked at the dirty potato at her dirty feet. Was this what she had become? She told the others that she found it humiliating to pick up food off the ground. "It goes against me," was all she could say. She was remembering how some women had behaved in the camps, fighting in the mud over a scrap of food.

In the camp, keeping their dignity had been primary. None of them had pushed or fought over food. They were proud of how they served one another, divided food equally, and maintained their civility in such an uncivil place. It had kept them strong when others became more and more like animals, lost their sense of themselves, and fell into dark despair. And so for Lon, it was as if the potatoes weighed more than she did.

They all stood there for a moment, pondering the existential question of whether to gather up the potatoes or not, and remembering those days in the camp as if they were still standing inside the barbed-wire fences.

Jacky's words broke through their trance. "It's food, for God's sake! *Merde!* Have you forgotten we nearly starved to death? Imagine in Ravensbrück, would you have stuck your nose up at a potato?"

They went to work, each one looking around herself on the ground for more potatoes. They had their heads down and were not looking at the hamlet of Reppen, with its scattering of yellow and beige homes with sloping red-tile roofs, and the church with a slate-gray onion-shaped dome in the distance.

"Soldiers," Nicole suddenly whispered to Hélène. During her years in the Résistance, Nicole had learned to be ever alert for danger. She had spotted two soldiers with rifles, apparently guarding the entrance to the town. They were staring at her.

"Soldiers," she repeated to the others, raising her voice just slightly. They stood up and looked at the soldiers, who looked back curiously. A German woman leaned out of her window, the shutters banging like gunshots as she opened them. She called out angrily to the soldiers, "Hey! What are you good for? Shouldn't you shoot them? Look at those vagrants! Thieves! Shoot them! Shoot them, now!"

The soldiers slowly lifted their guns, pointing them directly at the women.

Nicole felt a wave of fear course through her veins. Clutching their potatoes, they turned and hustled down a side street, behind a wall.

Their injuries from the camps—crushed feet, blistered skin, broken ankles, hip pain, and months of starvation, not to mention the past few days of ceaseless walking—made it physically impossible for them to run, but they could move quickly when necessary. The side street led them back out of the town. They found a ditch by the side of the road and stopped to catch their breath. Everyone was rattled.

"I think, as a group, we call too much attention to ourselves," Hélène said at last.

"We must look awful," Zaza agreed. "I would be scared of us."

"It would be better to send just two scouts into town. I think it should be Hélène and Lon," Nicole said. All agreed. The two of them were the most fluent in German. They would try again, but this time in disguise. Hélène wore her civilian dress with its pageboy collar. Lon was given the next-best items of clothing, a skirt and one of the tops whose stripes had almost completely faded. Zaza quickly fashioned a belt out of a rag.

"I won't make it too tight around the waist. I don't want them to see how thin you are," she said.

Zaza was a good seamstress. In Ravensbrück she had knitted socks for herself and Hélène, using metal nails she found in the mud as knitting needles and unraveling the woolen underwear they had been given for the yarn. Back in Leipzig, when Hélène had insisted that they attempt an escape, Zaza, frustrated by her constant pestering, said, "Why don't you just go on without me?" Hélène had responded in her usual cool way: "Because I can't sew. I need you. You have the needle and thread."

After cleaning themselves up, Lon and Hélène went in search of shelter and a place to cook their newly gathered potatoes.

Without a watch, it was hard to gauge how much time passed. But to Nicole it felt like hours. The seven women waiting in the ditch grew anxious and their easy chatter quieted. The memory of those soldiers and the angry German woman replayed in their minds. What would they do if Lon and Hélène didn't return?

Nicole was beginning to feel the chill of the early spring evening. Zaza felt a lump of fear rising in her throat. Josée said out loud what the others dared not: "I don't think they're coming back. What if they've been taken to Naundorf? What if they've been shot?"

"We'll wait a little longer," Nicole said, but then wondered: how much longer?

To their immense relief, Hélène and Lon returned soon after with blank, ambiguous expressions. The women peppered them with questions.

"What is it?"

"What did you find?"

"Will we need to walk more tonight?"

"What shall we do now?"

The two scouts said nothing. The group was getting really exasperated with their silence. "Open your bone boxes, dammit!" Jacky growled.

At last Hélène and Lon broke into sly smiles. "Hurry up! There's an inn where we can have some dinner," Lon said.

"And they've offered us a barn for sleeping tonight," Hélène added.

"That wasn't funny," Zaza said, even as she laughed with relief.

As the women walked past the church, Hélène explained that she and Lon had kept their story vague: they were refugees in search of food and a place to sleep. The less said the better.

Soon they came to the imposing *Gasthof*, with a gabled step facade. Inside it was warm and cozy, bathed in honey-yellow light. There was the smell of food and a low din of conversation. It was all so normal, as if there weren't a war going on. In their past life this was the kind of place they would have found "quaint," with its Germanic décor, lace on the piano, and a decorative ceramic heating stove. Many years later Nicole wrote of the strangeness of their situation, adding, "And still now I wonder if it is a dream, if I invented it or if it existed."[2]

The nine women were seated at a round table set with linen. A young waitress with blond braids coiled on either side of her head, like earmuffs, asked them if they were planning to eat. The question was so absurd. But of course, they would have to pay for their meal. Inspecting the handwritten menu, their treasurer, Josée, said that the money was for eating. It would be silly to save it, for Germany was losing and soon the money would be worthless. They quickly discussed the prices among themselves and decided the noodles were within their budget.

They sat silently, looking around warily. It felt as if they had gone straight into the lion's den. There was a table of German officers. "Remember the soldiers we met on the road just after we escaped?" Hélène coached them in a low whisper. "Act like you belong here."

The innkeeper arrived with a steaming plate of noodles, just as three of the German officers approached their table. The highest-ranking one, wearing a monocle, looked, Lon later wrote, "like he could have walked out of a film."[3] He was around forty, with a large military cap and his chest loaded with medals. He wore high leather boots and carried a whip in his right hand. He was flanked by two younger officers who kept exactly one step behind him. All of them were blond, with sharp blue eyes, clean-shaven faces, and a look the women feared to their core.

The Monocle, as Lon later nicknamed him, tapped his boot with his whip and stopped sharply at their table. There was a dreadful pause.

Then his face opened into a delighted, almost silly smile, and he asked, "Is it true? I hear that you are French girls. From Paris?"

"So, you know Paris?" Jacky asked nonchalantly.

"I love Paris!" the Monocle responded in his heavy accent. He had been there once, in 1942 during a brief furlough, because the Führer had declared that all German soldiers deserved one visit to Paris. Hitler had spent only three hours touring the city and later said, "It was the greatest and finest moment of my life."

"Who doesn't love Paris?" Jacky responded, practically purring.

Mena joined in. The two began to flirt, talking about how much they too missed their wonderful city. It didn't matter that the women spoke in French and the Germans responded in German. All three, especially the Monocle, were completely taken by the beautiful Parisiennes. Lon would later explain, "Here was French charm at its highest and most refined, seductive and deceptive, but oh such subtle flirting. A sweet smile here, a modestly turned-away head there, and meanwhile glances from under the lowered lids of demure but very keen eyes."[4] Miraculously, Jacky did not gasp for breath once—and perhaps her breathy voice made the flirtation all the more effective.

The Monocle asked, "And Paris? Is it still the same? Is the Champs-Élysées still there? And the Eiffel Tower? And the Moulin Rouge? Are all the girls there as beautiful as you are?"

"Well, you will just have to come to Paris," Jacky said. She shrugged flirtatiously. "Come and see for yourself."

It was clear the women did not have to be afraid of these German officers, but they had something else to worry about. During their time in the camp they had eaten as fast as possible, out of a crude tin bowl with their fingers or with a rudimentary spoon, as a guard stood over them with a whip. Now they found themselves seated in front of real dishes, with real cutlery, being served by a smiling German girl. Their biggest fear as they began to eat was not the German officers leaning over them but the forks.

Josée whispered to Nicole, "I'm going to poke myself with this thing."

With great force of will, they ate slowly, politely, trying to recall the table manners from their former lives.

Josée, making a show of her innocence in front of the lingering

Germans, carefully pulled out their money and gently folded it on the table. The Monocle raised both hands in a defensive gesture.

"No! No, this is out of the question, out of the question! It would be a real honor for me to pay for you gentle ladies after such a pleasant conversation."

There was very weak protest from the women, and Josée soon put the precious money away. The women ate their noodles and pretended to enjoy the company of the Monocle and his two fellow German officers. When the meal was done and the Germans bade them good night, clicking their heels and bowing with absurd politeness, the women were at last shown to a nearby barn where they could rest. The straw was fresh, and they were grateful to lie down. But they could still feel the cold. Jacky suggested that they sip a little schnapps to help warm themselves up. The bottle made the rounds. Soon they were sleeping soundly.

———

Among the bills briefly put on the table by Josée was a five-mark note. Lon remembered that specific bill and how she had come to have it. One day in Leipzig, she found it on the ground between the bunks. Because they were not allowed to have money, and because, as she herself wrote, she was a "silly girl," she tried to return it to the *Lagerälteste*, the prisoner who oversaw the other prisoners.

The brilliance of the concentration camp system (and perhaps all prison systems) was that some prisoners were put into positions of relative power over others. Those in power had a stake in maintaining the status quo, and soon they wanted to keep the system working as much or even more than the Nazis.

The *Lagerälteste* at Leipzig was Joanna Szumańska. Upon their arrival they had seen her standing next to Commandant Plaul. Szumańska was a complicated character. She was beautiful and knew it. She was twenty-eight, and it was rumored that before the war she had been one of the great actresses of Warsaw: a striking, cool woman, whom Lon reported was never seen smiling. Of course, she had reasons not to smile. She had been imprisoned since the beginning of the war. She was the daughter of a geography professor from Lwów University. Before the war she socialized with Jews, and according to her postwar testimony she was arrested for being part of a smuggling ring to help Jews escape the ghetto. However, others claimed that under interrogation she informed on her network. She was sent to Majdanek, where she served as the *Lagerälteste* of the women's camp.

Some of her fellow Poles testified at her war crimes trial that the prisoners chose her for the post because she had the courage to resist the authorities and had shown integrity and loyalty. Others reported that after being chosen at Majdanek, she asked to be excused from the position, and for that the SS nearly beat her to death. But the Jewish survivors of Majdanek tell another story, one of her harsh treatment and brutality. They called her "tiger" because she bared her teeth when she beat them. It was rumored that she and Commandant Plaul had a "romantic relationship." That is, he sexually exploited her, and Szumańska traded on this to make life easier for herself as well as the others.

She did protect some Jewish prisoners. For example, Maryla Reich, who passed as a non-Jewish Pole in Majdanek, said that Szumańska knew she was in fact Jewish and saved her from the big selection of Jews in 1943. But many Jewish prisoners felt otherwise. Dora Sroka said, "If there had been a crematorium there, Szumańska would have been the first stoker."[5]

When Lon went to Szumańska to turn in the five-mark bill, the Polish woman blanched. "Are you crazy?" she hissed. "If it gets out that you found money, the *Aufseherinnen* will all get into trouble collectively."

Lon realized she was right: letting money fall into the hands of prisoners was a serious offense. And since the Poles were the only ones who were *Aufseherinnen*, they were known to the Red Cross and sometimes received packages from home. Most likely money had been hidden in an *Aufseherin*'s package and she had dropped it without noticing. Instead of taking the bill, Szumańska insisted that Lon keep the money herself. She closed her hand over Lon's fist. "Keep it well hidden."

Later, after the war, Lon was called to testify on Szumańska's behalf when she was charged with war crimes in Paris by former Jewish prisoners. Lon was seen as an absolute outsider, not a Jew, not a Pole, not a friend of Szumańska's. And she did give testimony in her favor. Remembering the incident with the five-mark bill, she said that Szumańska did the best she could under the circumstances. Szumańska and the Poles in general, Lon argued, kept things running smoothly. This kept the German brutality at bay as much as possible. Szumańska was also accused of sleeping with the commandant. Lon pointed out that, first, that was not a war crime, and second, it was easy to imagine how she had been forced into that position and had little choice in the matter. Joanna Szumańska eventually was released and immigrated to the United States with her husband, a Jewish pianist.[6]

———◆———

Primo Levi has written that we must remember the story is being told by the survivors, and survivors were the lucky ones who almost always had some form of privilege in the perverse camp hierarchy. Privilege could be as little a thing as having a good pair of shoes, getting into a less deadly work detail, or getting assigned to a fair-minded *blockova*.

Furthermore, National Socialism was built on ideas of racial purity, eugenics, and social Darwinism, ideas that were popular in the general culture. Those ideas had proponents across Europe and America. Racist philosophers such as Joseph de Maistre, Louis de Bonald, and Arthur de Gobineau in France, Houston Stewart Chamberlain and Sir Francis Galton in England, and the American eugenics movement directly inspired the German Nazis.

The concentration camp system reflected those popular beliefs taken to their logical extreme. It reproduced a ghoulish internal hierarchy. At the bottom were the so-called *asozial* prisoners. This group included Sinti and Roma, Jehovah's Witnesses, homosexuals, sex workers, and common criminals. These survivors were seemingly forgotten by history until very recently. Only in February 2020 were these "green triangle" and "black triangle" prisoners recognized as being victims. They did not join survivor groups. They had no political organizations advocating for their rights after the war. They were not seen as heroes or noble victims. Among the prisoners, there was disdain for this group.[7]

Indeed, Tante Hélène and some of the other women's descendants I interviewed confirmed that the group of nine women hated and feared the "Gypsies" and civilian Russians, whom they described as brutal and criminal. Hélène seemed to have accepted the German propaganda that most of the women in the camps who were neither political prisoners nor Jewish were there because they were prostitutes. Many who were working in the sex trade were widowed homeless mothers whose husbands had died in the war. Although thousands of so-called *asozial* prisoners were murdered, not a single one was called upon to give testimony at the war crimes tribunals afterward.[8]

In her memoir, Juliette Bes, the young *ajiste* arrested in the same roundup as Zaza, describes how after her arrest she met and befriended a prostitute named Murielle, with whom she shared a cell in Fresnes. The military police had been looking for a young German soldier who happened to be a deserter and found him with Murielle, who had been arrested but expected to be released because she was "just doing her job." But instead she was deported. After the war, Murielle, like many sex workers, was put on trial for collaboration, for having had sex with German soldiers. Juliette was able to come to her defense, arguing that Murielle had suffered and behaved bravely in the camps, in solidarity with the political prisoners, and so she should not be punished.[9] To be forgiven for being a prostitute, she needed a political prisoner to speak on her behalf. After the war, prostitutes were often tried by a mob, who shaved their heads to make their perceived offense visible to all, paraded them through the streets, and hurled insults at them. These women were known as *les tondues*, "the shorn."

Immediately after the war, few historians wrote about the Porajmos, the Shoah of the Sinti and Roma. Of the tens of thousands of victims from these ethnic groups, 200 young girls sent to Ravensbrück were forcibly sterilized in medical experiments. Some of the girls were as young as eight. Most died from the operation, which was performed without any painkillers. Fritz Suhren, the commandant of Ravensbrück, later defended himself at his trial by saying, "Not only did we sterilize women, but also men and children, but they were Gypsies."[10] The Porajmos was not recognized by the German government until 1982.

The silence about homosexuality in camp life makes it difficult to get a clear picture. Lesbians, as *asozial* prisoners, were shunned by everyone, and often the most sadistic guards were put in charge of them. Political survivors would talk about the "special customs" of certain "pestiferous" women who dressed as men and were called *julots.* Their blocks were overcrowded, and they were subject to brutal beatings. There are accounts of young lesbians throwing their bodies against the electric barbed-wire fence, the preferred way to commit suicide. Their bodies were left hanging on the wire as a warning. There is no record of their names, no way of knowing who exactly they were. Others recount that in the *asozial* block, where crowding and violence were worst, some prisoners used sex to console themselves. There are descriptions of loud lovemaking that shook the beds, and reports of others who traded sex for food. Homosexuals were often blamed for crimes such as theft of food from the kitchen, even without proof, and they would be punished as a group.

In general, the French political prisoners found homosexual behavior morally depraved. They claimed that though homosexuality was commonplace among the German criminal underworld and among some political prisoners from other countries, among French political prisoners it was extremely rare.[11]

There are a few stories of genuine partnerships. Milena Jezenská, who had been Franz Kafka's lover and translator, met and fell in love with Margarete Buber-Neumann. Milena would not survive, but Margarete wrote, "I was thankful for having been sent to Ravensbrück, because it was there I met Milena."[12]

Buber-Neumann recounts her moving relationship with Milena in a book she wrote after the war. The book she and Milena had promised to write together about the camps is a testament to the importance of female solidarity. This camaraderie may account for why women on average survived longer in the camps than men did. The vital role of friendships and even romantic love between two women was a subject that Lon would write about as well.

———◆———

Lon, whose full name was Madelon Verstijnen, spent her childhood in Scheveningen, where her father was a notary. She moved to Leiden to study Assyrian with Professor Franz Böhl, a leading scholar in Near Eastern studies. She was his sole student during the war years. After her arrest, Lon's father and Böhl tried unsuccessfully to bribe Nazi officials to release Lon and her older brother, Eric.[13]

Eric was six years older than Lon and a law student in Leiden. The

Verstijnen family had a prominent past. They were bourgeois farmers, and later active in the Dutch East Indies. Lon's parents' generation enjoyed a remarkable period in which the artistic, literary, and intellectual avant-garde came together in Holland. The next generation, including Eric, Lon, and their cousins, was more politically committed.

Lon adored her handsome older brother. Once when they were in a pub in Leiden, Eric and Lon were chatting when a tipsy tattoo-covered sailor entered and took the stool just next to them. The sailor kept saying something that sounded to Lon like "Poseidon."

Eric got angry and said, "Sir, this is my sister!"

Lon quietly asked Eric, "But why do you care if he calls us a sea god?"

Through gritted teeth, Eric explained to his sister the man was saying not "Poseidon" but "Port Said," a place infamous for its easy access to prostitutes.

Then the man drunkenly asked Eric, "How did you find such a catch?"

Eric angrily repeated, "Sir, this is my sister. And now I want you to leave this establishment at once."

"Yes," the drunk mumbled, "Port Said." He took another sip of his drink.

Lon described how her brother carefully took off his jacket and hung it on the back of the chair, removed his cufflinks, and rolled up his sleeves. Then he put his glasses on the bar, which rendered him quite blind. He had taken a few boxing lessons, but she knew he wouldn't even be able to see what he was swinging at. Lon began to worry about the rapidly deteriorating situation. She knew that in any fight her brother and she would lose, no matter how drunk the sailor. She was relieved when the sailor stood up, paid his bill, and made for the door, saying, "I'm going already, Lord, I'm going!"

She was touched that Eric would fight for her honor, even though the result would have been disastrous. She remembered another time, when she visited him in his student room in Leiden when he was twenty-five and she was nineteen. As he lay on the bed with his hands behind his head, out of the blue he suddenly said to her, "All things considered, I love one woman and that is you." Lon felt that they alone understood each other perfectly. Perhaps Eric was the only man Lon ever loved. When she came to study in Leiden in 1940, Eric a bit gruffly warned her that with her newfound freedom she should not have sex with every guy she met. Lon was shocked; she told him that she was still a virgin. He put his hand on her head and said, "Keep it that way. Keep it that way."[14]

As the occupation and oppression solidified, the Nazis demanded the resignation of all Jewish professors from the university at Leiden. The dean of the law faculty gave a protest speech and the students went on strike in November 1940. Lon and her friend Guigui would have been part of this student movement. Fifty-three out of sixty-eight professors resigned in protest, and the university was closed. Eric was friends with Peter Tazelaar, who led a group working with the Dutch government-in-exile in London to set up an escape route for Jewish families and stranded Dutch airmen. Inspired by his friend's engagement, in 1943 Eric left Holland to join his friend and fellow law student Victor Swane in Paris. Lon longed to follow her brother. In her account Lon mentions that she had a fiancé, but Eric was clearly the focus of her yearning.

She and her friend Guigui met in their comfortable student house for young upper-class women. Guigui's calm demeanor was a perfect foil for Lon's fiery urgency. They bonded over a shared purpose. Shocked and ashamed by accounts of Jewish families being rounded up, Lon couldn't bear to feel so helpless. They agreed they would go to Paris, find Eric, and join the Résistance. His last letter had said he was staying at the Hôtel de Montholon, by the Gare du Nord.

Guigui at age thirteen, when her family was falling apart

Guillemette Claudine Daendels (Guigui) came from an aristocratic Dutch family. Guigui's father, Laurentius Henri Daendels, was born in Arnhem after the Daendels family had returned from making their fortune in the Dutch East Indies colonies. He appears to have lived off the remains of the family fortune. When he married Guigui's mother, Clara Van Rijck, their wedding announcement, in French, described him as a reserve lieutenant in the Hussards. They moved to a family estate in Hezenberg, where they raised horses, cows, dogs, and chickens. They had three children in quick succession; Guigui was born last, in 1920. The family hosted elaborate cross-country hunting outings. Prince Hendrik and Queen Wilhelmina spent time there. And the Daendelses were known for their largesse, giving money to the municipality, donating to town festivals, and organizing public events.

On the vast estate, they had a special house for the groom and another for their chauffeur, plus a country cottage for the head gardener. The children were raised with nannies and taught by a governess. Because Clara had been born in France and her sister married a Frenchman, and because it was chic, they often spoke French at home. It was a luxurious life that could not be sustained. Between 1930 and 1933, when Guigui would have been ten to thirteen years old, her parents separated. Much like what happened to Nicole and her family, Laurentius was going bankrupt and the marriage was falling apart. The liquidation of the family fortune was complete in January 1934. During the bankruptcy period Laurentius was ill in a sanatorium in Switzerland. He and Clara were divorced in September, and he returned to Holland in November 1934, dying only a few days later, when Guigui was fourteen years old.

During those crucial early adolescent years, Guigui lived through the dissolution of her parents' marriage, the loss of her childhood paradise, and the death of her father. Guigui seems to have learned from these events that nothing really mattered except love and friendship. According to her family, she was artistic and sensitive. She had a strong set of values and she lived according to them. Quiet and reserved, Guigui had no desire to lead, but she also didn't like to be controlled.[15]

On March 7, 1944, Lon and Guigui traveled from Leiden to Paris using false papers. They were full of idealistic hope. The trip went smoothly even though they had a few moments of fear when a suspicious German inspector took a long time over their papers. Perhaps he lingered because it was a chance to flirt with Guigui. At the Hôtel de Montholon, they met Victor Swane, Eric, and the rest of the group. They would wait for a few days at the hotel and then, according to the original plan, they would travel via Spain to England, to join the SOE. Neither Guigui nor Lon seemed too concerned with the details. They were just pleased to be finally doing something.

On March 8, Guigui and Lon went out to dinner with Eric. They talked about their parents and shared funny jokes and anecdotes that had nothing to do with the war. They discussed rationing and where one could get a decent cup of ersatz coffee. Lon told them about her studies with Professor Böhl. It would be their last meal together.

The girls were given a hotel room one floor above Eric's and went to sleep. At 6:00 AM on March 9, 1944, Lon and Guigui woke to the sound of banging fists. "Police! Open at once!"

There was nothing to do but open the door. A group of German police shoved Lon aside and stormed into the room. One trained a gun on the two women. Shivering in their nightgowns, they watched while the room was torn apart. To their utter astonishment, the police quickly found a removable panel in the closet. When they opened it, out tumbled stacks of German uniforms, rifles, and other weapons. The trove of contraband would have been used to sabotage German operations and to smuggle out desperate Jewish families. The police cleared the whole hotel, room by room. Everyone was arrested, including Victor, Eric, and a dozen others.

Their network had been betrayed. In February the Gestapo had made significant headway in uncovering several of the Dutch resistance groups. Sweeping arrests had led to the near decimation of the Holland–Paris escape line, led by Jean Weidner. The Hôtel de Montholon was the Paris meeting point for their organization. A letter warning Victor not to use the hotel any longer never reached him. He, Eric, Lon, and Guigui had walked right into the trap.

That morning Guigui's young French cousin James was coming to visit her at the hotel. He arrived by bicycle just as the group was being loaded into the police wagons. Luckily, and to Guigui's great relief, he was not noticed by the police and was able to turn away and get the bad news back to their families.

Guigui (far right) with her field hockey team

Outside the interrogation room, sitting on a bench next to Guigui, was a fellow Dutchman, Timen Willem Spijker. They came from different social milieus and had never met before. While Guigui had played field hockey with the university team in Leiden during her student years, Timen, a law student at the University of Nijmegen, had played the piano at silent-movie theaters to earn his living. Whether he was ever able to finish his degree is unclear, but he appears to have traveled to Paris in 1941, where he knew many people in the Dutch resistance.

In those intense times each meeting must have been freighted with meaning. Guigui and Timen didn't know what awaited them: Execution? Torture? Would they ever see their families again? They didn't know how they would withstand their fate. Sitting on that bench, they discovered they could speak to each other in Dutch. They found a kind of exhilaration and comfort in that moment of extreme fear and uncertainty. Timen was calmed by Guigui's gray eyes and touched by her gift of a handful of cigarette butts she had in her pocket.

Transported to Fresnes prison a few days later, perhaps they were able to continue to communicate despite being in separate sections of the prison. Juliette Bes talks about how her cellmate, the prostitute Murielle, would let Juliette stand on her shoulders so she could talk into the small louvered window that provided ventilation. Her message would be repeated from one cell to the next until it reached the right person.[16]

Timen would tell himself, "If I get out of here alive, I will find the girl I met in prison and I will marry her."

Timen was transferred to the Compiègne transit camp, which, like Romainville, was an antechamber to deportation to Germany. On June 18, 1944, he was put on a transport to Dachau. Eric, Lon's brother, was on the same train. Out of 2,143 men on that transport, there were only nine Dutchmen. Did Eric and Timen know each other? Did they discover that Eric's sister and the woman Timen had just met, whom he would later credit for getting him through the dark days of the camps, were close friends?

After Dachau, Eric was sent to Natzweiler-Struthof and then to a labor camp in Vaihingen. He had been given the designation *NN*, for *Nacht und Nebel* (night and fog). This was a specific form of punishment, created by Hitler in 1941. Seeing that Résistance leaders who were publicly executed had become martyrs, inspiring others, Hitler wanted the leaders of rebellion simply to disappear into obscurity and for their families to suffer years of uncertainty. Prisoners with the *NN* status were shifted from camp to camp, and their deaths were never recorded.[17]

One of the difficult things for Lon to bear in the camps was the bleakness, the total lack of any kind of beauty. Denied any color during the day, Lon found that her dream life grew especially vivid and wonderful. "It is remarkable that during those nearly fourteen months of imprisonment I never had one nightmare. The nightmares happened during the day. At night I led a very special life of my own in which all things I was or felt deprived of were fully compensated. One thing is sure. This dreaming in colors has been one of the most important factors to keep me going."[18]

Lon found beauty in her companions. She described how she would ask to look at Guigui's hands just to admire them, or into someone's eyes. There was no touching: "That non-touching also had to do with the fact that we were eternally and always packed together and pressed and could barely escape one another's physical presence. . . . But in that moment of contemplation of beauty, however paradoxical that may sound, privacy was considered almost sacred, and was always respected."[19]

Lon remembered an incident when another French woman rushed into the block and announced: "You must come immediately to the washroom. There is a Russian girl washing herself, you can't believe your eyes. Beau-ti-ful." They all rushed to see her, "a breathtaking Juno."[20] She was muscular and fit, not starved and skeletal. She had gorgeous skin without the blemish of boils and infected lice bites. The water pouring over her skin glistened. She was one of the Soviet army girls, and because of this she had special privileges, including using the washroom when it was off-limits to everyone else. They watched, mesmerized, as the girl quietly cleaned her perfect body.

The Soviet army women were cool, closed, and taciturn, a military elite. Lon admired their discipline and dignity, as did the others. They were an impressive group. She thought that perhaps they respected the French political prisoners who had shown solidarity by refusing the rewards for surpassing the quotas in the factory. But the Russians were powerful, and Lon imagined they must have felt contempt for the comparatively small and weak French.

The close-knit French communists impressed Lon as well. They were mostly former factory girls from working-class families. Proud and committed, they stood up for one another. The communists organized *les gamelles de la solidarité*, the solidarity bowls. Everyone in the block would contribute a spoonful of soup or a morsel of bread into a few spare bowls. Each day, these bowls would be given to those who were most in need. Perhaps someone was sick and needed extra strength, or someone had been beaten by the guards or injured at the factory, or someone had gotten news of the death of a loved one. Juliette Bes wrote of this act, "Charity is when you give what you can give; solidarity is giving when you have nothing to give."[21]

Friendship was vital to survival. After being separated in Fresnes, Lon and Guigui found each other again in Ravensbrück. They remained close their whole lives. If at times Guigui felt frustrated with Lon for her stubbornness, she always admired her toughness. It was Lon who elbowed her way through the crowd to make sure she and Guigui were on the same list for transfer to Leipzig. Lon was cunning and found ways to bargain in that hell. She sometimes lost patience with Guigui, who could be distracted and nonchalant. The friends complemented each other. When Lon was a little too pushy, Guigui the diplomat smoothed things out and knit the group back together.

------≋------

The nine had to count on one another to survive, and that bond was something they would find hard to replicate later in normal life. Like soldiers who feel a bond of brotherhood after being in battle together, the intensity of their friendships was an essential part of their experience. Mena and Guigui became extremely close and remained friends for life. Zaza and Hélène were inseparable. Nicole adored Zinka at first sight and credits her bunkmate Renée Astier de Villatte with keeping her alive. Lon formed a deep friendship with Alina, a Polish prisoner she met in Leipzig. They were on the same wavelength, she wrote. She met Alina in the *Revier*, where she was sent—much to her chagrin—soon after arriving in Leipzig because the long hours spent standing at the roll calls had brought on terrible swelling in her legs and she had collapsed from exhaustion.

Alina had a certain hardness to her, no doubt learned from the years she had already spent in various camps. She had been a political prisoner since 1940, when she was just twenty years old and a student at Warsaw University. Lon and Alina had long talks, some philosophical, but mostly about their childhoods. From Alina, Lon learned about life in Poland before and during the German occupation. There were no men left in Alina's family; Alina was her mother's only remaining child.

Lon was popular among the young Polish women, whose youth and education had been so abruptly cut short. Shut in prisons for years, they were starved for new ideas and stories. Lon brought a breath of fresh air. They hung on her every word. And she loved more than anything to be the center of attention. She gave lectures on Assyrian and art history. Since her father had often taken her to look at and buy antiques, Lon was able to talk for hours about antique furniture, crystal, carpets, and paintings from various periods and schools. She also taught English, which she admits she was not very good at. But it was something to entertain the girls and keep their minds occupied. Lon recounted the plots of novels she had read. For the bitterly cold Christmas of 1944, when she was in Leipzig, she created a booklet titled *Gems of Wisdom and Beauty*. It included Arabic calligraphy, poetry from Rumi, Hafiz, and Shakespeare, and passages from Somerset Maugham, all recorded from memory.

The more dangerous and precarious their daily situation became, the more Lon had an attentive audience longing for escape. Her favorite stories were from her own life, from the three-month period she had spent in Algiers when she was eighteen years old.

Near the end of March 1945, three weeks before the camp would be emptied for the death march, Lon lifted a bag that was too heavy and heard something snap in her back. She collapsed and was unable to get up, much less walk or work. She was carried by stretcher to the *Revier*, and luckily Alina, a trained nurse, was there to take charge. She pushed away the Russian doctors, who were useless, according to Lon, and set to work. Lon was freezing and in shock. Alina covered her with every spare blanket she could find and even added a hot water bottle. She ordered that Lon be given spoonfuls of hot turnip soup every hour. She gathered a group of the Polish girls who had so loved Lon's stories and they tended to Lon around the clock. But nothing seemed to be working. Lon appeared to be paralyzed and would surely be selected for extermination. She could talk and think but she couldn't do anything else, except curse her luck for dying in Germany.

At her lowest point, she recalled how Alina leaned over her during a massage and asked hopefully. "Can you tell me that story again?"

Lon realized that she couldn't even nod. She saw Alina's worried face above her and resigned herself to dying. But then she thought of the word "lame." Suddenly she felt such a rejection of that idea that the fight came back into her. On the fifth morning, she felt a tingling in her fingers, and when Alina came to look, she said, "I can move my fingers again!"

Alina sprang into action. She got Guigui and Mena to drag Lon out of bed. "Try to walk! To move! Continue! Do not panic! You'll get it!" Alina shouted. Lon hung stiffly between the two women, and with great effort they moved her around. This routine was repeated every hour.

By the sixth day Lon was able to take small steps again. But in the middle of the seventh night, Alina woke Lon in a panic. "Get out! Now! You have to get out of here right now!"

Without explanation Lon was lifted from her bed by two people—she was unable to tell who they were. In silence they hurried with her between them. She was dragged out of the *Revier* and through dark alleys between the barracks to be deposited in her own cot.

How she survived the *Appell* the next morning is a mystery. Undoubtedly she was supported by Guigui, Mena, and Zinka. And then she became more resilient. After ten days she was better. She knows it was because of the unremitting care of Alina and her Polish friends. Alina later told her that she had been informed that there was going to be a German inspection of the *Revier* that night to see who could be selected for extermination before the general evacuations. Alina had saved Lon's life.

CHAPTER FIVE

— ZINKA —

Renée Lebon (Zinka)

THE NEXT MORNING, APRIL 17, they woke lazily. The sun glimmered through the cracks in the barn's sides. They felt languorous in their straw bed. Zinka automatically reached for the cigarette case, the one she had spent so many hours carefully making from torn strips of her sleeping pallet in Leipzig. Tucked inside the case was her only photo of fat, healthy baby France. A guard had smuggled the photo to her, and she had miraculously been able to keep it all this time. She kept the case carefully tucked in her small sack, which she used as a pillow. Every morning, when she reached for the worn and smooth case, it served as a tenuous connection to her husband, Louis Francis. Soon she would hand it to him, she told herself. He would know with this gift that she had thought about him through so many months.[1] It was meant to be a Christmas gift last year, when they had hoped they would all be home by December.

———◆———

None of the women wanted to get up and start moving. They chatted drowsily, listening to the bucolic sounds of cows in the field nearby. They had just spent their second night of sleep in freedom. But that freedom was still tenuous. They needed to find the elusive front and the American soldiers.

"I wish we could hear cannons or something," Zinka said. "Then at least we would know what direction to walk in." They all knew that Zinka would defiantly walk toward cannon fire and bombs bursting if she thought that was the way home to her baby France. "Shouldn't the front be louder?"

"Maybe we are just not close enough yet," Hélène offered somberly. They had no idea how many miles and days of walking lay between them and the advancing Americans. She feared they would be recaptured by the Germans or the Russians would get them first. She wondered to herself if they wouldn't be better off in smaller groups. But she knew none of the others would accept this idea.

"This war is not like the others," Jacky said in her gravelly voice. "There's no stupid Maginot line, no trenches. *C'est le bordel.*"

Jacky was thinking of her late husband, Jean Aubéry du Boulley, who had died from tuberculosis contracted during his brief time as a soldier. She remembered how he described the chaos when the Germans invaded. He wrote that the French generals were old, doddering, and misguided; they seemed incapable of action. This new kind of war was nothing like the last one. No one knew what to do. This *drôle de guerre*, this funny war, had been a humiliating fiasco from start to finish.

Jacky worried that she was a drag on the group. Maybe they would be better off if she just took her chances and stayed behind in some village barn.

Mena's voice interrupted her thoughts. "Mesdames, mesdemoiselles, on this lovely morning I am going to serve you breakfast in bed," she announced with a dramatic flourish.

"Really?" Nicole asked. "With what?"

"I can tell which of the three eggs the Yugoslavs gave us was hard-boiled."

"How?" Nicole asked.

"By weight. Boiled ones are always lighter," she said with such self-assurance that even Hélène, who knew Mena's logic was not sound, had a moment of doubt.

Mena planned to divide the one hard-boiled egg on their remaining bread slices. She carefully weighed each egg against the other in her hands. She rotated the eggs to double-check. The women watched Mena with amusement. She was making funny faces of intense concentration. "This one," she announced, holding it aloft. "It's definitely lighter than the other two."

Full of confidence, she cracked open the chosen egg. It crumpled and began to ooze out through her fingers. Mena let out a tiny cry of surprise and shock. Luckily Zinka, who knew Mena all too well, had planned ahead. She had placed her tin bowl under the egg, catching the yolk as it slid through Mena's fingers. "Well done!" Lon called out to Zinka.

Now they all burst into uncontrolled laughter. They couldn't stop. It was a hysterical release of tension. How long had it been since they had truly laughed? Zinka imitated Mena's cry of shock, and that reignited another round of laughter, with Mena joining in.

"Never mind," Mena said. "I have a plan!"

She mixed the raw egg with the small bit of breadcrumbs and a bit of schnapps, the last of the stores given to them by the Yugoslavs, and spread this mixture on the bread. The result was delicious. Nicole proposed they call it *tartines d'oeufs durs à la Mena.*

———

Hélène laughed along with others, but she was concerned about the day ahead. She wanted a more substantial meal for the group and some indication, if possible, about the direction of the front. So far they had been lucky. She went in search of the guesthouse owner, with hopes that he would invite them back for breakfast. She found him banging pots in the kitchen, startling him. A skinny, nervous man, he clearly hoped that the women had already left. She could see he now regretted allowing them to sleep in the barn. He wanted to help, but he was terrified and wished she would disappear.

"We just were hoping for some warm breakfast before we go," Hélène said in her most polite, fawning German.

"Yes, all right," he snapped back nervously. "On the condition that you eat in the kitchen, not the dining room. And at once, and then you must go away quickly."

"I will tell the others—"

"You must understand," he interrupted her, "if you're discovered . . . A group of men escaped a few days ago from one of those columns of marching prisoners, not far from here. Some people from this village hunted them down and executed them in the field. They called it a 'Jew hunt.'"

Hélène nodded. She refused to register any fear. "We're not escaped prisoners."

He grunted, indicating that she could drop the charade. "Killed them, just like that," he said, snapping his fingers. "Many around here are not as sympathetic as I am. They say the Russians have entered Berlin. They're tearing the place down. People are scared."

He had another story to tell her. A German officer in the village had just shot himself that very morning. It wasn't a good sign. People were panicking.

He repeated the story of the suicide to the other women when they gathered in the kitchen. Quickly and silently, each ate a boiled potato and drank a cup of milk. Then they gathered their belongings and headed out onto the road toward what they hoped was the front.

As they left Reppen, an old woman leaned out of a small window and called down to Lon, "Where are you going, my child?"

"Where the sun is pointing us, madame." Hélène had suggested that until they got better information, they should simply follow the sun westward until they fell upon the Americans.

"Yes, but where are you heading to?"

"Home. To Holland," Lon answered.

The old woman did not seem surprised by this and added that she too was a refugee from Prussia and would like one day to return home. Looking at the pitiful sack slung over Lon's shoulder, she asked, "Is that all that you were able to save, my child?"

"No, madame," Lon replied. "I also saved my life."[2]

———❧———

Their early morning laughing fit kept the women's spirits high, despite the guesthouse owner's gloomy warnings. Lon wrote in her journal for that day, "I no longer feel my freedom as a crystal bowl in my hand but as a matter of course."[3] But they continued to be weak and worn out. Their feet were bleeding. Hélène was developing a terrible hip pain. Zinka did not know it, but she had tuberculosis; Jacky had diphtheria; Josée's feet were covered in infected blisters; Nicole was recovering from pneumonia. Mena had been pretending since the start of their escape that this was just a wonderful camping trip. But the reality of their situation seemed to be wearing on her nerves. She was acting strange, skirting the edge between madness and whimsy. It was unsettling. The others exchanged worried glances when Mena began to laugh and skip with delirious joy at the sight of a bumblebee.[4] She seemed out of control, shouting and pointing, "Look, look, look, a bumblebee. Look at it!"

They all remembered women who had gone mad in the camps, and it was frightening. It seemed cruel that now, so close to their freedom, Mena would crack. A few of the women felt angry with her. She needed to get a grip on herself. But Guigui smiled with understanding. She hooked her arm through Mena's, which served to calm her down. Guigui kissed Mena on the forehead and the two began to walk together at a steadier pace.

The landscape from Leipzig to Oschatz had been flat and monotonous, but now the land was dotted with trees and gently rolling hills. Little villages were tucked into the folds of small valleys.

Raitzen, the next village on their way, turned out to be only a few kilometers on. There they were immediately accosted by a policeman who said it was forbidden to walk in the zone between the two front lines. This news buoyed them. It was the first real information, however inadvertent, that they had received about the location of the front.

The policeman stuck his hand out with authority and demanded their papers. Hélène stepped forward. She had been expecting another confrontation with the German authorities. It was inevitable. Somehow she had to talk their way out of this one too.

The other women kept their heads down, avoiding eye contact. Mena began to giggle, but Guigui stopped her, squeezing her hand. Hélène made a quick decision to use the guestworkers story and explained to the man that their factory had been bombed. "Look at our clothes. We lost everything; we had no time to even get our things," she said. They looked desperate because they were. They had to flee. They were now simply trying to get home.

"We are only a group of women, meaning no harm," she said. "We don't understand war. It's not our business. We are just lost. Just women." She hoped this would awaken his pity. "Perhaps you could draw us a map of a route that will get us back to France without bothering the fighting men?"

He studied her, then scanned the group, and finally looked back at Hélène. He took a deep breath, and she could see he had softened. He asked her to follow him into his office, where he paternalistically drew a map for her, showing her where the current front lines might be, at least according to the last news he had received. He showed her how to best avoid that area. She praised his drawing, thanked him for being so kind, and peppered him with "innocent" questions. "It's just that I don't understand how war works," she kept repeating. "You understand. We are only women."

Inwardly, she was elated. He was drawing the map on letterhead from the Raitzen police station. The letterhead, she knew, would prove much more useful than the map itself. He didn't have a precise idea where the American troops were, but she didn't care. Knowing the German insistence on papers, she immediately recognized the importance of this official-looking paper and how they could subvert its meaning. They would be able to present it as proof that they had been given permission to travel; they had a *laisser-passer*—from the police of Raitzen, no less.

While Hélène was charming the policeman, the rest of the group waited outside, trying to soak up heat from the sun that poked out intermittently from behind the gray shroud of clouds. A group of German soldiers noticed the women sitting idly and laughing together. Learning they were French, they wanted to flirt and banter. They wanted the women to understand they did not see them as enemies. Gradually the soldiers learned that the women had escaped the SS, that they were not *Gastarbeiter.* The soldiers offered a trade: two breads, some margarine, cheese, a small chocolate, and cigarettes for twenty marks and one of the women's red triangles. It might come in handy to have proof that they had helped escaped French political prisoners. When the soldiers moved on, the women lit one cigarette, passing it from hand to hand. Taking a drag, Jacky was overcome with a spasm of coughing.

"I don't think that's a good idea," Zinka said. "Maybe with your heart, you shouldn't smoke."

"Merde!" Jacky snapped at her. "I'm fine. My lungs are out of practice. What's not good for my heart is this damn camping trip."

Mena took the cigarette and blew a series of perfect smoke rings. Her earlier delirium had passed and now she appeared apathetic, resigned. "Still, good or not, here we are on this damn camping trip."

———◆———

At the start of my search for the women on the "camping trip" with my Tante Hélène, I knew only their nicknames or noms de guerre. The archivist at the museum for the Nazi Forced Labor Memorial had given me the list of prisoners at HASAG Leipzig, and that had led me to discover the real identities of a few other women in the group of nine. But I had reached a dead end. The photocopied scanned page was hard to read, with smudges, pencil marks, and margin notes I could not decipher. If I was going to find out more about the nine women, I needed to visit the National Archives in Paris.

I would have to reserve the documents that I wanted to look at by going through the massive online inventory. I had no idea where to begin. I chose a box of documents belonging to someone named Odette Pilpoul, simply because it said she too had been a prisoner at HASAG Leipzig.

The files I had ordered were waiting for me when I arrived at the National Archives. They came in an old-fashioned canvas dossier, held together with cloth ties. Opening it, I smelled the familiar and comforting odor of old paper. I was transported to the attic of my father's farm, where I spent hot summer afternoons looking through boxes of letters and old magazines that dated from the war. As a boy, my father had a crush on the young Queen Elizabeth and he had collected magazines about her coronation. He had also kept the few letters and documents that remained from his father, who had escaped the persecution of Jews in Germany to later become a soldier with the American Office of Strategic Services during the war. There is a particular smell to papers from this time, and here it was again.

Pilpoul was a French political prisoner like the nine women I was writing about. They had lived, it turned out, in the same prison block in Leipzig. As a young woman in Paris, Odette had helped to print and distribute the clandestine paper *Libération*, the same paper that Geneviève de Gaulle worked on. In 1941 Odette became the assistant to the mayor of the Third Arrondissement. In that position she was able to provide hundreds of false documents to Jews and non-Jews, including false identity cards, birth certificates, and ration cards; she writes of always "forgetting" to use the stamp that marked a person as Jewish. She warned of coming roundups. She sabotaged investigations by the Gestapo and hid Jews in her apartment. She helped British and American pilots who had been shot down by the Luftwaffe, providing them with false papers. She placed Jewish babies with Christian families. But in 1944 she was caught with a Jewish family hidden in her apartment. She was sent to Fresnes, then Romainville, then Ravensbrück, and finally HASAG Leipzig.[5]

The box contained the notes she had kept in Leipzig, her meticulous lists, and the Nazi documents that she had managed to steal in the final days of the camp. Suddenly I was holding the original of that photocopied page from the archivist in Leipzig. I could now read all the faint markings. Next to my aunt's nom de guerre, Christine, Odette had written "Hélène." They must have been close friends if she knew my aunt's real name. Somehow Odette had saved this vital document from destruction.

Before stealing the Nazi list, Odette had made a makeshift notebook with scraps of discarded paper from the HASAG factory floor that she sewed together with scavenged thread. In it she recorded who was with her in the camp, who was transferred, who had been killed. She wrote everyone's full address so that their families could be contacted afterward, so they could know what had happened to their loved one. There is a list of her friends who died. There is a list that notes the arrival of a group in September that included Jacky, Nicole, and Nicole's close friend Renée, which explained why I hadn't been able to find them on the list sent to me by the archivist at Leipzig. All this clandestine record-keeping revealed a dedication to protecting the truth.

I had read that after the terrible terrorist attacks at the Bataclan nightclub in Paris in November 2015, people had created, as they often do, a spontaneous memorial near the site of the tragedy, a wall of photos and notes and drawings and cards. When it was time to clean this up and return to normal life, archivists carefully, lovingly gathered each piece of paper, each card and note, so that they could be preserved.

Looking around the reading room at the archives, I felt the presence of others before me, people like Odette who risked their lives to record and save what they could. Odette understood the importance of bearing witness. It felt as if that day she gave me permission to write this book.

———— ❧ ————

Even with the original Nazi list in my hands, I had no idea how I could find Zinka's real name. Zinka could be a nickname for the Yiddish name Myzinka, meaning "little finger" or "small one." Maybe it was a nickname given to her by other prisoners. What was her real name? And had she ever found her daughter? I wondered if there was a record of France's birth somewhere.

I searched for accounts of children born in the French prisons, and anything that could help me to find out what happened to those children. I also looked for any stories of escapes during the disorder of the death marches. There were quite a few, as the Nazi machine had been crumbling.

I came across the name Renée Guette on the same Nazi list of Leipzig inmates that listed Hélène. She was number 4036. She was arrested when she was just sixteen. In 1945 she was eighteen, around the same age as Josée. From her account she escaped from the death march the morning they first reached Wurzen, at the moment when they were bombed by Allied planes—the moment when Josée's bag was strafed with bullets. Renée explained that while others were running around madly, in the chaos she and a group of four ran toward a wooded area.

The SS guards shot at them. Renée lagged behind. A friend pulled her down into a ditch. Then a group of civilians passed by and they were able to use that diversion for cover to run to the woods, where they hid during their first night of freedom. She was found by the Russian army and handed over to the American refugee camp in Grimma on May 7.

Renée had been in Romainville, Neue Bremm, Ravensbrück, and then HASAG Leipzig—the same sequence as Hélène. After the war, a family sent Renée a photo of a little boy. They were looking for the boy and his mother, Pauley, who was their daughter and a friend of Renée's. Did she know what had happened to Pauley? She wrote on the back of the photo: "Pauley's older son, certainly dead. Last seen Pauley on the road just before liberation. Arrested pregnant. Her twins were drowned in a bucket in front of her eyes. After that she went crazy. She must have died on the road."

I thought there was little chance that Zinka's baby had survived. But then my search brought me to a newspaper photograph of five children born while their mothers were imprisoned in France. The photograph was taken after the war, and the caption explains that there were eight children born during that time. The mothers were kept apart from the other prisoners. Later these mothers were deported to Ravensbrück, and some went on to Leipzig. Their children had been taken away from them. Seven survived; Micheline and her baby Bébiette, who were Jewish, were sent to the gas chamber in 1943.

Lise London

Lise London was in the same group of mothers. After the war, she wrote a memoir, *La mégère de la rue Daguerre* (The shrew of Daguerre Street). Lise organized a protest against the forced labor of young French men in Germany, the STO. She stood on the busy rue Daguerre and made an impassioned speech to the crowd, followed by a confetti shower of political tracts and a passionate chorus of "La Marseillaise."

The protest was short-lived, as police soon descended on the crowd; Lise narrowly escaped. But she had made a fateful mistake, something that her husband had tried to warn against that morning. He had known she was heading into grave danger, so as they kissed on the stairs, he asked her, "Are you sure you have metro tickets with you?"[6]

She had not taken his worries seriously, or perhaps she had wanted to downplay them to reassure him. But at the critical moment when she was trying to escape, she did not have a metro ticket. She had to escape on foot and seek shelter at a friend's apartment nearby. But someone in the apartment building had seen her, and a few days later she was denounced and arrested. A newspaper article about the protest called her a *mégère*—a shrew. There was great pressure from the German authorities to give her the death penalty, but her pregnancy saved her. The French authorities, though fully collaborating with the Germans, were still hesitant to deport or execute a pregnant woman, since the child she carried was innocent.

Thinking of Zinka, I read Lise's description of what it was like to give birth in prison. The first time she went into labor, she was transferred to a hospital under armed guard and handcuffed to the hospital bed. Then as her labor pains increased, an agent from the French secret police began to interrogate her. They were sure that she had more information, that she knew names and heads of networks. The man began to slap her and beat her, even as she was having contractions. At last the presiding doctor had enough. He demanded that the police leave the room. But then her labor stopped, and so she was returned to the prison. When at last she did go into labor, her friends helped her give birth in secret. She bit on a towel to avoid making any noise.

Between April 4 and May 16, 1944, Lise and all the other female political prisoners were deported. The prison authorities promised the mothers they would do their best to reunite their babies with their families. On their last night, after giving up their children and before being handed over to the Germans, the women were given back their civilian clothes, their wedding rings, their watches. It felt strange to be back in their old clothes, which fit loosely, as everyone had lost weight. No one slept; their hearts ached with the loss of their children. A priest visited them in the early morning, and they were able to stuff his pockets with notes and addresses so that he could get word to their families to fetch their babies. As each group was sent off, they heard singing arise from the different buildings until everyone joined in. They sang the "Chant des Adieux" to the tune of "Auld Lang Syne":

> *Faut-il nous quitter sans espoir,*
> *Sans espoir de retour,*
> *Faut-il nous quitter sans espoir*
> *De nous revoir un jour*
> *Ce n'est qu'un au-revoir, mes frères*
> *Ce n'est qu'un au-revoir*
> *Oui, nous reverrons, mes frères,*
> *Ce n'est qu'un au-revoir*
>
> *Must we part without hope*
> *Without hope of returning*
> *Must we part without hope*
> *Of seeing each other again*
> *It's only a goodbye, my brothers*
> *It's only a goodbye*
> *Yes, we will see each other again, my brothers*
> *It's only a goodbye.*

They were led into a courtyard, surrounded by Nazi soldiers. The head of the prison read out the list of names. Lise London wrote that as the final name was called, and without a visible sign passing between them, the women broke into song again with "La Marseillaise."

"The SS raged, beat us with rifle butts, and pushed us to the trucks where we went without stopping the song." The SS, with their weapons in hand, stood on the backs of the trucks and pulled the tarpaulins over the women to hide them. The women could tell by the movement of the wheels over the paving stones that they were passing through the streets of the city. "We continued to sing 'La Marseillaise' to alert the passers-by and to make them understand what these German military trucks contained."[7]

———✺———

At the Romainville detention and deportation camp, they saw carved in the wooden bunks of their new block the names of some of their comrades along with "Vive la France" and "À bas Hitler!"

Someone found Danielle Casanova's name. They gathered round and felt the grooves with their fingers. Danielle, their hero, had passed through here. She had been trained as a dentist, but after the fall of France she had organized youth and then women's groups. She wrote for the underground newspaper *Pensée Libre* (Free Thought) and founded *La Voix des Femmes* (Women's Voice). Full of life and laughter, Danielle inspired many, many women to join the struggle. She believed ardently in absolute equality between men and women. Early on her husband had been taken prisoner in Germany. She had to move from place to place, hiding. Eventually she was caught, arrested, and sent to Auschwitz, where she worked in the infirmary. Because the Germans were so worried about infection and epidemics, those people they had to work closely with, such as the medical staff in the *Revier*, were given access to water and clean clothes.

Danielle brought news to the others whenever she could. When possible, she got them jobs to protect them—for one friend, for example, she created a job in the infirmary of scaring away the rats. When she came to visit the others at night in the blocks her face was wet with tears. She witnessed such horrific things each day. But to the women she brought hope. They were sure she would survive to tell their story—so sure that many gave her the only thing they had managed to save, their wedding rings.

Danielle died of typhus a year before the women were sent to

Romainville, and the word of her passing reached all the way back to the women in prison in France. Lise London wrote: "At the thought of her memory, tears formed in the eyes of all those women who loved her. We already knew that she was no longer, and yet we felt her close to us."[8]

From Romainville they were sent to Neue Bremm on May 30. That marked their true descent into hell. When the wagon was opened, they were immediately assaulted by a horrific sight. Lise wrote:

I always remember this first and unbearable image of skeletal men who, under the orders of a group of dashing and insolent SS officers, whips in hand, were forced to crawl running around a basin, endlessly for the joy of the sadistic brutes. The officers called it "sport." Two prisoners dragging a dead man passed in front of us, frozen with horror. One of them whispered to us, "See what they do to men here."[9]

Renée Guette also describes the first "sport" she was made to watch upon arrival at Neue Bremm: "We watched a skeleton of a man on all fours crawling toward a piece of sugar. He had to pick it up like a dog with his mouth, but at the last moment it was taken from him. Then the SS made him run like that on all fours as they whipped him."[10]

Zinka and Louis Francis, summer 1942

I found my first clue to Zinka's real name in Lise London's book. It turns out that they were close friends. Lise included a pencil sketch she made of a woman she called "Zimka," and in parentheses she added the name Renée Châtenay. I wasn't sure this was the same person as Zinka. But when I got hold of a copy of Lon's book, on one of the last pages she wrote that Zinka's real name was Renée Lebon Lebon. Searching for Renée Lebon and Renée Châtenay, I eventually found that they were one person: her maiden name was Lebon, her married name Châtenay. Her paternal grandmother was called Zinka, and in her honor Renée Lebon's middle name was Zinka.

Lon wrote, "Zinka—Renée Lebon Lebon—was a little doll, with curly hair and such a nice gap between her front teeth. She was the only one of us who had a child, born in Fresnes, France, who was handed over to the family."[11]

Zinka's father was Pierre Lebon, the son of André Lebon, who was minister of commerce and industry in the French colonies. His mother, Zinka's grandmother, was Zinka Paléologue; she was the sister of Maurice Paléologue, who was the last French ambassador to the tsar. Zinka came from a social milieu of aristocracy, powerful politicians, and diplomats.

In 1913 Pierre Lebon married Jeanne Crozet-Fourneyron, and they had two daughters; Zinka was born in 1914. Pierre fought in the First World War. Toward the end of the war in 1916, Jeanne fell ill and died of the Spanish influenza. Jeanne's unmarried sister Simone moved in to take care of the household. A few years later, in 1919, Pierre married Simone and they had four more children. Simone, Zinka's aunt and stepmother, died in 1936, before the war. In some ways, Zinka had twice lost her mother, first when she was two and then again at age twenty-two. She was left to take care of the other children, all her brothers and sisters. Perhaps for this reason she had not married earlier.

At the outbreak of the Second World War the family immediately joined the Résistance. The Lebon family was close to Charles de Gaulle, and Pierre, Zinka's father, would remain a faithful Gaullist for life. As early as 1940 Zinka was distributing journals, tracts, and propaganda. Her older brother Yves was part of the Free French forces and was killed at Bir-Hakeim in 1942. Zinka's father worked with de

Gaulle as a leader of Jade Fitzroy, a Résistance network. Her other brother, Roger, was head of the Gambetta network.

Concerned for the future of his unmarried daughter, Pierre noticed a nice young man who was the office manager at the ministry of supplies and provisions. Louis Francis Lebon (no relation) was two years younger than Zinka and had degrees in political science and law. Louis Francis was funny, with a sweet and goofy look: he was tall and thin, with large ears and a big grin. He towered over little Zinka.

Pierre was the matchmaker. He brought Louis Francis home to meet Zinka. There was no doubt about the importance of fighting the Germans in the patriotic Lebon family. One can assume that Louis Francis shared this fervor with Zinka, but he also could make her laugh. He probably worked with Pierre and other networks helping to get ration cards to those in hiding. Louis Francis fell in love with Zinka, and judging from the photographs, they were a happy pair. The two of them have their arms hooked tightly together, beaming, during the hardest years of the war. They were married on September 11, 1942.

In April 1943, along with Louis Francis, Zinka joined Comète, the network that hid downed British airmen and helped them escape back to England. Zinka was in charge of sheltering one large American pilot who was staying in a small *chambre de bonne*, one of those absurdly tiny apartments high in the eaves of Parisian buildings that were meant as maids' quarters. A Midwestern farm boy who had never traveled outside his state before the war, much less to foreign lands, the American was going stir-crazy in that tiny, stifling space. He told Zinka that he couldn't leave Paris without first seeing the Eiffel Tower. What would he tell his friends and family if he didn't? She took pity on him and agreed to take him to the place du Trocadéro, where he could see the tower. She hadn't thought about how big he would look next to her and next to the famished Parisians. They got a few stares from people on the metro. She explained to her American that he should say nothing, not speak a word, and if asked, he should pretend he was a deaf-mute. Once they were at the place du Trocadéro, to her horror Zinka saw that the place was teeming with German soldiers on furlough, snapping pictures of the sweeping vista down to the Seine and across the river to the Eiffel Tower. Her

American, overcome with the sight of the tower, exclaimed in his loud booming voice, "Wow! That's just fantastic!"

She grabbed him, spun him around, and pulled him quickly back down into the metro, hissing at him to shut up. Later she would laugh about his spontaneous outburst. The beauty of Paris was too much for him to contain himself. But at the moment she wanted to box his ears.[12]

Zinka's half sister Marthe and half brother Roger, aged twenty-one and twenty, accompanied pilots all the way to the Spanish border. They were also providing false papers to those in the underground and finding hiding places for people and radios. But by the spring of 1943 the Comète line had been infiltrated by the Germans and was seriously compromised. Multiple shelters were raided and agents hauled in by the Gestapo. Hundreds of US and Canadian pilots who had been in hiding were deported to Buchenwald. Nine months after their marriage, on June 23, 1943, Louis Francis was arrested.

Almost two months went by with no official word about her husband's fate. Zinka was desperate. Someone got word to her that he was being held in Fresnes and facing deportation to Germany. Adding to her anxiety, Zinka had discovered that she was three months pregnant. Wanting to share the news with her husband, maybe to help raise his morale, and worried that he would be deported or condemned to death, Zinka went to the Fresnes prison on August 12 to inquire after Louis Francis. She must have known she was taking a great risk, but Zinka was nothing if not brave. The Gestapo arrested her on the spot. She too became a prisoner in Fresnes.

She would have been deported earlier, and thus she would have had less of a chance of survival, but because she was pregnant the authorities kept her in the French prison, as they had with Lise London. Six months later, on February 8, 1944, she gave birth to her daughter, whom she patriotically named France. As noted earlier, she was allowed to keep France for eighteen days before the baby was taken away. We can't know if Louis Francis heard the news about his daughter's birth, but he was still in Fresnes at the time, so it is probable that he did. He may have been able to get a message back to Zinka.

Zinka's siblings Marthe and Roger had joined a network that worked directly with British intelligence. On March 20, 1944, while they were at work making preparations for another operation, their office was stormed by the Gestapo. They too were sent to Fresnes. Were the two sisters able to see each other? Were the men?

Louis Francis and Roger may have heard the news through the prison grapevine that Zinka and Marthe had been deported to Germany in May 1944. Many former prisoners from that time recount that on the mornings when a group of prisoners was readied for transport, waiting in the central courtyard, the whole prison would be on alert. And at a given moment, every prisoner in every cell would break into song together, singing at the top of their lungs the "Chant des Adieux," with the last line "It's only a goodbye." Louis Francis and Zinka, who probably never saw each other in prison, would have been thinking of each other as they sang those words.

Zinka was sent first to Romainville to await deportation. Some of the women's families had discovered that there was a hill above the prison where they could stand and see into the women's windows. Zinka last saw France, a fat, healthy three-month-old, in her sister Claude's arms on the distant hill. Somehow her sister also managed to smuggle a photograph of baby France to her.

Louis Francis was deported on June 3, 1944, to Sachsenhausen, a camp just north of Berlin. It was only a few stops before Fürstenberg, the town on the other side of the lake from Ravensbrück. I wondered if Zinka knew how close she was to him, at least in the first months of their deportation.

———⊸———

In the central courtyard at Romainville fifty names were called; Zinka's was among them. The prisoners were told to get their things, and each was given a Red Cross package. They waited for hours in rows in the courtyard, forbidden to talk. Then they were loaded onto trucks and driven to the Gare de l'Est, surrounded by soldiers. Upon arrival they tried to sing "La Marseillaise," but the guards reacted so violently that they stopped. They were surrounded by civilians, and the guards were especially determined that no insurrection happen now. They were led to the front cars, right after the locomotive, of a normal passenger train.

The train began to move, the blinds were ordered shut, and the windows were locked. It was forbidden to touch the windows or to speak, but soon word was passed: Go to the toilet, and you can drop a message out onto the tracks through the toilets. They each scribbled a final message to their families, and one by one these messages were "sent." Many of these notes were gathered by railway workers and in fact delivered.

An hour into the voyage, the train car shook violently. They had been struck by a bomb. The train stopped suddenly, and everyone fell from their seats. Then they heard airplanes. The Royal Air Force was targeting the train. Chaos ensued; people were shouting. Another pass by the planes could be heard above them, and the train was hit again, followed by the rat-a-tat-tat of automatic weapons fire. The girl next to Zinka had fallen on top of her and was badly wounded. She heard the Germans pulling some kind of weapons onto the roof of the train. They began shooting back at the planes. There was the sound of more planes overhead and exchanges of gunfire.

Zinka had wondered why they were in regular passenger cars and not the cattle wagons she had heard so much about. But now she realized the train was carrying German soldiers and weapons. The prisoners were being used as human shields.

When the planes flew away, silence descended, followed by the shouts of the Germans and the moans of the wounded. In her car, everything was topsy-turvy. The windows were shattered and the blinds the Germans had ordered shut were now in tatters. She was one of the few people to escape the shower of bullets. They had to carry the bodies of the dead out of the cars and place them on the side of the tracks while Germans shouted at them. Then a new locomotive was brought, and the train continued on its way.

After a long journey, with many stops and starts, sometimes even moving backward, they arrived in the middle of the night at a station where they were ordered to get down from the train. They were in Neue Bremm. They were led by guards with vicious dogs on leashes to a large hall where they were told to lie down on the straw mattresses and go to sleep. A female guard walked among them swinging her whip. But someone was brave enough at that moment to begin singing the beautiful strains of "Ave Maria." The guard at first tried to stop it, but the woman's voice was so beautiful, so crystalline and perfect, that even the guard was won over and allowed her to keep singing. This was Zinka's first night in Germany.[13]

The next morning, the guards told them they were there for their "education." They were led out to an area in front of a rectangular basin filled with water. There they saw a dozen male prisoners with their hands tied behind their backs; some of them were naked, and some of them had their feet tied loosely together as well. These men were forced to run around the basin, first in a low crouch and then upright, up and down and around like this without end. The guards whipped them as they passed and pushed and tripped them. When they collapsed, they were set upon by dogs and kicked by the guards. Some were pushed into the basin and drowned there. The guards amused themselves by pouring their paltry bowl of soup on the ground in front of them and making the men lick it up. The guards called this "sport." This would be the punishment that awaited the women if they disobeyed any order. This was the horrific world they had entered.

Zinka was the first of the nine women to be sent to Ravensbrück. She arrived in May 1944. While she was in Neue Bremm, she had heard about German losses on the Eastern Front and in Italy. Hélène, Zaza, Lon, Guigui, Josée, and Mena would arrive in June. They knew about the Allied landing in Normandy. Nicole and Jacky would not arrive until August, just as Paris was being liberated. Even as the war was turning, the nine were being sent deeper and deeper into Germany and away from liberation.

In Neue Bremm, Zinka was sure that at any moment she would be liberated. She knew it was only a matter of time before the Germans capitulated. But when she was once again put onto a train car, this time to be sent even farther east, Zinka felt her heart sink. Now she sensed she was in for a long struggle to survive. This time the women were stuffed into the wagons meant for animals. With no water in the heat of the summer, the women's thirst was almost unbearable. In May, the nights were still very cold, but during the day the cars heated up. There was only a tiny window for ventilation, and soon the car smelled terribly of urine, feces, sweat, and fear.

On the women's arrival in Ravensbrück, the usual dehumanizing ordeal was once again enacted. Zinka was stripped of her clothes and her wedding ring. She whispered a plea to the German-Czech prisoner working in the *Effektenkammer* to keep her one photo of baby

France safe. With barely a glance between them, the woman slipped the photo into an inside pocket of her striped jacket. A few days later, she surreptitiously handed it back to Zinka without a word.

After all the sinister formalities of the German killing bureaucracy were followed, Zinka became number 42106. She would be selected along with Hélène and the others for the large transport of women to the HASAG Leipzig labor camp in July, and there she would be assigned the number 3892.

———≈———

Outside the police station in Raitzen, a suspicious peasant woman approached the eight women while they sat smoking and waiting for Hélène. "Who are you? What are you doing here?" she barked at them. They felt both annoyed and frightened by her manner.

Lon patiently repeated the story they had heard Hélène give the policeman, but the woman wasn't interested. She interrupted Lon: "I saw you made a deal with those soldiers. You want to buy some of my potatoes?"

Lon agreed to buy fifty kilos if half were precooked. The farmer delivered them to Hélène as she left the police station: there were only thirty-seven kilos of potatoes, and none were cooked. The gruff, unfriendly manner of the peasant gave them all a bad feeling about Raitzen.

"Maybe we can sleep in the field, under the stars, and have a campfire and cook our potatoes over the fire?" Mena suggested enthusiastically.

"Campfire, *merde!*" Jacky growled. "Stars and fucking fields—God, give me a real roof over my head."

A few kilometers farther on they came to a large farmhouse, with a barn surrounded by rolling fields. They realized that as a group, they presented quite a spectacle, frightening to behold: rag-clad, limping, emaciated beggars with a big iron pot on a tripod and a sack of potatoes. So seven of them hid behind a wall while Hélène and Lon tried their luck.

They returned with such contrite looks on their faces that the others said nothing. No questions this time. They wordlessly began to gather their belongings, wondering how far it might be to the next village. At which point Hélène said, "Why are you walking away?"

Lon and Hélène burst into laughter. They seemed to love to play this trick.

"It's wonderful," Hélène explained. "We met the owner of this farm, Ernst Reitzer, and his daughter Annelise."

Blonde, smiling Annelise had not hesitated even an instant to invite them for a meal. When they entered the farmhouse, they found a large, bright kitchen featuring a beautiful table with flowers in a vase. The women, despite their hunger, felt moved by the simple beauty. They had lived so long in a place of no color, bereft of any beauty, that they stood for a moment in pure wonderment, tears in their eyes.

Annelise invited them to sit. There was a big, steaming pot of soup, a bowl of cooked potatoes, cream cheese, jam, coffee, and bread. She and Ernst were gracious hosts. And as the women ate, Annelise and Ernst asked questions, more or less discreetly. Mostly Annelise spoke, perhaps because she was the same age as the women, in her twenties. She wasn't actually a farmer, she explained. She had been in school when the war broke out. Then both her brothers died in the war and her mother died of a broken heart. She had to leave her studies to help her father run the farm. She played with the napkin in her lap as she spoke, smoothing it and resmoothing it across her knees as if she could iron out the wrinkles of her story. Once upon a time she had had big dreams, but then the war came. They all nodded in agreement. They knew exactly what she meant. Annelise looked up at the smiling faces around the table listening attentively. They were all so thin and drawn, their clothes in rags, their visages haggard despite their smiles. She could tell that these women were not bohemians or vagabonds, and she was genuinely curious how they had come to be in their current state.

The women would remember this evening, the generosity of their hosts, the feeling of calm and true kindness. Not the begrudging kindness they would receive from others who sensed the war was almost over and so wanted to end it on the right side of history. With Annelise and her father they felt genuine hospitality. When Annelise asked what had happened to them, they knew her question was sincere. Hélène spoke for them all. Her voice was poised and neutral.

She told them about the nightmare of the transports in the cattle cars, the crowded and unclean conditions. She told them about the exterminations, and the crematorium, the choking ash in the air that they knew had been their bunkmates just yesterday. She spoke of the terrible stench of burning flesh, human excrement, and rot, how it stuck to your skin and in the seams of the clothes that also held countless lice.

She told how they were forced to eat meals beneath the bodies of their friends who were hung from nooses in the rafters of the canteen. How they were made to stand for hours in the cold. How during these roll calls you might be executed for nothing at all. How they had to watch friends being murdered by firing squads. How they were whipped, beaten, tortured. How some were selected for the brothel for the SS guards. She told them about the baby taken from Zinka's arms, about those who were worked to death, about those who went crazy with hunger and fear. She told them about the *Kaninchen* (rabbits), the young Polish girls in Ravensbrück who were used for medical experiments.[14]

Clandestine photograph taken in Ravensbrück
of one of the *Kaninchen*, showing her wounds

A Nazi doctor, Karl Gebhardt, savagely cut open their legs, or broke their bones, or amputated their feet, and then infected them with different strains of gangrene-producing bacteria, staphylococci, and streptococci obtained from a nearby laboratory. They limped through the mud of the camp on makeshift crutches. They became mascots for the prisoners, who felt the "rabbits" had to survive to show the full scale of the Nazi horror. Near the end of the war, when the SS ordered the extermination of all the surviving "rabbits," the other women in Ravensbrück risked their lives to save them by switching their numbers with those of women who had already died, and then getting them smuggled onto transports to other labor camps. A few had arrived that way at HASAG Leipzig in the final months of the war.

By the time Hélène finished speaking, Annelise had begun weeping and Ernst was visibly moved. The women had never really believed that the Germans did not know what was happening in the camps, but that evening they understood that perhaps there were some Germans who truly did not know.

Hélène changed the subject to their nationalities. "So here we are: six French, two Dutch, one Spanish. Almost all of us were students or secretaries. One of us was learning to sing."

"Which one?" Annelise asked, her voice brightening, "Will she sing for us?"

Josée could not refuse. She hadn't refused all those Sunday afternoons in the camp when her friends begged her to sing for them, even though she had been told by her instructor not to sing when she was tired or worn out, because she was still very young and could overstrain her vocal cords. In Leipzig she had sung popular favorites of the time: "La Truite de Schubert"; "J'attendrai," Rina Ketty's big hit; or Lucienne Boyer's "Que reste-t-il de nos amours?," with the women humming along during the choruses and letting their heads sway with the music. On the bunks they hooked arms and smiled at one another. Her songs gave them one of those rare transcendent moments when they could feel their humanity again.

Now, in front of Annelise and Ernst, Josée blushed and whispered to Hélène, "What should I sing?"

"La Truite," Hélène suggested. It had been a camp favorite. Josée was able to give it a crystalline freshness. They listened as they had so many times before, weeping quietly as they remembered the people they had lost. But this time as they listened to Josée singing in the warm kitchen with their stomachs full, they wept openly and as free women.

CHAPTER SIX

— JOSÉE —

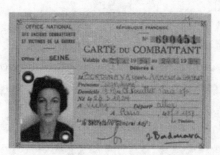

Joséphine Bordanava (Josée)

WHEN THE WOMEN WOKE UP on Annelise's farm on the morning of April 18, they could not have known that the infamous Abtnaundorf Massacre was taking place at the Leipzig-Thekla camp. Most of the several thousand men there were forced out on a death march with the women on April 13, but close to 300 were too sick to walk. Twelve SS soldiers locked up the sick prisoners in a barracks, doused the building with gasoline, and set it afire using grenade launchers and machine guns. Of the prisoners who managed to escape the inferno, many were shot; under cover of the dense smoke, a few did manage to make their way to the nearby living quarters of the Polish civilian workers, who took them in and hid them, but others were shot or beaten to death by local residents. The US Army arrived only a few hours later and discovered the still-smoldering site packed with charred bodies. Horrified, they filmed the crime scene, collecting the testimonies of the few survivors. These documents would be used as evidence at the International Military Tribunal in Nuremberg after the war.[1] If the Americans had not arrived in time, this likely would have been the fate of the women who remained behind at the HASAG Leipzig camp's *Revier.*

That same morning Annelise served the women an ample breakfast and showed them the laundry room, where there was a sink with running hot water. They washed their faces and hands and shared a rag to give themselves quick sponge baths. Hélène found a toothbrush on the windowsill.

"How do you know it's clean?" Zaza said, looking at it suspiciously.

"Who knows who it belongs to?" Lon added.

"It probably belonged to the cowherd, but I don't care," Hélène declared. Her teeth, brutally damaged in Ravensbrück, ached and troubled her. She longed to clean them properly.

Annelise and her father refused payment for their hospitality. They asked the women to "tell the French that not all the Germans were like the ones you knew before."[2] The women gave Annelise one of the red triangles that marked them as political prisoners. On the back, they signed it: *In remembrance of a generous welcome, cordial and unexpected, given to nine prisoners.*

The women felt buoyed as they walked to the next village, a tiny and picturesque place. There a German woman came to the gate of her garden and offered them a pot of cooked chickpeas. They happily accepted the gift and poured it into the heavy pot that Nicole had been carrying. They were moved by the woman's spontaneous kindness. Maybe this adventure they were on would turn out just fine, they mused. "Everyone is being so nice to us!" Zaza exclaimed.

Nicole felt uneasy about all this good fortune. It was hard to believe everyone would be so friendly and welcoming. Only a few days earlier they had been the Germans' prisoners. She wasn't surprised when a group of men appeared in the road, bristling with hostility and blocking their way.

Hélène stepped forward and began to speak, but she was interrupted by yet another red-faced, screaming *Bürgermeister*. "There have been others just like you who tried to pass here. It is forbidden!" he yelled.

Hélène took a deep breath, and with her tongue she felt the place in her mouth where her tooth was missing; it had become a habit when she was confronted by angry Germans. She exhaled and coolly responded: "For others it is normal, but we are not like the others."

"What do you mean? You all look the same." He practically spat at her. "Vagabonds . . ."

She pulled out the piece of paper with the Raitzen police station letterhead. "You see, we have been given permission to pass."

The *Bürgermeister* and the other men gathered around to have a look. They were instantly transformed. It worked like a charm, noted Zaza in her account, "as do all official papers on the Germans."[3]

Taking no chances, the women quickly left the little village behind them and found a spot away from the road to stop and eat under a shade tree. They laughed at how a piece of stationery had transformed those men from puffed-up, angry hotheads to demure, dutiful officials. They took turns scooping up heaps of chickpeas with their crudely fashioned camp spoons.

Zinka said, "Who would believe we could eat so much?" as she swallowed another spoonful.

And Nicole answered, "Yes, and who would believe that we ate so little for so long?"

———❦———

After a few hours' rest, they continued to Ostrau, the next village. This time Lon and Hélène headed directly to the gendarmerie. They reasoned that since they had "permission" and the document to prove it, they must report to the police to be allowed to continue and to the mayor to find a place to sleep. If they didn't announce themselves and were discovered, they risked looking like they were hiding, and then they would be sent to one of the camps or worse.

In Ostrau, the seven other women remained outside the police station and listened from a distance with growing dread. It sounded as if their strategy might fail. They could hear terrible shouts; had the magic document not worked? They couldn't understand what the policeman was saying, but they could get the gist of it.

It was different for Lon and Hélène, somehow not as frightening. They were used to such treatment. The man's screams had little effect on Hélène. She felt the space where her tooth was missing and calmly waited for him to finish. He was full of insults and curses about who they were and how their kind needed to be handed over to the SS; his orders were clear about this. They had already captured other "whores and Jews," and this was what they did with them. Those were the rules and he must obey the rules.

"Yes, we understand," Hélène responded evenly when he paused his tirade to take a breath, "but you will see, our case is different." She handed him the precious paper. "As you see, we have been given permission. We have this *laisser-passer*."

He took the document and for a long moment there was silence as he studied it. Then the miracle happened again. "Ah, yes," he said, his voice dropping. "Reitzen. I see. Yes, your case is different."

"We are only women," Hélène continued, happy that the paper had the wished-for effect, but not wanting him to study it too closely. She gently took it back, folded it, and put it in her coat pocket. "We don't know anything about the war and the front. Please tell us, will it be frightening?"

He obligingly gave her patronizing advice about how to continue through this no-man's-land between two fronts. "You must be quite careful," he explained. "It is dangerous, especially for a woman like yourself."

The more Hélène smiled and played the role of an ignorant woman, the more his attitude changed. It was a delicate balance of flirtation and feigned helplessness. It worked perfectly—until it went too far.

He had been eyeing her up and down while he talked—obviously he enjoyed the sound of his own voice—but she made the mistake of keeping eye contact with him a moment too long. He lowered his voice and said, "I have a place for you tonight. But just you. Not your friend." He nodded his head in Lon's direction, dismissing her. "You and I can get to know each other so much better," he said quietly, winking. "I have plenty of food," he added as a lure.

Hélène felt the smile freeze on her face.

Lon spoke up. "Yes, but we are a group. Of nine. There's a lot of us, you won't have enough food for all of us, so we will be moving on. We have quite a distance to travel. As you yourself have said."

Lon took hold of Hélène's hand, and Hélène gave her a grateful squeeze.

"But she can decide for herself," the policeman protested. "I will make it worth your while." He grabbed Hélène's other hand and pulled her toward him. "I can protect you in these dangerous times."

Hélène pulled back and felt a sharp pain in her hip as she tried to pivot out of his grasp. Lon stepped in between them and tried to pry Hélène out of the policeman's hold.

"It's my duty to stay with the group," Hélène said from behind Lon, forcing a smile, pretending that they weren't physically struggling. "Duty," she repeated the word. "You must understand, as a policeman." She took another step back and pulled free.

"We need Hélène," Lon confirmed; she stood like a wall blocking him.

"Good day!" Hélène turned to go.

He called out to her, but only Lon responded. "Sorry, we really must be going," she said, putting her hands up. Both of them knew he could just take Hélène at gunpoint if he wanted. She would have no defense. They walked away from him as fast as they could.

Once outside, Hélène said under her breath, "I want to get out of Ostrau now!"

"I think we should avoid the big towns. Here there's more risk of bombardment."

"And more of those types," Hélène hissed.

When they got to the group, they told everyone they were moving on right away. They didn't have to explain why. The look on Hélène's face was enough.

———————

They arrived at Delmschütz just as the daylight was dimming. The *Bürgermeister*'s house was atop a steep hill. Hélène looked at it and felt overwhelmed with pain. She wasn't sure she could climb up and back down. "I can't," she confessed to the group. "I can't go on." Her voice trembled. It was the first time she had revealed weakness, let down the mask of her cool command of the situation.

"It's my leg," she said, and felt tears welling in her eyes. Hélène's right leg was badly swollen and her hip radiated pain with each step. Ever since the long interrogations at Angers, she had had a problem with flaring pain in her hip joint. The encounter earlier in the day had set it off. After the day of walking it had grown almost unbearable.

"You don't have to," Zaza said immediately, putting her arm around Hélène. Hélène burst into tears and then apologized as she wiped them away.

"Guigui can go with me," Lon offered, and spoke a few words in Dutch to Guigui.

"Of course!" Guigui agreed, saluting Hélène playfully. Then in German she said, "I will have a lovely meeting with the *Bürgermeister*," which made Hélène laugh with relief.

Hélène settled in the ditch with the others. She felt grateful to have these friends. Zinka promised to massage her leg later with some of the liniment the Yugoslav prisoners had given them. Hélène had thought it would be easier to escape on her own, or just with Zaza, but now she realized they all needed one another. The women begged Josée to sing for them, and she did.

Hélène felt her anxiety ease. These were her friends. She could rest among them and allow herself to feel safe.

———————≈———————

Josée, Joséphine Bordanava, was the child of immigrants who arrived from Spain in the years before the war. Spanish refugees had flooded into France seeking shelter from the global economic depression of the 1930s and the civil war. But once in France they found themselves in a precarious position. The Spanish government did not acknowledge their citizenship once they fled the country, and the French authorities refused to recognize them, especially since many had entered the country illegally. They ended up scattered in refugee camps around the south of France. These same camps would later be used by the Nazis for their own purposes. Josée's father was a laborer. When she was ten, Josée was placed in a foster home in Cannes, where she stayed until she was fifteen. She may have been sent there for economic reasons or because of problems in her family, but it is clear that being a child of Spanish immigrants placed her on the margins of French society. She went back to her family briefly, but then returned to the foster home at age seventeen and stayed there until she was eighteen and went to live with a Mme. Sauvageot in Cannes.[4]

The Rayon de Soleil foster home where she grew up was founded by Alban and Germaine Fort in October 1935; two months later, young Josée moved in. By 1939, when she left briefly, there were twenty-four children living with the Forts. With the German occupation in the north of France, Jewish foster children were sent south to Cannes for their protection. In November 1942, Alban and Germaine Fort welcomed thirty-three Jewish children with false papers. This was the beginning of their clandestine work with the Marcel network, created by Moussa Abadi and Odette Rosenstock and one of the main rescue circuits for Jewish children in the southern zone.[5]

Moussa Abadi was a Syrian studying the fables of the Middle Ages at the Sorbonne until 1940, when the anti-Jewish laws drove him out of the university. Odette Rosenstock was a young doctor in Paris. At the end of the Spanish Civil War in 1938, refugees fleeing Franco crossed the mountains into France. Odette went to the Pyrenees as part of a medical charity to help them. There she witnessed the opening of the first internment camps for the refugees. She was appalled by the conditions and inhumane treatment and quickly became involved in clandestine actions. She used medical trucks to smuggle refugees out of the camps. She made quite an impression on Moussa when they first met through mutual friends.

The anti-Jewish laws caught up with Odette, and by October 1940 she was forbidden to practice medicine. She joined Moussa in the free southern zone, helping the many Jewish refugees who had fled there. The region was still under Italian control, and the Italians were not applying the anti-Jewish laws of Vichy and the Nazis. Jews from all over Europe under Italian occupation felt free from the fear of deportation. In the sunny Mediterranean towns along the coast one could almost ignore what was happening in the north of France and the rest of Europe.

But all was not fine. In April 1942, on the promenade des Anglais in Nice, Moussa witnessed a Jewish woman being stomped to death by a policeman while a crowd watched. Her six-year-old sobbed as he watched his mother's murder. The crowd looked on impassively. When Moussa asked what was happening, a man in the crowd said, "He's disciplining a Jew."[6]

In early 1943, Moussa met the chaplain of the Italian troops on the Eastern Front, who was passing through Nice. Don Julio Penitenti described the pogroms and persecutions of the Jews in eastern Europe. He told of children being lined up and shot as if for target practice, of whole villages executed and dumped in mass graves. Moussa refused to believe him. The priest took out his crucifix, put it in Moussa's hand, and covered his hand with his own. "I swear on the blood of Christ that what I have told you is true."[7]

Moussa ran home to Odette. They talked late into the night and came to a decision. They had found the cause for which they would risk their lives: the rescue of Jewish children. Together they established the Marcel network, saving the lives of 527 children between 1943 and 1945 by creating false baptismal papers, changing the identities of children, and hiding them with families in small villages and convents. They received help from Quakers and from the underground branch of the Jewish Scouts. Alban and Germaine Fort, the directors of the foster home where Josée spent her formative years, allowed Moussa to use their place as a safe house. They kept many children while Moussa looked for more permanent family placements.

In April 1944, Odette was arrested and sent to Auschwitz. She was one of the few from her convoy who was not sent immediately to be murdered. She was appointed as a doctor in the *Revier*. This was the same *Revier* where Dr. Josef Mengele performed his ghoulish experiments on twins. Somehow Odette survived; she was liberated from Bergen-Belsen by the British on April 15, 1945.

Though Moussa and Odette remained deeply in love with each other, immediately after the war they lived apart. Moussa suffered from terrible depression and was haunted by the traumas he had witnessed with the children. It was even harder after the war when he had to tell many of the children that their parents were dead. Eventually Moussa and Odette were married on November 3, 1959.

Alban and Germaine Fort introduced young Josée to the Résistance.[8] Her military records state that she was active in the Résistance in Cannes from the early part of 1942, when she would have just turned eighteen. But she had probably been involved from a younger age. She worked in the social services section of Combat, organizing the allocation of small pensions, goods, and food to the families of Résistance members who had been captured or killed. It was important for people to see that the movement would not forget their sacrifice and that the soldiers could count on their families being looked after should the worst happen.

When the Italians signed the Armistice of Cassibile with the Allies on September 3, 1943, essentially flipping their allegiance from the Axis powers to the Allies, the Germans moved quickly to occupy the southern zone of France, and immediately Josée and the others in her network felt the urgency of their work increase. The first roundup in Cannes took place in 1943, brought on by denouncements from members of the pro-Nazi *Milice française*, a paramilitary Vichy organization of French fascists. Six people who had been in hiding were arrested and deported. Denunciations and persecutions of Jewish refugees accelerated. Josée and her network had been uncovered. Fleeing imminent arrest by the Gestapo, Josée moved to Marseille.

In Marseille, she made contact with Jean Moulin's newly formed Mouvements unis de la Résistance (MUR). Under the pseudonym "Severine," Josée was put in charge of the distribution of social service packages from late 1943 to March 1, 1944. In the small hamlets around Marseille, she would have met families who were hiding children for the Marcel network.

Perhaps there was a family sheltering Jewish children along with their own in a tiny hamlet in the hills above Cassis. Their eldest two sons had joined MUR and could not help their father with the farm work, and Madame had her hands full. Josée was used to pitching in and during her visits insisted on helping in the garden or the laundry. After they finished working, Madame always urged Josée to have a cup of tea. It wasn't real tea, but herbs she gathered in the woods— herbs that she insisted were good for a young woman like Josée. They would make her lovely black hair thick and silky.

Once Madame put her hand on Josée's and said, "When my son comes home, I want him to marry you. You will see he's hardworking."

Josée blushed and laughed. "But I have never met him."

"Trust me," she said, "trust this old woman."

The children had been trained to stay in hiding whenever there were visitors, but sooner or later during Josée's visits they would emerge, thrilled to find her there. Maybe they sensed how much she craved their affection. In her later years in the foster home, she had often carried one of the youngest in her arms or on piggyback all day long. She was used to constant touching and warmth. Now in the Résistance, she had to live alone, move every week, not talk to others about her life, not mingle with her old friends. She was lonely. These visits were a restorative joy.

The children would beg her to sing for them. The youngest foster child would crawl into Josée's lap and lay her head on her chest. She had sweet ringlets and large dark eyes. Josée knew that the little girl's mother had been deported to one of the terrible camps in Poland, about which they had heard the worst rumors. When it was time for her to go, the little girl would start to cry, and Josée would say, "I'll sing one more song if you promise not to cry."

There was that awful visit when she had to deliver the news that the eldest son would not be coming home. "You can be proud; he died valiantly for France," she said. The words sounded flat and automatic because right then she wasn't sure if she believed them. Monsieur put his hand on Madame's shoulder and said softly, "Yes, that's right. Thank you, mademoiselle."

She left the couple alone in the kitchen and went to find the children in the barn. She let them hang on her like puppies, and she sang to them. The little one in her lap wiped away Josée's tears with her tiny fingers. The small girl said in her sweet, soft voice, "If you stop crying, I'll sing for you."

On March 1, according to Bernadette Ratier, regional and national Résistance leader,

The Gestapo came to arrest Jews who had previously lived in the place where now MUR local social services were keeping their offices. And there the Gestapo by accident discovered the liaison officer Jean-Pierre, who had on him all the mail of the region, and there was Miss Bordanava, pseudo "Séverine," who had with her the prepared packages of the prisoners and the envelopes containing the monthly payments for the families and all the mail of the social services that she was about to hand to Jean-Pierre. He was at that time very much sought after by the Gestapo and so everyone was arrested.[9]

Josée was transferred to 425 rue Paradis, headquarters of the Gestapo in Marseille, for questioning.[10] She was held at the Beaumettes prison in Marseille and then moved to Romainville. On June 14, 1944, she was one of the fifty-one women deported from Paris's Gare de l'Est to Saarbrücken. They were interned at the Neue Bremm camp at first. She was one of forty-six women, along with Mena, Lon, and Guigui, who were transferred to Ravensbrück on June 23, where she was assigned the number 43220.

———◆———

It was getting cold in the ditch in Delmschütz where the women waited, and Hélène and the others began to worry. Perhaps the *Bürgermeister* in his big house at the top of the hill had arrested Lon and Guigui. Perhaps this was the end of the road for them. After some discussion, they decided to send two more scouts. Zinka and Nicole would try to find out what had happened. The remaining five would mark the wait time by counting to 2,000. This would distract them from their fear. If Zinka and Nicole did not return by the time they had finished counting, they should assume the worst and get away as fast as possible.

But within a few moments, Nicole met up with Guigui on the footpath. "Where did you go?" Guigui exclaimed. "I have been trying to find you forever!" Typical of Guigui, who was always misplacing things, she had forgotten where she had left the group.

There were shouts of joy when the rest of the group saw a smiling Nicole return with Guigui in tow. Guigui told them in a rush that Lon was waiting for them at the *Bürgermeister*'s house. They needed to get a move on; a meal awaited them.

Nicole and Zaza supported Hélène on her slow walk up the hill.

They were led to an imposing house that dominated the valley below. The house was flanked by large barns, three stories high, with sloped red-tile gambrel roofs. The walls were plastered white with half-timbers in the Tudor style. The elegant main house was painted a creamy yellow, whereas the barns were massive, brooding hulks. The huge entrance hall was paneled in dark wood above black and white stone tiles. Life-sized paintings of what must have been the family's ancestors stared austerely down at them. Above the door was an adage in German, which Hélène translated: "Trust in God, but also in yourself. God blesses those who take care of themselves."

"Sounds about right," Nicole said.

Lon greeted them in the massive entrance. She seemed to know her way around the house already. She led them to the kitchen, where they could wash their hands. Here they were confronted with a huge sink that was so high it was reachable only when they stood on the tips of their toes. Everything was out of proportion. Seeing the giant-sized chairs at the table, Mena whispered to Guigui, "Have we shrunk or is this truly a giant's house?"

Zaza added, "We will need to ask for a thick book to sit on."

"Imagine how I feel!" tiny Zinka said. They had to help her scramble up into one of the chairs. They giggled at their dangling feet. The laughter eased their fears about this strange, colossal place.

"You'll see," Lon said ominously, "why everything is so large."

As they waited for their hosts to arrive, they felt like children playing at being adults. But they grew immediately silent when the owner, his wife, and their two daughters walked into the room imperiously. The *Bürgermeister* and his family were giants, all four over six feet tall, broad-shouldered and muscular. The daughters had their hair up in tightly braided buns. They wore long black dresses. They did not smile; they simply nodded in acknowledgment of their guests. The table was nicely set and there was a generous amount of food, but their hostility was palpable. This would not be like the meal they had shared with Annelise and her father. Not all meals could be like that, Zaza reasoned later; if they were, then there never would have been a war in the first place.

It was clear to Hélène and the others that the giants, with visible disgust on their faces, were deigning to eat with this ragtag group

of women for one reason only: the front was near. The giants understood that tomorrow their fortunes could turn, and it would be wise
to be kind to these refugees from the winning side, even if they were
filthy and smelly. Barely a word was spoken during the meal. Their
hosts did not ask a single question about who they were or where they
came from, and they offered no information about themselves. After
the food was served, the only sound was the clinking of their spoons
on the soup bowls.

The father pushed away his empty bowl to signal when the meal
was over, and a servant mysteriously appeared to clear away the bowls.
One of the sisters instructed the servant to show the women their
sleeping quarters. The women whispered a thank-you and followed
the servant out.

They were led to an immense barn. The women decided to climb
to the very top hayloft—they were scared that the farmhands might
come in the next morning and skewer them with pitchforks. And
after the earlier close call for Hélène, they were worried about farmhands coming in the night as well. Furthermore, they were afraid of
the contraption near the barn door that was meant to roll the hay
into tight bales. What if in the middle of the night it started to roll
them into tight bales? The barn was full of all kinds of weirdly shaped
machines. Everything was massive. And a feeling of ominous doom
hung around the place. None of the women came from farms, and
the giant tractors and plows frightened them.

No one slept that night. The wind howled. The barn creaked and
groaned, as if they were on an old ship sailing directly into a storm
at sea. Even as they kept up a brave front with one another—that this
was a "camping trip," as Mena liked to call it, or that everyone was
"being so nice," as Zaza exclaimed—they knew they were heading
toward grave peril.

CHAPTER SEVEN

— JACKY —

Jacqueline Aubéry (Jacky)

ON APRIL 19, THE NINE women watched as the day dawned through the slats of the giants' barn. Each one was lost in her private thoughts. Jacky prayed that she would find the strength to make it through another day. Nicole thought of all the times she'd awakened in the Leipzig camp next to Renée—their first gesture had always been to grab each other's hand—and felt a stab of grief. Zinka reached for the cigarette case that she had made for Louis Francis. Stay alive, she said to him in her thoughts. Josée began to hum a little song. The women loved this gentle wake-up. They did not know it was Josée's ritual of prayer that the children she had been helping to hide were still safe.

It was a cold, gray day, with spitting rain. The spring weather was unpredictable, one moment lovely and the next bitterly cold and wet. They stayed for a long time in the straw until a servant from the main house came to announce that there was warm water available in the laundry.

The laundry was located in its own building. In a clean white-tiled room they found an actual shower and large ceramic basins with buckets, which the women could use to pour water over their heads. They stood beneath the warm water as if stunned. Since Ravensbrück, the whispered word "showers" had been a punch in the gut. It came with the memory of women drenched with freezing water and made to stand naked in the snow until they collapsed and froze to the ground. They all knew about the gas "showers." And there were the rushed, painfully cold showers each morning at Leipzig, when their bones ached. The only hot water that they had known in many months had been in the munitions factory in Leipzig. There the red-hot shells coming from the forge were submerged in large barrels of water to cool them down. After the shells were removed, sometimes the women would quickly plunge their heads into the barrels of heated water, hoping that the guards would not see and that the scalding water would kill the lice that bit their scalps.

Lice had been the center of their nightly rituals in Leipzig. In the evening before going to sleep, the women searched one another's heads and then worked down, looking through the seams of their clothes. They became good at trapping the little beasts and crushing them with their fingernails. They did not want to be caught with lice and get their heads shaved again. Lice was feared by both the prisoners and the SS. All around the camps, one could read the signs: *Eine Laus, dein Tod* (One louse, your death). Lice led to scabies, infected bites, and typhus. Typhus was epidemic in the camps and often deadly. The nightly hunt was crucial to survival.

While they worked scrupulously trapping lice they would talk over whatever rumors they had heard that day. Those who spoke other languages, such as Hélène, reported news from other blocks. Being the most privileged, the Polish and Russian prisoners often had the best information; perhaps they had heard something about another city that had fallen. But the rumors were often false, and soon refuted by other rumors.

They told one another how wonderfully chic they looked. Most of them were French women, after all, and style mattered. They joked about how slender they were, but they could use some color in their cheeks, they remarked. They no longer saw daylight. The morning roll call happened in the cold dark of 4:00 AM, and they returned from the factory in the dark. Then the conversation would often turn to food.

Nicole found relief by describing in detail all the steps of a recipe, ingredient by ingredient. It had started with an olfactory hallucination at work. The molten iron ore coming out of the forge and burning the grease smelled of steaks cooking on a grill, or roasted chickens. The sensation was marvelous and fleeting. Then she was left with an overwhelming hunger and panic. She found that talking about food helped. Initially, most of her recipes were cakes, with lots of sugar, butter, and eggs. Nicole began to recite these feasts to her friends during the nightly lice hunt.

She described how to make a bavarois with strawberries. It was a dessert she had prepared many times with the family cook. "Step one," she said, and everyone grew quiet. "Pour a quarter liter of milk in a saucepan and add vanilla. You can add the whole pod, or you can open the pod and crush the vanilla seeds, then add them. The house will smell of vanilla."

She paused and took a breath to smell it, just barely—the vanilla scent.

"Step two: In a bowl beat four egg yolks with seventy grams of sugar, until the yolks are thick and lightened in color."

"We had such lovely eggs at my grandmother's farm," someone offered. There was a murmur of agreement. An egg—if only they could have an egg, it would sustain them for weeks.

"Step three: When the milk has just begun to boil, you pour it into the egg mixture, stirring all the while." Nicole remembered how she would stir while the cook poured. Her young hands had been fast and didn't tire.

"Step four: Pour this mixture back into the casserole and very,

very slowly heat it up just to the point that it stiffens, but then pour it back into the bowl to cool it. You do not want to overheat because the eggs will curdle and separate. It's very important to pay close attention.

"Step five: You can add chocolate bits to the mixture and stir a little to let them melt. My mother preferred white chocolate, so the color stayed pearly and smooth.

"Step six: Now you take some cream and you whip it to thick, stiff, shiny peaks." This was also Nicole's job because the cook would get too tired. It took patience to whip and whip. For a long time it seemed as if the cream would never stiffen. But it always did, like magic.

"Then you fold the cream into the egg, milk, and chocolate mixture. And you let that chill." Nicole was silent, remembering how the cook would let her lick the beater after she was done.

"Keep going," a woman called from the dark corner of her bunk.

"Yes, we need to soak the strawberries in kirsch. I would chop them up fine and cover them with kirsch. What step are we on?"

"Seven!" they called out.

"Right. Step seven: Butter the tart tin and arrange the ladyfinger cookies around the rim and along the bottom of the mold. Place them tightly one right up against the other."

"Like us!" someone called, and there was laughter. The women were beginning to lie down and arrange themselves on their crowded bunks. To have enough room on the hard, slender planks, they often lay alternating head to foot. They had caught enough lice for the night; they were tired. And they sensed the bavarois was almost done. The trick was to fall asleep with the memory of the smell and the flavors before the hunger surged back and gripped your insides.

"Step eight," Nicole continued. "Pour first a layer of the cream and then sprinkle a layer of strawberries. Then more cream, then more berries, until the whole thing is full.

"Step nine: Let it cool in the icebox for at least four hours and then you can serve it."

When she finished there was silence and then muffled applause.

"I could taste it!" Jacky said, her eyes bright with fever. "The strawberries and the cream . . ."

The next day they wanted another recipe. Nicole recounted a

Spanish paella, in Josée's honor. Then she made a chestnut cream and puffed crêpes. The description was an event, a performance. They wanted more. And the other blocks wanted them as well. If she wrote the recipes down, they could be passed around. Someone gave her scraps of paper stolen from the camp offices. She needed a pencil. She risked talking to one of the civilians who worked near her in the factory. He was scared to help her. But the next day she found a small pencil stub carefully perched on a machine where she would find it when she came to work. She began to record and share her recipes with other blocks. Other "cooks" wrote and shared their recipes. It became a favorite pastime, imagination mixed with saliva.

Nicole's recipe notebook from Leipzig

It seems counterintuitive, but the recitation of recipes and the making of small recipe books appears to be a nearly universal reaction among the starving.[1] Being hungry was said to be more painful than being beaten. Not only was it physically painful, it was psychologically harrowing. Hunger could reduce people to animals. Fights erupted over the soup distribution. The women had witnessed prisoners, insane with hunger, steal food and beat one another. They had seen women rolling in the mud over a scrap of bread. They did not want to be reduced like that, to lose their dignity. Instead they found temporary relief in the sharing of recipes. On Sunday afternoons, the only rest period of the week, they would share "Sunday dinner" together.

Nicole tore some of her mattress cover and with a strap she scavenged, she sewed a cover to protect her recipes. Guigui made a recipe book using long, thin strips of paper that bear the HASAG stamp on them. Not one inch of paper is wasted. The recipes are full of sugar and caramel, butter and flour, all rich in calories and childhood memories. Their recipe books mattered enough that they took them along when they escaped. Since they were not mentioned when Hélène asked them to make an inventory of their collective items immediately at the beginning of their escape, I imagine they saw their recipe books as intimate personal possessions, precious objects that had sustained them through their hunger.

After the war, they rarely spoke of the recipe books—almost as if they were shameful. They were simple recipes and not political pamphlets. Perhaps they felt they would be misunderstood. No one would understand how much they risked to create them. It would have been different if the risk was for "noble things" like poems, songs, or politics. Those things were talked about and shared after the war, because they conformed to a heroic narrative. Homemade cookbooks were banal and domestic.

In the precarious world of the camps, the orderliness and structure of a recipe—the list of ingredients, the step-by-step sequence—was a temporary reprieve. It allowed for the illusion of control. The sharing of meals was a way to share memories without it being too painful. Thinking about a lost child, partner, or parent was dangerous. You could lose your mind in the grief. Dark memories could push you into a downward spiral. But sharing the memory of a meal allowed the women to feel human without it hurting too much. Recipes were a link to the real world, to their lives before, and to their lives in the future. And they formed a link with the other groups in the camp. Everyone eats. Everyone has a favorite meal. Not everyone can write a song or poem, but to remember a good meal is universal.

The French women were running out of recipes when a group of Hungarian Jews arrived in early 1945. Nicole remembered that a few of the women tried to participate. These women were given worse food than the other prisoners; their soup was watered down and mostly just cold liquid. Hungarian was a language that few others spoke, but with the help of someone who could translate—maybe one of the Hungarians spoke another language—the Hungarians recited their own favorite dishes. The women felt that with these new arrivals, they now had a whole new cuisine to "taste."

In the laundry at the giants' mansion in Delmschütz, the women luxuriated under the flow of hot water. They shouted with delight at the discovery of a block of soap. They scoured their bodies, their filthy feet, their fingernails. They scrubbed each other's backs and rinsed the soap from each other's hair with buckets of warm water. The water streaming from their hair was dark brown with filth. Gradually, they came out of their daze. They sang, splashed each other, and laughed as dirty water ran down the clean tiles into the drain.

Everything about the giants' house was immaculate. When they arrived, they had noticed with shame that even the animals were cleaner than they were. "Now," Zinka said, "at least we are as clean as the giants' cows."

Steam rose from their bodies as they put their old clothes back on. They lingered late into the morning hoping for a second meal. At last a servant came to get them. "Madame has prepared your lunch and then she requests that you leave," she said with an unconcealed sneer.

But they didn't care; they were clean, and it was food. After the meal of boiled potatoes and warm milk, they headed down the hill toward the next small village, unsure of which direction to go. Being thrown from a place of such luxury back into the biting wind, they suddenly felt overwhelmed with hopelessness.

"Don't you think a front should make more noise?" Josée asked, grumbling, as they trudged. She often voiced what the others were thinking but didn't dare say.

"I wish we could hear a cannon," agreed Hélène. With each step, her left leg felt a jolt of pain. The blisters on Josée's feet, now scrubbed clean, bled and stung as they rubbed against her wooden clogs.

Jacky's diphtheria seemed worse; perhaps it had been exacerbated by the steam of the showers followed by the cold. She repeatedly stopped to cough and could barely catch her breath or keep up with the others, despite their already slow pace. When she bent over with a hacking seizure, the others would pause, looking on helplessly. Zinka insisted on carrying her sack. Hélène knew they couldn't go on for much longer.

The quiet was worrisome. Hardly anyone was on the road. The

large barns they passed were all shuttered. They were thrilled when they met a French POW working in a farmer's field. Hélène asked if he knew the location and direction of the front. Instead he gabbed on about how he had once tried to escape. They could see that he had been well fed. His story was full of bravado, but they guessed that he had never been in much danger since being taken prisoner. He had never seen a woman beaten to death during the roll call nor seen another whose belly was torn open by guard dogs.

At Hélène's persistence, he finally said, "I heard the front was now near Leisnig. But it's not over. The Germans are preparing a strong counterattack in the woods before Leisnig. That would be a place to avoid in my book. This war will go on a long, long time. They're tough, these Germans."[2] He spoke with admiration.

"We have to go now," Lon said at the same time that Nicole said, "We can't linger here."

As soon as he was out of earshot, they all began to vent their frustration.

"What a useless person."

"We need to forget everything he said."

"Nothing he told us was helpful."

"*Merde!* He'd never stop gumming on!"

"We must not let him frighten us about Leisnig."

Nicole concluded with her adamant refrain: "The war will end soon, and the Germans will lose."

The country they walked through was wide open, with steep rolling hills. There was nothing to stop the gusts that battered them. They were exhausted, a limping ragtag group. They found a sort of lean-to hut on the edge of another field where they collapsed to rest, out of the wind.

Even though they kept telling one another to ignore what the French POW had said, his words continued to aggravate them. They needed to find the strength to carry on. They began a ritual they had gone through many times since the beginning of their escape: one by one, each person gave her opinion of the situation. Stating the obvious was Nicole: "It's about time we find the Americans and end this little camping trip of ours. I'm fed up, as much as I like all of you."

Zaza suggested, "Let's find a village and stay put for a few days.

We are too exhausted to keep going like this. And Hélène, you can barely walk."

Hélène looked at her friend and acknowledged her concern with a feeble smile. "I think we should carry on. I don't think stopping is wise."

Lon jumped in: "Right, what if we try instead to finish this as quickly as possible? I say we force ourselves to get up and leave early in the morning and we don't stop at midday. We just push on."

There was a general outcry from the group. They all thought that suggestion was funny coming from Lon, who was one of the most difficult to rouse in the morning. And besides, their strategy of lingering in the morning until eleven and even twelve meant that they almost always were fed again.

"We can't stick our nose up at chow," Jacky exclaimed.

"We've only gone a few kilometers today and already I'm beat," Josée said. "I can't imagine what 'pushing ourselves' would feel like!"

Nothing was decided. They huddled inside the lean-to, trying to keep warm for an hour or so. But the cold was creeping in and they were shivering. When the howling wind around the hut seemed to calm for a moment, Nicole took a deep breath and stood up. "It's too cold to stay here," she said. "We need to keep moving."

Groaning, they slowly rose to their feet and began trudging up the next hill. A short distance later, they came to the village of Obersteina, the steeple of its church peeking up from the top of the hill. Once again, they noticed some potatoes that had fallen on the ground. Zinka and Mena began to gather them. But Nicole and Josée protested: "Stop! We have enough. We still have the raw potatoes from that witch in Raitzen. And they are heavy enough."

"No," Mena said. "Remember the first potatoes we found outside of Reppen and how those potatoes gave us our first real meal, with noodles and forks, paid for by the Monocle? Our first meal sitting at a real table!" The potatoes, she was sure, had been good luck, leading them to that moment.

"Think how much we wanted a potato like this only a few weeks ago! We've made it this far," Zinka agreed. "We shouldn't let good food go to waste no matter how heavy." They gathered the potatoes.

Once again the group found a ditch to rest in by the side of the road while Lon and Hélène went into the village in search of food and shelter. Villagers passed them and remarked rather rudely on their pitiful condition. But the women would not let Germans get away with such remarks. They answered back that they were just fine, thank you. They were simply taking a short rest.

A small German soldier marched up and peered into the ditch at them. They realized he was small because he was incredibly young. His uniform was oversized. His jacket was made for a man with wider shoulders. The pants were held up with a string and rolled up at the bottom. When he asked them assertively who they were, Guigui asked, "How old are you?"

Near the end of the war, most of Germany's grown men had been sent east to the Russian front. Soldiers deployed back at home were underage, some as young as thirteen or fourteen. The boy soldier was flustered by Guigui's question. Officiously he asked again what they were doing in the ditch. Guigui answered patiently, as an adult would explain something to a child: "We are going to France since this war of yours is basically over. You've lost. We're headed in that direction." She pointed westward.

The boy soldier, slightly crestfallen, said, "Yes, it's true, Leisnig has been taken by the Americans." But then, noticing how these words made the women practically cheer with joy, he yelled, his voice lifting an octave, "But it's not done yet! And there is no way you will be allowed to stay in this village!"

"Why not?" Guigui asked in a gentle voice.

"Because the general will never allow it."

The women laughed. Mena told him, "Hélène will have your general wrapped around her finger in no time."

"He's no match for Hélène," Josée agreed.

The boy soldier grew impatient with them: why were they so nonchalant? His face turned red and he stamped his feet like a child throwing a tantrum. It was half amusing, half unsettling. They were tempted to tease him more, but it was dangerous to push him too far. He did have a gun.

At that moment Hélène and Lon returned. "Hey, did you see the famous general?" Josée called out. "This one says his general will kick us out of the village at once." She nodded to the boy.

"We met him, and in fact we're sleeping at his home tonight," Hélène responded in French. Then she repeated it in German so the boy could hear.

As the women laughed, he turned quickly and left.

But as soon as he was gone, they let their true feelings show. "Should we be staying with a general? That sounds like it could be an awful trap," Nicole said anxiously.

"I don't like damn generals," Jacky put in, coughing.

The others agreed; the soldier, though just a boy, did seem especially fierce in his hatred of them.

Hélène reassured them, "He's a retired general. He's offered us his barn, and we can dine at the children's home, which is next to his estate."

"Children's home?" Josée asked as she helped Jacky to her feet. Having grown up in a children's home, she was curious.

"What I understood," offered Lon, "is that his children's home was an agricultural school before the war, and it's now a kind of home for war-orphaned children."

"But he wants us out by five tomorrow morning," Hélène added. "And if we're discovered there by his servants in the morning, we'll have problems."

The women gathered their belongings, but the news of this early departure upset Josée. "Wait, five o'clock? Can we at least wash ourselves in the morning before we go?"

"Really? At five?" Jacky responded with a smirk.

"Yes!" Josée was angry, almost petulant. "I want to know if there's a pump or something for the morning."

"Josée, be honest. Tomorrow morning you will not want to splash any goddamn freezing water on your face."

Guigui understood that what was really bothering Josée was the terrible pain in her bleeding feet. She moved to her side. "Lean on me," Guigui whispered. "It's only a short walk to our château, my lady." The group was beginning to bicker; they were frazzled. And Jacky's tendency to be brutally frank wasn't helping.

❧

Jacqueline Aubéry du Boulley, née Petit, was born in the Charente region of western France in 1915, in the middle of the First World War. Jacky's was an old Protestant family. Her father was a merchant marine and often away at sea. There was some sort of falling-out between her parents, and she was raised by her uncle and paternal grandmother. The uncle was the mayor of Blanzac, a small village in the Charente. When her father retired from the sea, Jacky went to live with him and his new wife, Emma, in Paris. She did not stay in contact with her mother or her brother.

After finishing lycée at sixteen, she worked as a secretary until she met and married Jean Aubéry du Boulley in 1939. He came from a bourgeois musical family in Normandy. They were together for only a short while before he was mobilized to fight in the war, but she had good memories of that brief honeymoon period. Every weekend they would go to the *guinguettes*, the outdoor bars along the Seine and Soane Rivers, just outside Paris, where you could swim, eat and drink, listen to live music, and dance late into the night.

Jean's father had been the general minister in the French colony of Gabon. He was wounded in the First World War and died of his wounds when Jean was a small child. Jean's mother, Flore, was a flamboyant character, whom Jacky loved. Flore had traveled and lived in many different countries in Africa. After her husband's death she moved to Palestine and then Egypt, where she met her second husband. Together Flore and Jean's stepfather established a high-end leather-goods store in Paris where they sold crocodile-skin handbags. Jean worked there before he was drafted.

Jean had contracted tuberculosis during his military service, and in 1940 he was sent to the thermal baths at Cambo-les-Bains to convalesce. He stayed there while Jacky returned to Paris to run the leather-goods store. During the occupation this would have been no small feat. At the time women could not have a bank account or access money without their husband's or father's permission. Flore had moved down to Antibes, on the southern coast of France, to live in the free zone, away from direct German occupation. Jacky, with her toughness, managed to get by on her own.

With his health slowly deteriorating from TB, Jean was transferred to a sanatorium in Grenoble for the fresh air of the Alps. In 1943 there was no real cure for TB; doctors simply tried to surgically remove infected parts of the lungs, and after such an operation Jean died from internal bleeding. Jacky moved to Antibes to live with Flore. It was here that she started working with the Résistance. She and her mother-in-law provided a safe house for downed British airmen. Gradually Jacky became an *agent de liaison*, and eventually she moved back to Paris.

Through intermediaries, Jacky joined the Brutus network, one of the first important intelligence networks set up directly under the orders of de Gaulle. It had more than 1,000 agents, many of whom were eventually killed or deported.

Her boss, Gaston Vedel, had served in the First World War. A pioneer in aviation, he flew for the postal service in Africa. In 1941 he joined the Résistance with his wife, Odette. In 1943 he escaped capture by the Gestapo when they came to his home, but his wife was taken in his place. After brutal interrogations and torture, she was deported to Ravensbrück.

Vedel continued his activities, working clandestinely in Marseille until it became too difficult to stay hidden. He traveled north to Paris, where he moved into Jacky's apartment at 21 boulevard des Batignolles. The Brutus headquarters was just a short walk away.

Jacky carried out several missions in Versailles, but she also traveled to Toulouse with information for the networks there. On July 4, coming back from a mission, she was arrested with Vedel and another agent at the entrance to the Brutus headquarters. The Gestapo had been waiting for them.

After lengthy interrogations, Vedel and Jacky were deported on August 15 from the Gare de Pantin. Vedel would be sent to Buchenwald and then to Mittelbau-Dora, the rocket factory built in a former gypsum mine by forced labor. Nine thousand French deportees would die at Dora, which was known as *le cimetière des français*, the French cemetery.

———✒———

Hélène and Lon led the way across the general's well-tended grounds. Josée, with her aching feet, was grateful to lean on Guigui's arm. Zaza carried the bag of potatoes, Nicole lugged the heavy pot and tripod, and Zinka had Jacky's bag. Zinka paused from time to time to wait for Jacky to catch up with the rest of them. It was getting dark and cold. A mansion at the end of a tree-lined lane, the children's home was flanked by large barns. On the ground floor of one of the barns was a long, wide hall. Entering, they saw bunk beds neatly made up with blue-and-white checkered blankets. The bunks and the insistence on order made the women feel uneasy; it brought back memories of Ravensbrück. Farther down the same wide hall they came to a long room with vaulted stone ceilings and tables running the length of the space. The women were seated at a table in the corner, and soon they were served a simple soup. It was not enough to sate their overwhelming hunger, but it was tasty. Slowly they felt themselves revive, and they looked around the room.

The atmosphere in the dining hall was unnerving. Children were running and chasing one another. Their chatter echoed against the stone. One or two would periodically approach the women's table and giggle, pointing their fingers at them, then dart away, as if each one was daring the other to go farther, to get closer to these strange beasts. Their governess didn't stop them and indeed encouraged their behavior, laughing along with the children at the pathetic spectacle.

The nine felt as if they were watching some kind of performance. The children were playing at being carefree, perfect German children. They were making flower decorations for something, perhaps a party. The women were reminded of the geraniums that bloomed in the window boxes of the *Revier* in Ravensbrück. Then a child sitting in the window overlooking the central courtyard saw the general approaching and shouted, "OK, start!" The children quickly assembled into rows and began singing. After a short period of inspection, the general left the dining area, nodding in approval.

Soon Lon and Guigui realized with disgust that the governess was Dutch and that these were Dutch children, orphans whose parents had joined the German cause. The Dutch governess sang German songs with the children, some of the same German songs the women remembered hearing the guards singing. Though the sound of the children's sweet voices was agreeable, the entire scene was sinister—the perfect children with their blond braids and nice clothes, laughing and giggling, mocking the women.

Three boys who looked about fifteen entered the dining hall dressed in Wehrmacht uniforms. They looked as if they were play-acting, but they had real grenades hanging from their belts. They marched toward the women's table. Lon had her back to them as they entered, but she saw the startled looks on the others' faces. She turned slowly to find the barrel of a gun directed at her forehead. She broke into a cold sweat.

The soldier holding the gun, desperate to prove he was in charge, screamed at her, demanding their papers. Lon was aware that the singing had stopped. The children were watching, grinning. This was great entertainment.

"Who are you? Where do you come from? What are you doing here?" the soldier barked in German. His face was red-hot with excitement.

Lon thought: This is it. This would be the place, after all that they had been through, where the story ended. They would be taken outside and shot by these boys.

"You belong in a camp for foreign prisoners!"

"Or executed," the soldier standing just behind him interjected. "That is the punishment for attempted escape."

Lon's instinct for survival pushed through her fear. She stood and tried her best to look calm and stern. "We have more than papers. We have a *laisser-passer* from the police. And the general himself has invited us here as his personal guests."

Her bravado worked, and the soldier holstered his gun. The three boy soldiers walked away without even looking at the famous Raitzen police paper. Trembling, Lon collapsed back into her seat. She had lost her appetite. She felt as if the others did not understand how close a call that had been.

But they were now watching another disquieting scene. The soldiers had gone over to the young Dutch governess. One kissed her neck while the other kissed her fully on the mouth. They fondled her openly, with their hands all over her, even on her breasts. She seemed delighted by their attention, by the open public display.

The women had seen the SS and the guards behave this way in

Ravensbrück. They would do whatever they wanted to a woman in front of other prisoners. Prisoners were not human, just *Stück*, things. But to see these boys do the same in front of children felt deeply disturbing.

Anxious to get away, they walked in silence to the barn, where they hoped to rest.

The apprehensive feeling didn't ease. Just as they lay down to sleep under the rafters, they were visited by another French POW. They couldn't get a good look at his face because he stayed in the shadows. Nicole told him that they were tired and needed to sleep. But he ignored her. He wanted so badly to speak in his native tongue.

He chatted away, telling them that French political prisoners in the camps were being used at the front to walk across land mines to clear the fields. Zinka and Zaza, lying side by side, squeezed each other's hands at this news; their husbands were both in camps somewhere.

He went on, "But the political prisoners in general have it good— they just have to stay put in a camp and wait for the end of the war. We soldiers had to work on farms. They just sit in the camp and get fed."

The women bit their tongues.

Then he said, "On Tuesday in Riesa, I saw 300 women in a long column dressed in tatters, guarded by women in uniform."

"Riesa," Nicole whispered to Hélène. "Is that near here?"

"No, I remember," Hélène said, "that's well to the north of the Leipzig–Dresden line; we're south of there."

The POW continued talking, laughing at the memory of the sight. "You should have seen how they were dressed! No pants, wooden clogs, striped clothes, really pathetic. I could barely tell they were women! Filthy Jews, I'm sure. Or whores."

Zinka almost stood up to face him, but it was Nicole who spoke, unable to hold her tongue any longer. "We were like that. We were guarded by the SS men and women with whips and dogs—"

He interrupted her. "So, are you all prostitutes?"

This was too much. Mena blurted out loudly, with the full force of her anger, "Have you never heard of the Résistance?"

He stuttered and stammered.

"I doubt it," Nicole answered. "He probably volunteered to work in Germany."

That finally did it; the POW retreated. As he did so, Zinka taunted, "While you were farming for the Germans, we were fighting for our country."

A bit later, Hélène said to the others, "Before you fall asleep, I need to tell you what the general told us. The front is fifteen to twenty kilometers away, and we can cross it. He says the end is near."

"The general thinks we should cross at night because in daylight it's dangerous," Lon added.

Zaza questioned this reasoning. "Maybe for a soldier or an army, but perhaps for nine women it's better to try to cross in broad daylight so they can see who we are."

Hélène continued, "The general says it's best to walk in the early hours, between five and eight in the morning, because the planes don't fly before eight o'clock."

"I think maybe he doesn't want us to be seen by his servants," said Josée.

Whatever the general's true reasons were, it did not matter, because long before 5:00 AM, the women would be awakened to find themselves in grave danger.

CHAPTER EIGHT

— MENA —

Yvonne Le Guillou (Mena)

"Aufstehen! Schnell! Raus!"

They were startled from their sleep by shouting. They thought they were somehow back in the camp and the SS had surrounded them. The women jumped to their feet.

"You have to leave at once!" the general cried. His voice was shrill with panic. "The police are coming. They know you are here! Someone has tipped them off! Please, you must be quick, or we will all be shot. Even me! They will shoot me!"

The women scrambled to gather their things. "You want your pump with cold water now?" Jacky said to Josée.

"Just shut up!" Josée grumbled.

Word of the nine had spread, or perhaps the French POW from

the night before had told the police about them because they had insulted him.

They slipped silently out of the barn into the darkness and bitter cold. They were frozen and hungry, and the wind was blowing harder than the day before. They moved swiftly, their hearts pumping with adrenaline, forgetting their aches and pains. They skirted the edge of the road, hoping they would not be seen.

Off in the distance, they saw a group of soldiers waving flash-lights, heading toward the children's home. With a quick exchange of glances, quietly they stole into the darkness of the woods, one by one. The cold and the fear reminded them of many mornings when they had marched through such weather, accompanied by guards with whips and dogs, to the factory to begin another twelve-hour work shift. There was no jovial banter. They were rattled, jarred back to the reality of their situation.

A few hours later, they emerged from the woods at the tiny village of Kiebitz, just as the sun was rising. At the center of the hamlet they discovered a small café and leaned their foreheads against the glass to peer through the window. Inside were velvet benches, round tables, caned chairs, and even a piano.

"Let's go inside," Mena pleaded. "Let's pretend we're in Paris."

"I think we have enough money to buy a coffee," Josée agreed.

"Maybe Mena can even get her bowl of potato and leek soup," Jacky offered, trying to make up for the meanness of her remark about the water pump earlier. They all laughed, because whenever anyone criticized German cuisine, Mena came to its defense, saying the Germans made an excellent leek and potato soup.

"Or we can pretend we're eating your famous camping soup," Josée said.

"No! It's not the same," Mena insisted. "My camping soup is sup-posed to be made on a wood fire with dandelions."

"So you don't want to go inside?" Nicole teased. She was feeling grateful to have survived their near disaster. This was her team, her group of friends. In some ways she would never feel this close to a group of people again. Together, she felt, they would make it.

"Come on, come on." Lon impatiently pushed past them and through the doors.

They followed her, and each found a place to settle. It was a relief to sit down for a moment, out of the weather.

Hélène brushed her hair back and straightened herself up, trying to look like a proper lady. She felt the gap in her mouth with her tongue and approached the café owner, who was standing off in the corner, his arms crossed, watching the women as they settled into his shop.

She addressed him politely, smiling. He uncrossed his arms and the dimmest of smiles passed over his face. She carefully negotiated with him, explaining the amount of money they had and asking for the price of a coffee and soup. Eventually the grumbling café owner served them all soup and coffee. He waved his hands, refusing their payment. Hélène thought it was a sign that they were getting close to the front. People were more and more scared about the future and inclined to be kind to them. Soon they would have the power of the victors.

They stayed in the café for several hours, letting the sun rise and hoping it would bring some warmth to the day. As the soup filled their bellies, they began to tease one another.

"I didn't know Guigui could move so fast," Jacky remarked wryly. Everyone chuckled. Guigui was famously slow to get ready in the mornings. She had an unhurried way of moving that sometimes frustrated the more impatient.

Guigui laughed, but she added, "Or you! I saw how you jumped!"

"I thought we were done for back there," Josée confessed. "I was shaking all over. I could barely tie my bundle. I was shaking more than when the Gestapo arrested me the first time!"

"Oh, God, me too! I was sure that was it," agreed Zaza.

"And Zinka," Josée asked, "were you this once just a little bit scared?"

Zinka gave them her gap-toothed grin and shrugged. "It got my heart beating."

They teased one another about who had been most frightened, who had moved the fastest. For a little while in the café they recovered their old camaraderie. The pressures of the past days had been wearing it thin, but it hadn't broken.

———— ≈ ————

After Kiebitz they trekked on to Zaschwitz, and once again seven of the women waited in a ditch by the edge of the village while the two scouts, Lon and Hélène, went to look for the *Bürgermeister*, or general, or whoever was in charge. The women were now realizing that as much as they longed to find the front, it posed its own set of problems. What would they find there, and would they be allowed to cross safely?

As the seven of them waited in the ditch, they discussed what they knew about fronts; most of their knowledge came from novels.

"What if it's like Waterloo?" Zaza asked.

"Exactly! Who was it, Stendhal? Wasn't it at Waterloo where he was disappointed because nothing happened?" Guigui said.

"I'm not sure it was Waterloo," Nicole said. She was suddenly remembering her family's lovely library of fine leather-covered books. That had been before her father went bankrupt and all the books were sold.

"It had to be, there was Napoleon," Zaza said.

"Also, shouldn't it be louder, with bombs and shooting? I mean, who ever heard of a silent front?" Zinka asked. The front should have flames and havoc, they thought. They had memories of their fathers or grandfathers talking about the trenches of the Great War. Would there be trenches they had to cross? Fields of mud and barbed wire?

"This war is nothing like the last one," Jacky said in her raspy voice. "No trenches. Just bombs dropping on us from above."

Their discussion of modern warfare was interrupted by the return of Lon and Hélène. They had met with some men in the village, and though the men offered no place to eat or sleep, they had shared some information.

"We were informed that our plan is folly because the Germans will never let us cross the front," Hélène reported somberly. Then with a shrug she continued, "But there were two young girls who had just come from the other side. The Americans let them cross over to get back home."

"The Americans?" Josée asked.

"Yes. They confirmed that Colditz has been taken by the Americans." Lon grinned as she delivered the good news. "If we can get there, we will find them."

They were cheered by this information. At least there was a confirmed spot on the map where they could find American soldiers.

"How far is this Colditz?" Jacky asked. But no one knew.

Nicole stood up. "We can't stop," she said. "And the fact that they say the Germans won't let us pass means we need to keep going. It means we're getting close." She gave her hand to Josée, pulling her up. Josée in turn helped Jacky.

"Somehow we need to cross the front, when we find it, and without getting shot," Hélène said. "I suggest we take smaller roads."

"Maybe this will come in handy," Zinka said. Jumping to her feet, she pulled from her pocket a mysteriously clean white handkerchief. She waved it in the air as if waving for surrender.

"Zinka! Where did you get that?" Nicole asked incredulously.

"How is it so clean and white?" Josée asked, clapping her hands.

"It's perfect," Hélène said, laughing.

"I'll keep it in my pocket, to keep it clean until we need it to cross this famously silent but dangerous front!" said Zinka.

At the crossroads near the village of Eichardt, they were greeted by a handsome young man on a bicycle who was missing his left arm. Hélène asked him for directions toward Colditz, but explained they wanted to use smaller roads. He offered to go along with them to show them a shortcut on a nearby back road.

He walked his bike alongside them, chatting with Lon and Guigui. "But you're students, aren't you?" he asked. "Before the war I was working on my master's degree. Instead I paid this price," he said, and nodded at his missing arm. "But it's not over for you. Your life is still ahead of you."

"It's not over for you either." Guigui smiled at him, her gray eyes peering from beneath her bangs. They discovered that he was from a town near the Dutch border where Guigui was sure her family was staying. She asked him if he was going home; when he said he was, she requested that he take a letter for her mother, and he agreed.

"Do you have anything to eat?" he asked.

"Just some potatoes," Lon answered. "But no way to cook them."

"Wait one moment here," he said. "I'll be right back."

The women watched him get back on his bike and head off in the direction they had come from. He took a side lane toward a farm in the distance. They sat on the side of the road and let the sunshine warm their faces. He returned in a little while, out of breath. "Would you like some *Erbensuppe*?"

They laughed. They kept being asked: Were they hungry? Would they like something to eat? Back in the café they had agreed that this question was absurd. "Never again," Zaza had said, "will I turn down an offer of food."

They followed the soldier back to the farm, where they were greeted boisterously by a band of a dozen German men, dressed in a strange combination of rags and uniform parts. Hélène was startled by the sight of them. She assumed they were soldiers, and she worried they had been led into a trap. She grabbed hold of Zaza's hand. She was terrified of situations where they were outnumbered by men.

The men had obviously been living at this abandoned farm for a while. The farmhouse had been bombed and was missing most of its roof. In the ruins the men had constructed a makeshift camp, with a small shelter built out of the blackened bricks. They had furnished it with broken tables and wobbly chairs. They had built an outdoor stove over an open fire pit. And not far from their encampment was a large pen of pigs snorting and rooting through the mud.

The men seemed relaxed and certainly pleased to entertain a group of women. "Welcome!" they called out with open arms. "You are friends of Hans, and now you are friends of ours!"

"Hello, ladies. Please, come sit."

The women hesitated, exchanging nervous looks. The men took turns presenting themselves, giving their full names and bowing politely. This civility helped some of the women relax. They then introduced themselves. When it was Mena's turn to present herself, she curtsied and twirled, and a few of the men applauded.

"Here we go again," Zaza said in French, rolling her eyes. "Mena playing with hearts."

"Arrêtez!" Mena said with a laugh.

The men, charmed, laughed along, not understanding the French but enjoying the sight of the lighthearted banter between the women.

The hosts arranged benches and chairs for them to sit around the fire. They made an attempt to wipe the chairs off, as if the women were delicate flowers and the rags they wore were spotlessly clean.

The men's courtly manners in such a hovel were both touching and sad. It was a remnant of a world that no longer existed, not after everything they had seen.

The cook was a large man with a pirate-style eyepatch covering his left eye. His one good eye looked over the women with a fierce gaze. Had they met him in any other place or circumstance, they would have been terrified. His hair was shorn close, either by himself or someone who had no idea how to cut hair. It stood out in all directions, and there were nearly bald spots where it was cut too close to the scalp. He had the rough beard of a man who has temporarily given up shaving, and he was missing one of his front teeth. He wore an apron fashioned out of scraps of a uniform, and he waved around a large ladle. He was big and enthusiastic, and almost ferocious. Another man passed around bowls and spoons.

"You need to eat! You look hungry," the cook bellowed. Hélène felt wary as he fixed his one-eyed gaze on her and told her, "You are much too thin." He served her with the attentiveness of a loving nanny. "Take a little more. There, there. Let me give you another piece of meat. Some with a little fat on it."

The cook sloshed more into their bowls without asking. He watched them eat as if he were gazing at his children.

"I'm giving you good advice," he said, his one eye fixing on Hélène. "Whenever you see soldiers cooking, you need to go there and demand to be fed." Hélène was trying to translate for the other women, but she was having a hard time keeping up with him.

"He says, 'The best cooking is a soldier's cooking,'" she reported.

They all nodded in agreement.

This was real soup, not the watery fare they had eaten while in captivity. It wasn't the camp soup made out of vegetable peelings, the kind they dismissively called "Pétain" after the collaborating leader of the Vichy government. Nor was this the thin soup they had been fed in Reppen. This was a thick, hearty pea stew with chunks of meat and potatoes.

"Remember all your meals in Leipzig?" Jacky said softly to Nicole.

"I remember," Josée said. She was sitting on the other side of Nicole.

"And that Hungarian goulash," Nicole said. It had come from one of the Hungarian Jewish women. "She was so happy to tell us about it."

"That was delicious," Jacky agreed, as if they had actually eaten those meals, not just listened to the recitation of the recipes.

"But nothing was as good as this," Nicole said, and they murmured in agreement. They had eaten the first bowls fast, but now, on their second serving, they could slow down to savor it. Hélène gradually relaxed.

"What? What are they saying about my food?" the cook asked her. "They don't like it?"

"He thinks you don't like his soup," Hélène translated. She was trying not to get rattled by his frantic attention.

"Oh, no!" they protested. "This is very good!"

Lon and Guigui told him in German, "It's delicious."

The other women made a thumbs-up sign.

"Nothing is as good as this," Mena said in French. She turned to the cook and said carefully in broken German, "This is very good." She kissed the tips of her fingers. "Perfect." The cook blushed beet red.

"Poor soul," whispered Guigui. "Mena," she added more loudly, "give the man a break."

"What? What am I doing?" Mena asked coyly, her head cocked.

Mena, the enchantress, had evaded me for a long time. In my search for the identities of the nine women, Mena was the last person I was able to identify. When I began corresponding with Guigui's grandson Olivier Clémentin, I asked him if he had any idea who Mena was.

He wrote back: "Yes, my mother knew Mena well. She married and lived in Paris after the war. I'll find the details." He soon got back to me to let me know that Mena's real name was Yvonne.

I studied the Nazi list. There were two possible Yvonnes in HASAG Leipzig who were both born in 1922, around the right age. I wrote back to him, "Could Mena have been Yvonne Le Guillou or Yvonne Rolland?"

He responded immediately, "Yvonne Le Guillou, yes, that's the one. She was Breton."

———— ❧ ————

Yvonne Le Guillou was born on April 26, 1922, in Paris to a working-class family originally from Brittany, in the far northwest of France

on the English Channel. Her parents had been peasant farmers with a tiny plot of land next to their own parents' plots. Like so many young people, in the years just after the First World War they packed up and moved away to the city to seek out a better life. Her parents spoke Breton, but Mena would have felt herself to be 100 percent a city girl and proud of her working-class background.

Laurence, Guigui's daughter, told me, "We visited Mena's family home in the north, Saint-Jacut-de-la-Mer. I know in Zaza's book she talks about Mena being the perfect Parisian, but she also was really from Brittany. When I was a young student, I had dinner with her and her husband twice a week in the Seventeenth Arrondissement. She was pretty, very vibrant; she loved to tell stories."

Sad to say, Mena's daughter, Edith, had died young of cancer, but Laurence gave me the address for Mena's son-in-law. I wrote to him, and Jean-Louis Leplâtre called me only a few days later. He was a cheerful man who was interested in the story of his mother-in-law, whom he described as being a truly beautiful woman: "Une vraiment belle femme, élégante, charmante."[1]

Jean-Louis was clearly still in love with his late wife, Edith, Mena's daughter. He spoke mostly about his wife: "She was an excellent mother. I have to say, she did everything well. She was pretty, she cooked well; she was very intelligent. She was chic. She loved to go to Saint-Jacut-de-la-Mer to visit her grandmother."

But when I asked him about the war, and about Mena's story before marriage and childbirth, he said he knew nothing. That was all between mother and daughter. "They told each other everything," he said. He wondered aloud if Edith, who had been a prolific diarist, had written about her mother and Mena's stories from the war. He suggested that I speak to his son, Mena's grandson, Guillaume. "He took an interest in these things, and I think his mother told him quite a lot about his grandmother."

A few days later I got an email from Guillaume Leplâtre recounting anecdotes he had been told about his grandmother. She had died when he was only two and half, so the stories had come from his mother "with a certain feeling of sacred transmission."[2] Mena had hardly ever spoken about the war. There were members of his family—his cousin, for example—who had no idea that she had been in Ravensbrück. But, according to his mother, even though she never spoke about it, the memory of what she had lived through was always present. Mena had taken the coat she wore as a deportee—the coat marked with the white X, the coat that saved her life during the exceptionally cold winter of 1944–45—and made a quilt out of it for baby Edith's crib, and later that quilt had been transformed into a teddy bear for her only child.

Mena said she joined the Résistance because of love for a boy. She minimized her role, claiming not to have done much; she had just passed messages. She said she had had no idea of the risks she was running and wondered if she would have joined had she known. She had done what she had done simply because she was a foolish, romantic girl in love.

The Dutch resistance fighter Albert Starink mentions Mena in an unpublished account that he wrote for his children and later sent to Guigui.[3] He met Mena (whom he knew as Yvonne) in 1943 in Paris through another Dutch friend. Starink describes her as "a dreamer, sweet, funny and a beautiful woman." One night she invited him to her place in Montrouge, in the suburbs of Paris. To his great surprise, Albert arrived to find her in the company of another man, Jan van Brakel, who was obviously her lover. In fact, they were living together. The Dutch artist Mena Loopuyt had loaned her apartment to van Brakel, and Yvonne would take Mena's name as her nom de guerre.

Mena and Jan were part of a network escorting Jewish families from Holland and Belgium across France and Spain to Portugal and safety. I could not find her military record. After the war, she must not have applied for *déporté résistant* status. When I asked Guillaume about this, he wondered if she might have been scared to do so. She and Jan had been betrayed by a friend or a neighbor; the French government in Paris had collaborated with the Nazis. Mena knew how quickly things could turn, and so, Guillaume said, she had a certain paranoia. She probably didn't want to call attention to herself.

Sometime in early 1944, Starink writes, the two lovers, Jan and Mena, returned to Paris together to a hotel on boulevard Montparnasse, where several Dutch people were in hiding and awaiting passage across the Pyrenees to England. Jan and Mena fell into a trap and were arrested by the Gestapo. Mena was relieved during her interrogation not to be tortured but "only" beaten. She worried that if tortured, she would have told them the many names of people she knew in the Résistance. She got through the interrogation by playing the ignorant peasant from Brittany—"faisant sa bretonne," laying on a thick Breton accent. Jan van Brakel would die in the camps.

As for the stories from the camps, Guillaume knew about the wild hats the older women at HASAG Leipzig had made out of scraps for the young women to wear on St. Catherine's Day. He knew about the way they had danced the farandole all night. His grandmother had talked about the strong support network among the women. Those with an education and diplomas gave classes to the others. They recited poetry and whole plays they had memorized. Mena came from a simple background and did not have more than a basic education, but she admired the many women who gave lessons. The women who came from the haute couture trade taught her to sew. The politically active women, such as Lise London, talked about the ideals of the revolution and women's suffrage.

Guillaume remembered stories about the brutality of the guards, common criminals who ruled over the women. Mena had told Edith how the Germans were scared of the Sinti and Roma. "They would not enter the Gypsy blocks unless armed with dogs and whips because those women were fierce," Mena had said proudly. "If given half a chance, they would have torn out the Germans' eyes with their nails."

Mena was very modest about being seen naked. Edith wasn't sure why, but after the war she was adamant about her privacy. Guillaume wondered if it was due to a tattoo that she was hiding, but I knew the prisoners at Ravensbrück were not tattooed. However, there was the endless humiliation of being paraded naked in front of the SS. Mena must have reclaimed her body and her privacy just as fiercely as the Roma she admired. Marceline Loridan-Ivens, who was best friends in Birkenau with the famous feminist Simone Veil, movingly wrote about the lasting trauma of being naked in front of Nazi officers: "I don't like my body. It's as if it still bears the trace of a man's first look at me, that of a Nazi. I had never been naked before, especially in my new skin as a young girl who had just grown breasts and everything else. So getting undressed for me has long been associated with death, hatred."[4]

Mena had told her daughter about a child born in the camp and how they all worked together to keep the baby alive. Lise London wrote about a baby born to a Jewish woman who had managed to hide her pregnancy right up to the moment when she gave birth to a rosy little girl with blond hair. She was taken to the *Revier*, and there the baby was put in a box since they did not have a crib. The French prisoners decided to "adopt" the baby. They shortened their hems or took in the seams of their clothes to get scraps of material. With those scraps they made dresses and booties and a quilt. They were constantly searching for a pretext to go to the *Revier* to see the baby. As soon as she had given birth, the mother had to return to the twelve-hour work shift in the factory. When her shift was done, she would rush to see her child and try to feed her, but exhausted and starved as she was, she had no milk. The Polish nurses asked the SS for milk, but the response they got was: "No, not a drop of milk for the baby of a Jewish dog."[5]

The French went from block to block asking for donations of the sugar, margarine, and powdered milk that a few of the Poles received from their families. But they were not very successful. After just a few weeks, the baby, who had been so rosy and sweet, was just a skeleton that somehow clung to life. Two months passed, and she was still alive. Her fingers were thin as spider legs and her eyes were covered with large scabs—she was blinded by malnutrition. The French prisoners no longer made excuses to go see her; it was too painful. Lise remembered her own children at that age, how beautiful and plump they were. This one had turned into a haunted, ancient-looking person. Yet all during this period the commander had a puppy that was given bowls of milk by the kitchen every day.

Another selection was announced: mostly Jews, and the sick and weak. The mother and the baby were selected. They were to leave the next day. Lise recounts how, as she was walking up the stairs to the infirmary, she heard the angry cries and shouts of the Polish nurse. The mother, hoping to spare her child the terrible suffering of the journey ahead, had tried to kill it by banging its head against the wall. The Polish nurse held the child, who was still alive, only now its head was all blue and bruised. The mother sat in the corner, in a state of utter despair, while the nurse insulted her: "Here you are with your Jews! They are not women, they are animals."[6]

———◆———

In Ravensbrück, children and babies were simply forbidden. This meant they would be taken from their mothers upon birth and killed—or, if sufficiently "Aryan"-looking, they might have been given to Nazi families to raise. Abortions were carried out up to eight months. Any baby born alive was killed at birth, asphyxiated or drowned in a bucket in front of the mother. Because newborns have a strong, reflexive resistance to drowning, this could sometimes take as long as twenty minutes.[7]

In the late summer of 1944, around the time Jacky and Nicole arrived at Ravensbrück, huge numbers of women were arriving from Warsaw. Other women were coming from countries where the Allies were gaining ground and the Germans were evacuating prisoners in a hurry. Many of these women arrived in the early stages of pregnancy. According to the staff records, one in ten Polish women arriving at Ravensbrück at that time was pregnant because of the mass rapes by German soldiers that had occurred in Warsaw.

Women were giving birth at *Appell*, in the bathhouse, at work, in the mud of a tent. Something had to be done to deal with this influx. In an extraordinary shift in the regulations, a *Kinderzimmer*, or quasi–maternity ward, was created at Ravensbrück in block 11. It seemed as if the Nazis had had a miraculous change of heart. The starvation of the mothers during pregnancy caused the babies to have a high water content in their tissue at birth, which made the newborns, like the baby Mena remembered, appear plump, rosy, and healthy, but this was an illusion. The mothers had to go back to work immediately but were allowed to come to the ward four times a day to attempt to feed the children. The new mothers—starved, traumatized, and depleted, with an utterly deficient diet—simply could not produce the milk necessary to nurse their children. They were soon wild with hunger and fear for their babies. They begged for milk but were refused.

The *Kinderzimmer* was crowded with forty babies and only two bunk beds. There was no hygiene, no bottles, no milk, no diapers.

The babies became covered in boils and sores. The mothers tried to wash cloth scraps in the dark watery liquid they were served as coffee in the morning and then tried to dry the scraps against their bodies, but the babies were often wrapped in wet or damp makeshift diapers.

Adding to this cruelty, the rule was that the babies would be locked in the ward alone at night, and a window was deliberately left open, even in winter. One mother was able to steal the key to go see her baby boy. The sight that she confronted was horrific: "Vermin of all sorts jumping on the beds and inside the noses and ears of the babies. Most of the babies were naked because their blankets had come off. They were crying of hunger and cold and covered in sores."[8]

The babies lived only a few weeks, maybe a month. Most of the records at Ravensbrück were destroyed before liberation, but some prisoners kept their own records. Zdenka Nedvedova, a Czech pediatrician, had been put in charge of the *Kinderzimmer*. She worked with a young French Résistance fighter, Marie-Jo Chombart de Lauwe, fighting as hard as she could to save the babies, even risking confrontation with an SS senior nurse who was hoarding powdered milk she had stolen from the Red Cross parcels.

Marie-Jo and Zdenka hoped the war would end soon, in time to save some of the children. Zdenka kept a secret birth journal, which she managed to save. She recorded that 600 babies were born in the camp between September 1944 and April 1945. Most of the babies who were still alive in February 1945 were sent to Bergen-Belsen, where they were exterminated. But babies were being born right up to the end. The Foundation for the Memory of the Deported (FMD) found that thirty-one babies survived until liberation.[9]

In the final chaotic months of the camp, children arrived with their mothers. At least 900 boys and girls ages two to sixteen were recorded as prisoners in Ravensbrück. Some of these children were adopted by camp mothers if their own mothers had died. Children were separated from their parents and records were lost. In 2005, on the sixty-fifth anniversary of the liberation, Julius Maslovat, a child survivor of Buchenwald and Bergen-Belsen, wore a plaque around his neck with a photograph of himself at the age of two and the question, "Do you recognize me?" He was searching for anyone who might know who he was.[10]

———

In the makeshift camp of the German soldiers, Guigui elbowed Mena. She had put down her spoon and seemed to have drifted into dark memories. "Eat," Guigui urged her friend. Mena nodded and resumed eating the thick stew.

Hélène surmised that these men had deserted and were waiting for the war to end. They were happy to have female company and were probably harmless. They gave the women a few cans of German field rations, which they called "monkey meat." The women found it quite tasty.

Hélène asked about how they might cross the front. The men drew a map in the dirt, explaining possible routes. They thought the front was probably about twelve kilometers away, which meant the women could be across it by tomorrow. But things could change quickly, one man emphasized. Another warned the women that the final days of war were always the most dangerous.

"We've lost contact with our unit," explained one man, who was wearing strange blue worker's trousers that were obviously several sizes too large.

"Plans kept changing and no one bothered to tell us," added a young man with closely cropped blond hair. His eyes were fixed on Mena.

Lon, who was translating, added in French, "I get the feeling he wants us to understand he's not a coward."

The men asked Lon and Hélène about their story, but the women were evasive. Their factory had been bombed, they said, and they were trying to get home.

The soldiers too kept their story vague. It was somehow impolite to talk openly about what they were doing there; it might remind everyone that they were enemies. But at one point the cook blurted out, "I didn't agree with many things about this war. I will say it now. I'm not going to hide it anymore. The SS, they are the criminals!"

"You don't like the SS?" Hélène asked. She looked at him intently. She thought of Fritz Stupitz, the foreman at the munitions factory who had done so much to try to help her. She remembered when he had admitted to her that he didn't like Hitler.

"They preyed on us, just as they preyed on you. Everyone was scared to speak the truth, and that's how we got into this mess." The cook was getting angry, his already ruddy face turning a deeper red. "Everybody had to lie and turn one another in. They made people behave badly."

"What's he going on about?" Jacky asked, alarmed by the cook's sudden anger and his mad gesticulations. Hélène translated the gist of the cook's fury at the SS.

"In fact, you must avoid them on your way to the front," the young boy with the blue eyes said earnestly, speaking to Mena.

The cook continued to rant. "The SS are shooting and killing everything now, like trapped animals. We saw a group of prisoners from one of these camps, about thirty, all of them hung from the tree branches. The SS did it. They are just animals," he said, waving his ladle.

When Lon translated his words, the women became visibly upset.

"Hey, let's not talk that way when we have such charming company," another soldier said to the cook. "Look, you've upset them. Calm down. The war will be over in a few days." Turning to the women, he told them, "You're tough and beautiful."

All the men agreed. "Very brave," one said.

"And so beautiful," the young blue-eyed soldier said to Mena.

"They're telling us we are beautiful," Hélène said with a smile.

"And strong," Lon added.

The women were happy to hear this. Even after everything they had been subjected to, they still hoped to be admired as women.

The weather was fabulous. The sun had come out and their bellies were full. Their morale was boosted by the encounter. It was Hélène who stood up first and said, "We are so grateful for your hospitality, but we can't stay. We must find that front."

The men were disappointed, but they respected Hélène's words, and everyone stood up to say a formal goodbye. The men bowed and wished them well.

"Avoid the SS!" the cook called out as they walked away.

The sun was shining, the ditches were green, and the trees were beginning to bloom. As they traveled, Hélène felt she needed to explain her decision to leave the soldiers' camp. "Mena," she said, "I know you didn't want to leave, but we can't stay there after dark.

Those men are fine in daylight, but who knows if at night they might get the wrong idea."

"And we need to keep moving," Nicole agreed.

"OK, I understand we needed to leave the men. But," Mena sighed, "I thought we aren't supposed to walk in the middle of the day. Doesn't it make us a prime target for bombs?"

"I agree," Jacky said. "Let's rest somewhere. No men, just rest and sun."

A little farther on there was a beautiful ditch. The ground was covered in a carpet of yellow dandelions. Hélène and Nicole both wanted to keep going; they felt they had already taken a long lunch break. But in the end, they had to acquiesce. After a few moments of quiet, Hélène asked Zaza, "Do you hear that?"

"Cannons?"

"No, birds!" The two friends smiled.

The nine lay comfortably in the ditch. Mena was braiding wreaths of dandelion flowers for their heads. They must have been a strange sight in the midst of a war and so near the front. Several carts passed carrying peasants, wounded soldiers, and the elderly. Most of the soldiers were young and curious, calling out: "Hello!" They wanted to know how a group of French girls had gotten there. When told about Josée, some added, "Oh, there's a Spaniard? Which one is she?"

"And two Dutch," Lon would call out. This easy banter back and forth made the women smile as they breathed in the delicious scent of green grass. Who knew that the front could feel so much like springtime?

Then Hélène and Nicole stood up. It was time to move on. They certainly couldn't spend the night in the ditch. They needed to pick up the pace.

An old peasant with a wagon loaded with potatoes and a wounded soldier stopped to chat as they were getting ready to move on. The soldier was no more than twenty years old. They asked for his opinion of the front, its location, and the difficulty of crossing it. He told them the front was now at the Mulde River.

"You probably won't be allowed to cross," the soldier said. "But I would go to the next village and wait."

When Hélène translated his advice, the women began to argue.

Zaza worried about staying in one place. As a general rule, the Germans were organized people, she argued, and the most organized of the Germans were the SS. If they didn't keep moving, it would be as if they were just sitting there waiting to get picked up and sent back to a camp or hung like those men the cook had described.

Nicole was impatient. She had been deported only nine days before Paris was liberated. She had been that close to freedom. Instead, she had spent the past nine months in hell. She wasn't waiting around to be recaptured by the Germans.

Hélène, Zaza, Zinka, and Josée agreed with Nicole that they should keep moving. But the others complained; they were exhausted. Why not just find a nice place where they could lie low and wait for the end of the war? Why risk being shot at?

This reasoning made Nicole furious. If they stayed, she argued, they were "just as likely—no, *more* likely—to get shot by an SS getting a last-minute sadistic thrill!"

The soldier, hearing them speak in French, interrupted. "Take these," he said in thickly accented French as he tossed potatoes to them. "When I was in France the people were so kind to me. They gave me potatoes to eat."

And, vaguely understanding that the women were quarrelling about whether or not they should cross the front, he added, "If you continue in this direction, I can tell you, you will come to Altenhof. There is a company of soldiers there. What you should do is go there and present yourself to the commander. He will take care of you."

His words did not settle the argument. Why would a German commander help a group of escaping women prisoners to cross the front?

———⟨⟩———

They reached Altenhof in the late afternoon, and once again the seven women waited in a ditch by the edge of the village while Hélène and Lon went in search of the commander in question.

After crossing a small bridge, they found him overseeing a group of boy soldiers; not a single one appeared older than fourteen. They were going through a marching routine. An older man, the commander watched over the group of boys with an almost protective gaze.

"So you are a group of French women," he commented flirtatiously. He spoke a little French. But Hélène stuck to the point: they needed a place to sleep that night and permission to cross the front tomorrow.

"For you? Or for all nine?" he asked.

"All of us together."

"Nine pretty girls want to cross the front?" He was smirking.

"Yes, we just want to go home," Hélène insisted.

"You know it's crazy, don't you? You will be shot at by both sides."

"We're willing to risk it," Hélène assured him.

He seemed to find this audacity fascinating. He turned for a moment to assess his group of child soldiers, who were marching sloppily across the field. The two women waited for him to respond. When he turned back around to address them he was smiling.

"I will give you what you want if you do something for me. A simple trade," he said. Looking directly at Hélène, he winked.

He shouted orders, and the boys marched over to where they were standing. He shouted more orders, and they snapped their feet together at attention. He spoke loudly, with a serious expression on his face. He asked if Hélène and Lon would do him the honor of "inspecting the troops."

For a moment the two women thought they might burst into laughter, for the situation was absurd. And although the commander's demeanor was serious, the slight glint in his eyes told them that he too knew it was absurd. Was this really the "simple trade" he had referred to?

Of course they would, they said seriously.

Lon had the impulse to straighten collars, button shirts, and smooth down the boys' hair. They were so young, so fierce, and so scared.

Though Hélène kept up a brave front, she was worried that the commander would want something more from her than this charade.

———— ❦ ————

On the opposite side of the bridge, the other seven settled in, expecting the wait to be thirty, maybe forty minutes. No one had a watch, of course. Finally Zaza spoke up. "It's taking them a long time."

"Yes," agreed Nicole grimly. "This wait is longer than the one in Delmschütz when Guigui lost us."

The sun would soon set. They felt a chill in the air. But, immobilized by fear, they could not decide what to do.

Finally Lon and Hélène returned, worn out and limping.

"Do we have a place to eat and sleep?" Zinka asked, ever practical.

"Yes," Lon responded. But both women looked worried.

"Will they let us cross?" Nicole asked.

"We'll tell you the whole story, but really, we need to cross the bridge right away before it's closed," Lon answered vaguely.

The seven others obeyed quietly. Close by they found a picturesque bridge made of stone with a series of lovely arches over a small river. The bridge was guarded by two soldiers who were at the most fourteen years old. The boys had strung as many grenades as possible around their belts. They compensated for their extreme youth by being especially nasty and aggressive to the women. In the distance the women saw more baby soldiers in helmets that were too large for their heads, practicing with *Panzerfaust*, the very weapons they had made in the factory in Leipzig. The women felt a bit nervous observing those exercises, knowing that they had sabotaged so many of those *Panzerfaust*. At any moment one of them might just explode.

———

When I was writing about the boy soldiers, I was talking with my neighbor, an elderly Austrian man who is a war journalist and acclaimed writer. He has covered wars all over the globe, but he had only been a soldier once, he said. He showed me a book about this career in war journalism, and there in the photographs was a picture of a group of thirteen-year-old boys in short pants, their hands up in the air, surrendering to American soldiers.

"That's me," he said, pointing to one of them. "That's when I was a soldier."

"So young," I said.

"Yes, and we were told to fight against the tanks with heavy *Panzerfaust* that we could barely lift."

———

Hélène told the boy soldiers guarding the bridge that they were expected for dinner, and the boys reluctantly let the women cross. But almost as soon as they had crossed, a group of soldiers on bicycles caught up with them and announced that the commander wanted to speak to them, the whole group, at once. They turned back, crossing the bridge again under the glare of the two boy soldiers.

The commander asked the women to stand in a line so he could "inspect them." They had learned to decode the details on the collars of German uniforms, so they knew that he was not SS, but their last *Appell* was fresh in their memory, as were so many other roll calls they had had to endure. It was hard for them not to tremble and feel nausea while he carefully looked them over.

He spoke to Hélène and Lon. "So, this is your group of nine women who want to cross the Mulde? I will need more substantial payment from you if you plan to cross as a group."

"Payment?" Hélène asked, looking at him, hoping to shame him.

"We will give you what little money we have," Lon offered.

He laughed dismissively. "I'm sure we can work out a much more interesting exchange," he said, not taking his eyes off Hélène. "A nice sort of payment. We each have something the other one wants."

When the two women turned back to face the other seven, they looked grim. "We will go to the barn now, where he's told us to sleep. The people there will cook our potatoes," Lon told the others, barking her words almost like an order.

Zaza looked at Hélène's ashen face. "What?" she whispered to her friend.

"He won't let us pass. He says we still owe him payment." Disgusted, Hélène almost spat the word out. "He wants me to make the 'payment.'"

Zaza said nothing, but she took her friend's hand.

"But let's go. We can talk about that later," Hélène said.

They crossed the bridge again, under the now curious gaze of the two baby soldiers. Fifty meters farther along, the group of soldiers on bicycles again caught up with them and announced that the commander wanted to see just the "two women."

Lon and Hélène recrossed the bridge. This time they were led to a large building that served as the commander's office and home and were told to wait in a sort of vestibule. Hélène's hip ached. They sat down on a small bench, not speaking, just staring at the floor. It was like so many times in these past years when they had been stuck waiting to see what terrible thing would come next.

A man arrived and said that the commander would like "the French woman, alone, in his room." The word he used in German was ambiguous: *Stube*, which could mean an office or a bedroom. Hélène grabbed Lon's hand and nodded, indicating that she needed Lon to come with her. They entered the room together.

They saw a couch with a low table set with bread, cheese, fruit, and wine. The commander was standing with his back to them. He was no longer in his uniform, having changed into a clean white shirt, and he was shaving. He didn't realize Lon had entered with Hélène, and he started to speak playfully in French. "So, you haven't had much to complain about, have you? I'm not the big bad wolf?"

"No," Lon replied in German. "But the sheep would like to return quickly to their flock."

Startled, the commander turned to face the two women. One side of his face was still covered in white shaving cream. There was a long moment when they looked at one another. Then he burst into laughter. "Ah! I thought we had an understanding. My generosity would be met by your generosity."

"We simply want to cross the front lines," Hélène said.

"Please, help yourselves to some of this food and drink I had prepared for you."

"No, thank you," Lon said. "We have been hungry for a long time, but our sole desire now is to return to our home as rapidly as possible."

The commander kept his eyes on Hélène. He laughed a little, as if trying to lighten the moment. "Perhaps I misunderstood. But I would prefer to speak with the French woman alone."

"We are a group. We stay together. Whatever you say to her you can say with me present," Lon insisted.

He stared at Hélène, and she glared back at him. There was a long, tense moment of silence. At last he nodded and sighed. "All right. You will have your *Passierschein*."

"Thank you," Lon said, holding back a smile.

"And if you want to do something kind for us . . . ," Hélène added, feeling the bravery of rage.

He smiled at her boldness. "What more do you want?"

"Someone to accompany us to the last possible limit, to as close to the front as possible. So that your advance line of soldiers won't shoot at us by accident."

"You are courageous fools, but all right. Be here tomorrow, early, and I will give you an escort to the Mulde River." He waved his hands, dismissing them.

———❦———

While Lon and Hélène were with the commander, the others had settled on a long bench outside a small café just on the other side of the bridge. Mena and Guigui went inside to ask for some water. Mena was thirsty, but she could not speak a word of German. She turned any efforts to learn into a joke. When Guigui told her a word of German vocabulary, Mena would transform the word into French-sounding nonsense. Invariably this made them all laugh, and the language lesson would be abandoned.

The men inside playing cards and drinking beer had taken an interest in Mena and Guigui's story. "When you hear French you think of smoking," the men said, handing them cigarettes.

The women sitting outside were approached by a postman on a bike, who asked who they were and where they came from. When they told him, he replied, "What? One of you is Spanish? Which one? She doesn't look Spanish. She's just as pretty as you French girls."

They were annoyed with his awkward flirtation, but he too gave them cigarettes. Mena and Guigui came out of the café with their arms full of bread and sausages, and even coffee—a generous present, though they had no way of using it.

The women were worried about Hélène and Lon. Zaza had told them what Hélène whispered about the ambiguous word "payment." Feeling helpless and anxious, they were grateful to smoke. Instead of sharing one cigarette, they each had their own. In the camps, cigarettes had been used for trade; they could be used to buy more soup or an extra ration of bread. No one except the very privileged ever actually smoked them. One exception was when a woman was sure she was going to die—if she had given up or if she had been selected for death. Then she might smoke a last cigarette.

It was getting dark. There were baby soldiers everywhere. The town was poised, expectant. It was clear these were the final days of the war. The soldiers on the bridge did not look at the women anymore; by now the seven of them had become part of the land-scape. Instead the boy soldiers began to play with their grenades. The women hoped the grenades were fake, because if they were real, at any moment one of them could explode.

They sighed with collective relief when Hélène and Lon reap-peared and crossed the bridge one more time. The two seemed pleased with themselves.

"The commander?" Zinka asked Hélène.

"Fantastic news! Not only do we have a *laisser-passer,* but he will send some soldiers with us to get us across the Mulde River tomorrow morning." There were shouts of joy and many questions, but again Lon said, "We can't explain everything right here. We need to hurry to the farm—this close to the front there's a strict curfew."

The farmhouse room where they would spend the night had a fabulous view of the forest of pine trees, and nothing else. Just a hard wooden floor and one table. They missed their soft haylofts, even though the hay could be itchy and prickly. The hard wood planks reminded them of their old bunks back in the block. The owners of the farm were flustered. Though the commander had ordered them to shelter the women, they had no food to feed them. The women of-fered their potatoes, which the farmers were happy to cook for them.

The farmhouse was on top of a hill. Hélène pointed to the woods. "You see the middle, where it seems the pine trees are less dense? That's the Mulde River. That's what we shall cross tomorrow. And once on the other side, we will be on the liberated side of Europe."

The women wanted to know everything. What had happened with the commander? What sort of escort would there be? How would they cross?

Lon lay down, exhausted. "You tell them, Hélène. I am too tired to find the words in French. My brain's a scramble."

Hélène told them about their initial meeting with the commander and his offer of a "simple trade," which Hélène had feared would not be so simple. "And I was right," she said.

"What happened the third time you two had to go see him?" Nicole asked.

"He was expecting more 'payment' for the *laisser-passer*." Hélène described the scene with the couch, the food, and the commander shaving. And she explained how bravely Lon had defended her honor.

Though this was a good story and the escort welcome news, there were now new worries to talk over. Perhaps just being so close to their goal was frightening. Their conversation turned to the crossing of the Mulde River. How would it be done? The bridges had been bombed, so they thought it was likely they would cross by boat.

"What kind of boat?" Jacky asked. "I mean, can we trust it?"

"Oh, you're too crazy. A boat, a raft, that our escorts will give us," Nicole answered impatiently.

"Yes, but the Mulde appears to be the frontier. Once we are in our famous raft given to us by the escort, in the middle of the river, won't we be a perfect target?" Guigui asked.

"Yes," Lon put in calmly. "It's been days since anyone has crossed the Mulde because it is dangerous, and we will be sitting ducks."

"Well," Nicole said, frustrated by the wavering resolve of the others, "we can just stay here and wait for whatever happens—the grenades of children, exploding *Panzerfaust*—or we can finally cross the damn Mulde by swimming it if we have to!"

Her outburst quieted everyone down for a moment.

Hélène began talking about strategy. "The best way to not appear as targets, as sitting ducks on a raft, is to appear as much as possible as innocent ladies. No trousers. We wear our prison dresses, even in tatters. Those who have hair let it down so it can be seen from a distance. Jacky, you must take off your turban. We mustn't look like soldiers."

Zinka asked, "Who here feels comfortable swimming, even fully dressed?"

Five women raised their hands: Nicole, Hélène, Mena, Lon, and Guigui. They were strong swimmers. The other four, Jacky, Zaza, Zinka, and Josée, knew how to swim but didn't feel they could cross a river.

"OK," Zinka continued. "Those who feel sure of yourselves should take one of us as your responsibility."

"Drowning people are panicky, and sometimes their flailing can drown even a good swimmer," Lon said. "I've heard it happens."

"Whomever I am in charge of better keep calm," Hélène said.

"The best way to ensure that is to knock them out with a punch. Then it's easy to drag them to the other side," Lon said. This made everyone laugh.

"I'll take Zaza," Nicole volunteered, "since she's naturally peaceful."

"I once almost drowned," Zaza told her, "so I promise to behave. I will be as calm as a dove."

"No, to be safe, I think I'll knock you out," Nicole said, laughing.

When their hosts brought the cooked potatoes, the women found they had little appetite. They ate a few and saved some for breakfast; the rest Zaza would carry in her sack the next day.

Before settling down to sleep, Hélène explained the plan. They had to get up early the next morning and walk three kilometers to the Mulde. Once on the other side, they still had about fifteen kilometers to go to Colditz, where they knew there were American troops. They should try to do it all in one day because the commander warned that there were still a few German soldiers posted in the last villages and woods before Colditz. Tomorrow was the day they had to push themselves. It had to be the last day of their "camping trip."

CHAPTER NINE

— THE LONGEST DAY —

EARLY ON THE MORNING OF April 21 they woke and ate a few cold boiled potatoes. But they had no real appetite. Restless and frightened, they scrambled to leave. Would this be the day when they finally found the Americans? The rush to make their bundles and get going intensified the usual morning commotion. "Can you take this?" Mena asked Guigui, holding up a small folded rag. "I forgot to add it, and now my bundle is done."

"Yes, but where are my shoes?" Guigui asked. "Everyone is always taking my stuff." She said something like this every morning as she searched for her belongings, which she tended to leave scattered about.

"If you kept your things in order . . . ," Josée began, retrieving Guigui's missing shoes from the corner of the room. But she stopped herself. She had tried to train this group before, with no success, and today they were too excited to listen to her "orderly campground" speech again. "Oh, Jesus, Marie, and Joseph, let's just get going," she said.

Lon had lost the strings she used to tie up her bundle. "I know where I left them," she insisted emphatically when Zaza suggested she had perhaps packed them.

"It's going to be a long day," Nicole reminded them. "We need an early start."

They wanted to look as much like ladies as they could, so they spent a little extra time on their hair and their rags. But these were pathetic attempts to look chic. They had no mirrors; they had to rely on one another to confirm that they looked good. Everyone was lying, and everyone knew it. Jacky's worn-out striped dress looked like a sack. Zaza tried to adjust the waist, but all the fiddling got on Jacky's nerves, "Ach, leave it," she snarled.

Jacky needed a moment alone. She went out into the cold to smoke the butt of a cigarette she had carefully saved from yesterday. She wasn't sure she would survive another day of walking. She didn't want to bellyache, but her lungs burned, and her mouth and throat felt as though they were on fire. There were deep blue circles around her eyes. She felt feverish. Somehow, she told herself, she had to cross that damn river.

The others filed out of the barn, ready to report to the commander to get their *laisser-passer* and escort. They had to walk back down the hill past the boy soldiers and across the bridge once more. At the commander's quarters a younger officer came out to meet them. He was the same man who had announced to Lon and Hélène the day before that the commander wanted to see "the French woman alone." Lon remembered that he too had smelled of shaving cream, and now she saw that his room was next door to the commander's; no doubt he had intended to get "payment" from her in his room while Hélène was with the commander.

"You realize, don't you, that we treated you fairly," he began, winking at Lon. "In exchange, please treat us fairly when you reach the other side. Do not tell them too much about what you have seen here."

Hélène and Lon smiled. What they had seen was a bunch of children playing at being soldiers. "We are grateful," Lon said.

He handed her a piece of paper, on which was written:

Altenhof, the 21st of April, 1945

Authorization is given to six French women, two Dutch women, and one Spanish woman, under the guidance of the Dutch woman Madelon Verstijnen, to cross the front toward the west to return to their homeland.

Hélène read the note and translated it for the women gathered around her. When she got to the end, the wonderful phrase "return to their homeland," there was an intake of breath. The women, scared as they were, smiled. The officer nodded. "There you go," he said curtly. As a farewell, he added, "Good luck."

Their escort was a young soldier pulling a bicycle. He wasn't interested in small talk of any kind, even a flirtation with Mena. He was single-minded in his task. The bicycle handlebars kept getting hung up on tree branches as they walked through the thick forest that descended steeply to the river. They wondered why he would bring a bicycle when he would just have to climb back up the hill with it. But clearly their escort was terrified. At the slightest snap of a branch he jumped. They were worried he was going to turn at any minute and begin frantically pedaling back to town before getting them to the river.

"Keep him close," Lon said to Guigui. "If he turns to run, you're the fastest. You grab him."

"Yes," Hélène agreed. "We need to keep him with us up to the last possible moment."

"I'm a good runner too," Josée volunteered. "I'll help you, Guigui."

As they bantered anxiously, Zaza noticed that the forest was splendid. If they hadn't been so scared about what awaited them, she would have liked to spend time in these woods. They smelled of cool, fresh pine, and there was the hushed sound of birds in the canopy. "These are lovely woods," she said brightly. "Like in a fairy tale."

"Yeah, but while you're playing Little Red Riding Hood, Fritz could be anywhere in here, about to shoot us," Jacky quipped.

They scrambled onward for about three kilometers, the hill getting steeper as they approached the river. They could hear its roar and smell the water misting in the air. At last they arrived at the final German outpost, guarded by two bored soldiers. The *laisser-passer* and a word from their escort worked. The soldiers shrugged lethargically and indicated that the women could go on down to the river and cross it if that was what they wanted. At that, their escort turned and began frantically climbing back up the hill at record speed. The women watched him go and joked, "He'll be back at Altenhof before we're across the river."

Guigui asked the two guards, "So where do we cross? Is there a ferry or a raft?"

The soldiers laughed. "Just go to the old bridge and see for your-self how it's done."

At the river's edge the women had a terrible shock. The bridge had been blown up, and the Mulde River in April was in full flood. Rapids foamed around rocks and the broken cement chunks of the collapsed bridge. The river was running fast; there was no way a boat or ferry could navigate across it. And there was equally no chance a person could swim across.

A makeshift crossing had been rigged in a precarious way. At their end of the broken bridge was a wobbly ladder. In fact, it was several ladders strapped together to form a rickety, overextended contrap-tion. The long ladder descended straight down for fifteen dizzying meters. The bottom rungs of the ladder plunged into the swirling river. From the rung just above the surface, they would have to leap to an uneven chunk of concrete lying half submerged in the rapids. From there they could climb from boulder to boulder. The surface of these "stepping-stones" looked slippery, glossy with water and foam.

On the other side of the river, the other half of the broken bridge could be climbed with a smaller ladder leaned against the steeply sloping side. The ladders looked alarmingly fragile against the raging waters of the Mulde. At any moment the whole thing could easily be swept away.

The women had mentally prepared themselves to be shot at by snipers or to drown. They had wrestled with these fears all night. But they had not prepared themselves for this sort of gauntlet. Now they drew back, thinking that there had to be another way to cross.

"Maybe if we go farther downstream?" Josée suggested.

"All the bridges are blown," Hélène said. "We have no choice." This crossing had to be done before their fear actually caught up with them.

The problem was that each of them carried a package, small but not suited for going down ladders. They needed both hands free for that. Some were wearing wooden clogs. It was beginning to drizzle, so every step was slick. They were not prepared for these acrobatics.

"I'll go first," Zinka volunteered.

"No, I should go before you," Nicole said. "You're smaller. I should be there to help you." Furthermore, Nicole argued, she should go first because she was familiar with mountain climbing. She abandoned the heavy cooking pot and tripod, saying bravely, "Tonight we will eat with the Americans, so we don't need this anymore."

As Nicole descended, she felt the ladder sway and buckle under her weight. She took a deep breath and continued, pushing through her fear. At the bottom of the ladder she jumped to the broken concrete and waited for Zinka to climb down. The ladder rungs were far apart, too far for someone as small as Zinka to easily manage. At the bottom, where she had to leap from the ladder to the broken chunk of bridge, she slipped and fell halfway into the freezing river. The others gasped. Josée let out a scream. But Nicole lunged and grabbed Zinka just in time, pulling her up onto the rock.

Zinka was drenched. In the near disaster, she had lost all her things, including the one photo she had of her daughter, France, and the stuffed bear Mena had made for France's first birthday. Watching her bundle as it was carried away by the river, Zinka squeezed Nicole's hand. She was covered in spray from the river, so Nicole couldn't see that she was crying.

The two of them clambered over the rocks and boulders and carefully climbed up the ladder at the other end. Then Zinka turned to face the women on the other side of the river. She smiled and waved to them to signal that all was well.

Jacky and Mena crossed next.

"Wish we had a bit of schnapps or some of your famous eggs this morning," Jacky said to Mena as they approached the bridge. "A little liquid courage."

Jacky was worried that she would falter, but she was tall, with long arms and legs, which helped her on the first descent, long and dangerous. In the end, it was Mena who lost one of her clogs on the ladder. She kicked the other one off then as well. "What's the point?" she called to Jacky above the roaring water. "I can't walk with only one clog. Anyway, the ladder's easier with bare feet."

Once on the other side, Mena gave Zinka some dry clothes from her bundle. Zaza and Hélène went next, with Hélène going first. Zaza was chatting to keep her courage up, telling Hélène, "This isn't too bad. Just one foot after the other."

"Pay attention," Hélène called up to her.

Just then Zaza's foot slipped off a rung, and in the effort to regain her balance she lost her large bundle with the remainder of their cooked potatoes from the night before. It was quickly washed away by the dark waters of the Mulde. She let out a cry. "Oh no! What have I done?"

"Concentrate, Zaza! Don't look at the river!" Hélène called to her. Her heart was pounding. In her imagination, Hélène could see Zaza falling.

"I'm so sorry," Zaza cried down to Hélène. "I've lost everything!"

"It's not important. Forget it. Just be careful and get down the ladder."

In Zaza's lost bundle were all her clothes, including the sweater she had carefully deloused the night before and that very morning as she waited for the others to be ready. She was mostly angry about the potatoes. "Stupid, I'm so stupid!" she shouted above the rush of water. She kept repeating how stupid she felt as she and Hélène clambered over the boulders. Zaza's legs were shaking with fear at her near accident. She had only been halfway down the ladder. If she had fallen, she would have been just as likely to smash her head against the rocks as to drown in the river.

The women who had already crossed greeted them with relief. But Zaza was still upset about the lost potatoes. "What will we eat?" she cried.

"It's a good sign," Zinka reassured her. "Every time we run out of food since we've been on the road, someone arrives and gives us more. You did right by losing the potatoes and your rags. It means that soon we will get new clothes and something better to eat than potatoes." Zinka was holding back her own tears. She told herself that losing France's photo meant that she would see her baby soon.

Josée, Guigui, and Lon crossed last. The other women helped hoist them up the last embankment. Then they all lay on the ground catching their breath. They were soaked from the spray of the river and the drizzling rain, but they were finally across the Mulde.

———※———

"Right," Hélène said after five minutes' rest. "We need to keep moving. We're just getting wetter and colder by staying here in the rain."

The women walked into the forest following an indistinct path through the woods that headed west. Almost immediately they ran into a local German boy. He confirmed that he had actually seen American soldiers, and that they were indeed in Colditz.

"It's easy to get there. No one will stop you," he said. "But be careful about the artillery fire when you are walking on high ground. When you hear a whistle, get down. Take shelter, if you can, in a ditch."

They were buoyed by this news. The Americans were real. And they had now met someone who had actually seen them. But when they got out of the forest and found themselves walking on the high top of a hill, they began to worry about the boy's warning. What kind of whistle did he mean? Why hadn't they asked him to be more specific?

Halfway up a sloping hill they heard the first whistle. "It's just the wind," Nicole said confidently. She didn't want them to stop moving.

But immediately following the third whistle they saw black smoke rising from the ground not very far away. They hurriedly took shelter behind a small hillock. Pressing themselves flat on the earth, they waited. In the lull they noticed spring flowers poking out of the ground all around them.

The whistles came more often now. They sounded like silk being torn, and they were followed by the thud of an explosion in the distance. The sound rolled toward them like thunder. They could not tell if they were being targeted; it seemed like the shooting was aimed at something farther away. They lay there for a long time, waiting.

When they felt it was safe, they continued as fast as possible, wanting to get off the open high ground. The countryside was deserted. They passed through villages that were shuttered and appeared abandoned. They wondered if the inhabitants were hiding in their cellars and wine caves. They found no one to tell them the way, no one to offer them food. They were exhausted and drenched. But to cheer everyone up Zinka said, "The good news is since we've been shot at, and heard and seen bombs, it really does feel like the front we've been searching for. I thought we'd never find it."

"Well, here it is," Jacky grumbled. "Let's sell tickets."

It was early afternoon and they were hungry, cranky, and frazzled.

In one village they bumped into a *Bürgermeister* who was fleeing in the opposite direction with a small group of villagers. He asked them about crossing the Mulde, and they assured him it was possible although precarious. Zaza warned them about the risk of dropping their things into the water.

The man was frantic to get away. He didn't want to linger and chat with a group of strange French women. When they asked him for food, he said, "I can't do anything for you. Go to the next village— there is a man who has just killed a pig. He'll have something to eat."

As they trudged on to the next village, a man sped past them on a bicycle. Entering the village, they saw his bicycle leaning against a house. He had to be inside. They banged on the door. No one opened it. Lon, Nicole, and Zinka forced their way into the house, pushing the door open with their shoulders.

The man inside was alarmed to see them suddenly burst into his house. "This is a private home!"

"We just need something to eat," Hélène said.

"It's 3:00 PM. How can you expect lunch at 3:00 PM? And besides, we have no food. Go to the next village. There is a guesthouse. They have to feed you there. It's their job to feed people like you; it's not mine. I'm not an innkeeper."

Lon argued with him until Hélène pulled her away. "There's no point," she told her. "We need to keep going."

The weather had turned worse. Now they marched through a driving rain with wind blowing in their faces, making it hard to keep their eyes open. Every step was grueling. Hélène, who was usually undaunted, faltered. She somehow missed a turn, and eventually realized they had gone in the wrong direction. They had to turn around. Everyone had either tears or rain in their eyes.

"It's OK," Zaza said, trying to encourage her friend. "We all make mistakes. I lost the potatoes. The good thing is, you noticed your mistake."

"Would you stop it, Miss Everything-Is-Always-Rosy? You and your damn optimism. Shut your trap about those lost potatoes," Jacky snarled. "It just makes me hungrier."

Nicole snapped at Jacky, "Why don't *you* shut your trap?"

Guigui told Nicole that maybe she should try to understand how tired Jacky was, how hard this was for her. "You're always pushing, pushing, pushing for us to go faster."

"If I didn't push we would still be back in Altenhof, waiting for you to find your other shoe," Nicole answered angrily.

Josée defended Nicole, saying that maybe if Guigui had learned to keep her things in order and hadn't taken so long that morning, they would already have found the Americans.

"Yeah? Well, maybe if Lon hadn't argued with that man, he might have been inclined to be nice to us," Guigui said.

"Maybe, maybe, maybe," Mena screamed. "And maybe if Zinka didn't want to be shot at to prove she was at the front, we wouldn't have been shot at! And just maybe there would be no war. And maybe I wouldn't be here in the mud with all of you!"

Everyone went silent. Her screaming scared them. They were wary of the way Mena could veer quickly toward the irrational. But what she said was true. She was pointing out how ridiculous they were being.

"Let's just say Mena's right and it's all my fault," Zinka said. "But here we are at the front. It's no time to argue."

They nodded in agreement and walked on in silent despair. This moment was as bad as the long night of the death march between Wurzen and Oschatz before their escape.

———

They stopped at a farm along the road. Having promised themselves to keep going to the end of this day, instead of asking for food and shelter they decided to ask for shoes or old slippers. The feet of the women who still wore wooden clogs were bleeding from sores. Mena, who had lost her clogs in the river, was now walking barefoot, and a boot of mud had caked around her feet. Lon had thrown away her clogs and was wearing a pair of oversized men's boots donated by the Yugoslavs. In the rain and the mud, the pain in their feet became another torture. It was Zaza's idea to ask for slippers because she was wearing the slippers that had been given to her by the Poles in Leipzig. But the farmers shook their heads, barely hiding their disgust and fear. No, they had nothing to give them.

They reached the village that was supposed to have a welcoming guesthouse, where it was the innkeeper's job to feed weary travelers. The doors to the inn were open, but it was deserted. Suspecting that the owners were hiding down in the cellar, the women stomped heavily on the floor. They talked loudly, hoping to rouse someone. They searched through all the cupboards for a bit of bread or food. They found nothing. Twenty minutes later they heard the steps of the owners coming up from the cellar. The man wanted the women to leave at once. The Americans had been there in the morning. He was scared they would return and find the women there. If the German hadn't been too terrified to think straight, he would have realized that being caught feeding a group of French women would be good for him.

The women refused to leave before they had had a chance to rest and dry off a little. The man grumbled, but finally, after much negotiation with Lon and Hélène, he agreed to show the women to the stables, where they could take off their wet coats and outer garments.

Seeing the women shiver and tremble, the man's wife took pity on them and brought over bowls of hot coffee and milk. But there was no question of staying there for the night. Hélène reminded them, "We decided we would not stop until we reached the Americans."

Shivering, they put on their cold coats, heavy and damp with rain, and continued. The owners told them that they would find the Americans in Colditz, maybe even in the village before, Puschwitz. They could see Puschwitz in the distance; this gave them hope. They weren't far away. If they could pick up their pace, maybe they had only an hour or two more of walking. The rain had died down, but now the wind was blowing a full gale. "The good thing about this wind is soon our coats will dry," Zaza said, trying to make a joke of their misery.

"Jesus, Zaza," Jacky shot back. "If Fritz blew off your arm, you'd say, 'Good thing is I have another one!'" As soon as the remark left her mouth she regretted saying it. She was just cold, tired, and scared that she would not be able to hold on much longer.

At Puschwitz there were no Americans. Instead a white flag or sheet hung from every window—in fact, from every place that could hold a flag. The women knocked and then banged loudly on the door of the town café. Inside they found an old woman. She confirmed that though the Americans had not yet come to their village, they had definitely taken Colditz.

"But no one is allowed in or out. You will never get in. Even the women can't get milk for their babies. Someone went right to the entrance of Colditz and they turned him away," she told them.

She was happy enough to explain the route to Colditz through the forest. And no, she absolutely did not have any food to share. She didn't even have food for herself.

Walking out of Puschwitz, they were stopped by an old man. He gave them the same information and looked them over with a lecherous eye. "If you don't find a place to sleep, you can stay here with me," he offered, grinning. They could see his ramshackle cabin just off the path. He said he was happy to offer his bed to more than one. "Several at a time," he leered, winking and licking his lips. "We can keep each other warm until the war ends."

A few minutes later Jacky couldn't help remarking, "Well, looking on the bright side of things, the way you like to, Zaza, if you can't go on, I know a man in Puschwitz who will be happy to keep you warm." Zaza laughed, and the others joined in. The tension between them fell away.

They entered another beautiful forest of tall pines. It was a welcome relief to get out of the wind. The ground was carpeted with pine needles, and the place had the sacred feel of a cathedral. On another occasion they might have enjoyed the woods, but now they were worried. What if they startled a soldier and he shot them? It was one thing to fear the artillery whistles on the open plain. Here in the forest, anything or anyone could be hiding only a few meters away.

Suddenly they heard a bullet to their right. They dropped to their stomachs and tried to hide behind some trees. They began waving their white flags. Mena had stolen a large white dish towel from the village of the white flags. Zinka had her rag tied to a branch. They began to giggle nervously. Finally they stood back up. Mena and Zinka, being the brave ones, marched in front, waving their flags. In the back of the group was Lon. Her rag was more gray than white, but she had it on a very long branch. "You never know—they could come upon us from behind," she said.

They moved in single file, one following right after the other. They decided to sing to make it known they were not soldiers but just civilians, women caught at the front. They sang "Yankee Doodle" and "It's a Long Way to Tipperary"—the only two English songs they knew.

The shots continued, but soon they realized the firing was not actually close by. There was some kind of firefight going on off to their right a good distance away. The exchange of bullets continued, and they kept singing, brandishing their white flags. They felt ridiculous. They laughed, trying to appear fearless to one another.

The forest path led to a road, a sudden opening that cut though the dense green, and there they saw tire tracks in the mud. The rain had stopped. There was a bit of sunlight poking through the clouds into the clearing. Lon, Jacky, and Mena collapsed on the edge of the road, hoping the weak sun would dry and warm them. "We need to rest," Lon insisted.

"We shouldn't stop now," Nicole said urgently.

"Just go on without us," Jacky urged, waving her hand. She was panting, barely able to breathe. "We'll catch up."

"We won't do that," Hélène said. "You know that. We stick together. You're going to have to get up so we can all keep going."

"I've bellows to mend," Jacky said, gasping for air.

"Five minutes," Lon said. Everyone nodded uneasily. It was obvious at that moment that Jacky couldn't continue. Josée sat down too, and they winced at her bloody feet when she pulled them out of her wooden clogs.

Hélène's hip was throbbing. "OK, five minutes."

They sat in silence, looking up and down the road. In the hush, they heard the sounds of insects and wild animals. The smell of the mud and the forest rose from the earth as the sun briefly warmed them. Before the five minutes were up, they heard another sound: a motor in the distance, indicating an approaching car. A military car with a machine gun mounted on the front was heading toward them.

Hélène and Nicole jumped to their feet. There was pandemonium. Everyone spoke at once.

"What should we do?"

"Who has a car and gas?"

"Germans, SS retreating?"

"Americans, maybe?"

"Not common Germans. They won't have gas. It has to be SS!"

"The cook said the SS are killing everyone in their path."

"We should go back into the forest and hide!"

"I can't move."

"Get up!"

"I can't!"

Then it was too late.

Each of them thought: It's a German car coming toward us and they will mow us down, right here, when we were so close to finding the Americans.

Then Hélène stuttered, "But the license plate, the plate—it's yellow!" All the German license plates were white.

A few seconds later, the vehicle pulled to a stop right next to them. Two American soldiers sitting in the front of the jeep laughed at their white flags.

The women began to speak, but they didn't remember to speak in English. For a moment they were speaking German until Josée whispered, "They think we're Germans. They'll think we're the enemy."

Recovering themselves, Lon and Guigui remembered their English. "We escaped from a German prison camp," Lon said. They gave the soldiers a brief synopsis of their story, how they had been walking for days toward the front.

One of the soldiers pulled out a new pack of Camel cigarettes and opened it with his teeth. "Have a smoke?"

CHAPTER TEN

— RETURN TO LIFE —

American troops crossing Colditz bridge, April 12, 1945

COLDITZ IS DOMINATED BY A thousand-year-old fortress. Its outer walls are seven feet thick, and the cliff on which it stands is a sheer drop 250 feet into the Mulde River. The castle had been a Nazi POW camp for high-profile Allied officers who had repeatedly escaped from other camps. In April the castle had been taken by the Americans, who now used it as their military headquarters. The town below the castle was full of cars and big, loud American soldiers handing out gum and cigarettes and chocolate. The women were taken directly up to the castle courtyard, where they met the American commander. Moved by their story, he ordered a group of three soldiers to requisition a German house.

"A nice one for these ladies, Captain Abrams," he said, nodding and smiling to Hélène. She had impressed him already with her language skills.

They followed Captain Abrams and the other two soldiers down to the center of town. Once away from the commander's headquarters, the soldiers wanted to know everyone's name, and they introduced themselves. They had typical American names: Harry and Reggie and Ira. "Ira Abrams," the captain said, putting his hand out to shake Hélène's.

Ira and Hélène led the group, walking in silence, but there was chatter and light conversation between the other women and Harry and Reggie. The other soldiers were thrilled to talk to young women who were not the enemy. And the women were happy to talk as well, though they were beginning to feel the sheer exhaustion from the day's events.

Pointing to an impressive three-story house, Ira said, "This one looks nice. Wait here, ladies."

The soldiers banged on the door but did not wait for it to be opened. They went inside while the women waited in the road. Other passing soldiers waved at them and smiled. A few tried to speak with them upon learning they were French. "Bonjour," they said in their thick American accents. Everyone kept offering them chewing gum and cigarettes. One soldier had a phrase book. He was desperately trying to put a sentence together to speak to Josée until Hélène asked him in perfect English, "What are you trying to say to her?"

"Oh!" He grinned. "Ask her for me, please, if she'll be my gal."

"No, she won't," Hélène said sternly.

"Aw, come on. Please, just tell me her name."

Hélène was happy when Ira reappeared. Behind him was a German couple carrying suitcases. They looked dazed. The man was trying to talk calmly, though he was red in the face and obviously angry. His wife was sobbing, pleading. She grabbed desperately at Ira's jacket.

"What are they saying?" Harry asked Hélène.

"They're saying they have nowhere to go," Hélène told him. The women watched this spectacle of a wealthy German couple begging for their house.

"Well, did *you*?" Ira asked Hélène. "Did *you* have a place to go?"

Hélène looked at him. There was a fierceness in his eyes. "Here," she answered. "We were just trying to get here."

"Then go on inside." He nodded toward the door. "It's your new home. They can figure something out. Those two are acting desperate, but I've seen a few things."

It seemed to Hélène that he might have said more but stopped himself. She nodded, imagining that he had, like all of them, "seen a few things."

"Let's go inside," she said to the group.

"You can lock the door," Ira said in parting.

Hélène closed the door behind them, and the women looked at one another. They were stunned. They wandered through the house. There was a piano and books on shelves, rugs and lamps, cushions on chairs. It felt almost like a stage set, like make-believe. Within these walls, all during the time the nine of them had been imprisoned, normal people had lived their normal lives. They climbed upstairs. Nicole opened an armoire, and Josée started to cry when she saw all the clothes. They pulled out dresses and skirts and blouses. Mena spread outfits on the bed, saying, "This one is perfect for Hélène. And this green will match Nicole's eyes. . . ."

Zinka had found the large tiled bathroom. Immediately she and Guigui began filling the tub and playfully splashing each other. There was a cake of perfumed soap. Everyone had a turn at the bath, and then they dressed in clean clothes. They threw their old rags into a corner and vowed to burn them.

"We'll make a lovely campfire for you, Mena," Josée promised.

"I just want to keep my coat," Mena said, pulling it from the pile and holding it close.

They had looked but found almost no food in the kitchen, so they were happy when a few hours later the soldiers returned. "We thought you might want some chow. Are you hungry?"

When Hélène translated, the women laughed; there was that question again. The soldiers escorted them to the military canteen, which had been set up in a local restaurant. They were served a warm meal. But it was much more than they could eat. The women were distressed; they couldn't imagine leaving food on their plates.

The three soldiers they knew were joined by others, and soon there were soldiers swarming around the women, endlessly barraging them with questions. Ira made eye contact with Hélène and could see that she was overwhelmed. "Give them some air," Ira ordered.

"We're very tired," Hélène explained, grateful for Ira's help. The long day had caught up with them. Hélène asked Ira and the two other soldiers to escort them back to their new home. That night the three soldiers promised to stand guard outside the door, and the nine women slept together in a large, soft feather bed.

It is hard to know how much the American soldiers in Colditz understood about what the women had been through. By the spring of 1945, American soldiers from different units had seen and liberated various camps. As they moved across Germany, US soldiers discovered the corpses of victims of the death marches along the roads.

Knowledge of the magnitude of the Nazi killing was growing. Almost a year earlier, in July 1944, the Soviets had been the first to liberate a camp: Majdanek, near Lublin, Poland. But it was with the Soviet liberation of Auschwitz in January 1945 that the scale of the systematic killing became evident. Though the Auschwitz camp was mostly emptied, the Soviets found roughly 6,000 emaciated prisoners and ample evidence of genocide. More than 800,000 women's outfits and 14,000 pounds of human hair were discovered there.

The two soldiers who found the women on the road to Colditz were from the 2nd Infantry Division. They had landed on Omaha Beach in Normandy and battled their way to Belgium. They had tenaciously held their position in the Battle of the Bulge, preventing the Germans from recapturing Belgium. In April they uncovered the Leipzig-Thekla massacre. Just as the British would do at Bergen-Belsen, where they forced the SS guards to dig graves and bury the dead, the US military ordered the mayor of Leipzig to provide caskets, floral wreaths for the coffins, and crews of workers to dig the graves. One hundred prominent citizens of Leipzig were ordered to attend the burials.

Even hardened soldiers who had gone through battles on the beaches in Normandy and the Battle of the Bulge still were profoundly shocked at the discovery of the camps. The US Seventh Army liberated Dachau on April 29. Colonel William W. Quinn later wrote, "There our troops found sights, sounds, and stenches horrible beyond belief, cruelties so enormous as to be incomprehensible to the normal mind."[1]

In the camps, they would find bodies in piles. Some prisoners could barely walk; some were crawling on all fours. In Buchenwald a man was saved by the small movement of his little finger. His body had been piled on a cart of corpses to be dumped into a mass grave when an American soldier saw his finger move.

Soldiers were shocked by the silence. Though there were thousands of people everywhere around them dying, there was almost no sound. They described the terrible fetid odor of death that got worse as you went deeper into the camp and into the dark barracks. Many prisoners were half or completely naked. They looked just like skeletons. Everyone moved slowly as if in a daze, ghostlike. The word most often repeated as soldiers tried to describe what they had seen was "unbelievable."

Prisoners tried to hug the soldiers and kiss them. They wept. They thanked them in whispers. The soldiers gave them all their food. But because the prisoners' digestive systems could not cope with the rich food, sometimes eating it killed them. Because the prisoners were covered in lice and typhus was killing thousands a day, the military medical staff had to shave the prisoners again and shower them to clean them. This could retraumatize them. Even once liberated, the former prisoners still saved their food; the nurses would find bread hidden under their pillows.

Many former prisoners died in those first few days following liberation, 15,000 in Bergen-Belsen alone. Some had held on to life long enough to be liberated, then let go. There are accounts of families rushing to a field hospital, arriving only in time to say goodbye to the survivor.

The logistics were daunting. The typhoid epidemic meant that the former prisoners needed to be quarantined and treated. And the huge administrative task of repatriation had to be set in motion. Furthermore, the Allies, realizing the scope of the Germans' crimes against humanity, needed to gather evidence and capture the fleeing

SS guards to bring them to justice. All this was taking place while the war was still going on.

———❧———

Zaza's account of the escape ends with the American soldiers finding the women on the road to Colditz on April 21. In her final sentence, she declares that they were "nine who didn't want to die, and who fought together to return to LIFE."[2] But returning to life would be more complicated than the women could imagine.

For a week they stayed in the requisitioned house in Colditz, eating warm meals in the US Army canteen and helping themselves to clean clothes. Hélène told me that soldiers visited the house often, too often for her taste, always carrying a bottle of champagne tucked under their arm. They seemed to have an endless supply. She and Zaza took refuge in the upper rooms. My aunt was very strict about what was proper. And I imagine there was a divide in the attitudes of the women between those who welcomed the attentions of the soldiers and those who did not. Lon, for example, maintained a lifelong deep admiration for Americans in uniform who smoked, no doubt remembering their liberators. She felt profoundly grateful to and protected by the American soldiers.

The women learned the Red Cross was organizing a train back to Paris for returning deportees. They would have to wait a few weeks for the train to be readied. But in the meantime, if they wanted to be on that train, they had to go live in the Red Cross refugee camp near Grimma.

———❧———

Meanwhile, in the final days of April 1945, Nazi control of Ravensbrück was unraveling. Much of the history of this camp was forgotten after the war, lost behind the Iron Curtain and reframed by the Soviet narrative. The beginning of the liberation of the camp happened on April 21, the same day that the nine women crossed the Mulde. A message was sent to Folke Bernadotte of the Swedish Red Cross from Himmler agreeing to release the remaining women in Ravensbrück.

A Swedish diplomat and vice president of the Swedish Red Cross,

and nephew of King Gustav V of Sweden, Bernadotte had been nego-
tiating the rescue of prisoners from various camps. Initially the operations were limited to Scandinavians, but they gradually expanded.
In the final months of the war, from March to May 1945, the most
dramatic rescues took place in operations that became known as the
White Buses.[3] These rescue missions were a huge logistical operation, involving a staff of about 300, a medical team of twenty, hospital buses, trucks, passenger cars, motorcycles, a field kitchen, and
full supplies for the entire trip, including food and gasoline, none of
which could be obtained in Germany.

But the buses could only transport about 1,000 prisoners at a time.
When Himmler told Bernadotte he could take all the women from
Ravensbrück, numbering about 15,000, there was a scramble to get
buses assembled and to Ravensbrück as fast as possible.

Himmler was desperate. His last-ditch hope was that he could
negotiate a separate peace with the Allies behind Hitler's back. He
hoped that by excluding the Soviet Union, he could play on the long-
held belief among Western nations that communism posed a greater
threat than fascism. He asked Bernadotte to deliver his message to
the Swedish government to be forwarded to US general Dwight Eisen-
hower. Himmler also asked that the prisoner releases be kept out of
the press, because if Hitler, isolated and increasingly paranoid, heard
about them, he would order them to stop.

When Himmler's order reached the Ravensbrück camp commandant, Fritz Suhren, he initially refused to follow it. Even as the Soviets
were fast approaching the camp gates, Suhren was following earlier
orders from Hitler, which were to keep the prisoners in the camp and
at the approach of enemy troops to liquidate them all.[4] Suhren was
continuing with systematic gassings and executions.

Meanwhile, the camp SS were busy cleaning up: they were burning bodies, burning all the camp records, cleaning the blocks, and
removing the piles of corpses, but always continuing to execute the
sick and those prisoners marked *NN*, for *Nacht und Nabel*.

The Swedish Red Cross was able to rescue about 7,000 women
from Ravensbrück. But the Allies would not promise the Swedish Red
Cross safe passage through the war zone. Two of the transports from
Ravensbrück were bombed, and about twenty-five prisoners and one

driver died; the exact number of casualties is still unknown. On the final transport out, there was almost a riot among the women trying to get a seat on the bus.

Even as the Red Cross was liberating truckloads of prisoners, Suhren was ordering the murder of others by firing squad, poison, and provisional gas chamber.

The remaining SS looted the *Effektenkammer* that held all the jewelry and goods taken from the prisoners when they had arrived. They loaded up as much of the precious goods as they could on carts and wagons, changed into civilian clothes, and in the final days of April they fled, leaving behind thousands of seriously ill prisoners.

On April 30, the first Russian soldier entered Ravensbrück, followed by an advance unit of the Red Army.

The women greeted the liberators with tears and prostrations. Colonel Mikhail Stakhanov described the scene when he arrived by tank:

> We drove over barbed wire in our tanks and broke the camp gates. And then we stopped. It was impossible to move further as the human mass surround the tanks; women got under our tanks and on top of them. They looked awful, wearing overalls, skinny; they didn't look like human beings. There were 3,000 sick, so sick it was impossible to take them away, they were too weak.[5]

After the initial enthusiasm for the arrival of the Red Army, things soon took a dark turn. The soldiers went on a rampage, raping the women—even the sick and dying, even mothers who had just given birth, even women who weighed no more than sixty pounds. The narrative of the Second World War was different for historians from the Soviet Union. Because Ravensbrück would fall behind the Iron Curtain as part of East Germany, much of this part of the story was never told. Prominent communist prisoners and Red Army women did not speak of it. But there are multiple witness accounts. French survivors spoke of pleading that they were exhausted, to no effect.

Later Yevgenia Lazarevna Klemm, the brilliant Red Army leader, would tell how she begged the soldiers to leave her women alone:

"We are Red Army soldiers who have been at the front at Stalingrad, Leningrad, and the Crimea. We have been in a concentration camp for two years."[6]

German women suffered the most from the systematic Soviet sexual violence. When the Red Army crossed the German border they burned, looted, and raped with a vengeance. The Soviet journalist Vasily Grossman traveled with the Soviet army all the way from Stalingrad. "Horrible things are happening to German women," he wrote. "An educated German is explaining in broken Russian that his wife has already been raped by ten men today." A breastfeeding mother spoke of being raped in a barn. "Her relatives came and asked her attackers to let her have a break, because the hungry baby was crying."[7]

The anonymous memoir *A Woman in Berlin* described the systematic rape of women in that city; by some estimates, 100,000 women were raped by the occupying Soviets.[8] The memoir was fiercely condemned for besmirching the honor of German women when it was published in 1959. The author refused to allow the book to be reprinted until after her death. When it was rereleased in 2003, it became a bestseller. The Russians to this day maintain that the story of Soviet rapes is a Western fabrication and that the great sacrifice made by the Red Army to defeat the Nazis should not be sullied. By the end of the war the Russians had lost 26.6 million people, or 13.7 percent of the total population.

Though it was by no means on the same scale, it remains similarly taboo to talk about how the American GIs raped civilian women. US soldiers were presented with an eroticized France in propaganda. Many US troops believed that French women were willing and easy. *Life* magazine reported the widespread belief among GIs that France was "a tremendous brothel inhabited by forty million hedonists who spent all their time eating, drinking, making love, and in general having a hell of a good time." Some soldiers landing in Normandy seemed to think French women were their well-earned plunder. By the late summer of 1944 hundreds of women in Normandy reported being raped by the Yanks. In 1945 after the war, as soldiers gathered in Le Havre awaiting the troopships home, a local wrote, "This is a regime of terror, imposed by bandits in uniform."[9] One resident of Cherbourg wrote: "With the Germans, the men had to camouflage themselves—but with the Americans, we had to hide the women."[10]

Just as it is difficult to get an accounting of how many newly liberated prisoners were raped by the Red Army in Ravensbrück, or German women by the Soviets, the account of how many US soldiers raped women is equally unclear, and no doubt the numbers are vastly underreported. The US military dealt with the alarming reports of rape by placing the blame on Black soldiers: 130 of the 153 troops disciplined for rape by the army were African American, while African Americans were only 10 percent of the troops. US forces executed twenty-nine soldiers for rape, and twenty-five of them were African American. The executed soldiers, mostly Blacks, would be hung, as in a lynching, and this posed a problem in the land of the guillotine. A hangman was brought from Texas just to carry out the job.

Some of the political prisoners who returned to France reported that often the first question they were asked was whether they had been raped. And if they had not been, they almost felt guilty, as if they had somehow not really suffered. Marceline Loridan-Ivens reported that upon her return from Auschwitz one of the first questions her mother asked her in a whisper was whether she was still pure and could still be married. "She understood nothing. We were not women, we were not men, there. We were dirty Jews, things, stinking animals. They made us strip only to determine when to kill us."[11]

Perhaps we need to wonder about our tendency to form hierarchies of suffering, especially when those hierarchies are based on a concept of female purity. A more truthful accounting would recognize that women have had to bear the burden of war far more than has been acknowledged.

The narrator in *A Woman in Berlin* wryly remembers how, during the war, when men would come back to Berlin on leave, she made such a fuss over them, even if the soldier had been stationed in Paris or someplace relatively safe. Meanwhile the women back home "were under constant bombardment," struggling to find food and water and to feed children. Their hardships were not mentioned. She notes that the men can tell their war stories but the women "will have to keep politely mum; each one of us will have to act as if she in particular was spared. Otherwise no man is going to want to touch us anymore."[12]

The war was unraveling fast. On April 28, Mussolini was captured and killed by Italian partisans. Hitler killed himself on April 30. The nine would hear the news soon after.

On May 1 they moved to the Red Cross camp in Grimma, fifteen kilometers from Colditz. Next door was a US military camp, but the women were directed to enter the camp for refugees, former prisoners, and displaced persons. The refugee camp was barren and dusty, crowded with gaunt, frail ghosts. They were surrounded by guards and fences. The shock and letdown were terrible. Once there, they were greeted by a woman they knew, Line. They had spent nine months with Line in Leipzig. But now, just a few weeks later, she was completely transformed. She had cut her hair to look like a man's so she could travel incognito. She had gained weight. She was now acting the part of a harsh administrator, treating them in much the same manner as they had been treated by the Germans. She barked at them to fill out the forms with their names and numbers. They were given their ration cards. They were told the food was good, but they found that it was awful compared to the American meals they had been enjoying over the past week in Colditz.[13]

They were shown to a large, dark room full of a strange collection of furniture with a pile of hay on the floor at one end. There was a round table, a pool table, and a piano. They didn't mind sleeping on the floor in the straw if this meant getting home soon. But they did mind that they were in effect prisoners again.

Feeling desperate, they wandered the grounds to take stock of their new situation. The weather was fair, and someone was playing the accordion. But it was a lonely wheezing sound that only made them feel more dejected. A soldier in Colditz had played the piano in their requisitioned house, and other soldiers joined him with harmonica and guitar. After hearing Josée sing, one of the young soldiers had brought over a gramophone and played American songs for her. Nightly their house had been filled with joyful music. Here the lone accordion sounded like a dirge.

The Grimma refugee camp seemed just as gray as Leipzig. It was populated mostly by men: Poles, Russians, and a few French. After their years in camps, the men's faces were hollowed out and expressionless. Many of them were half out of their minds and made lewd

and offensive remarks and gestures toward the women. The few
women the nine met were equally troubling, and it made them wonder if they were just like them. Had they all been transformed into
lifeless, crude, desperate people? They returned to their room. Josée,
Guigui, Lon, and Mena went to bed feeling miserably sad. Guigui
tried to comfort Josée as she cried herself to sleep.

Zinka, Hélène, and Jacky sat outside on the steps at the building's
entrance, looking at the camp around them and feeling dejected.
Hélène and Jacky discussed how they might fix the situation. If they
could find work in the administration, they might gain some control.
After the past weeks of freedom, they would not be passive. Zinka
wondered if she could get a job, since she was a trained nurse. At least
then she would feel useful.

Nicole and Zaza spent an hour or so chatting with the American
guards for the sole pleasure of speaking English and interacting with
healthy and optimistic men instead of desperate refugees.

In the middle of the night a group of men forced open the locked
door of their room and stormed in. After all they had been through,
this was too much. Hélène in Russian and Zinka in French let out
the full force of their rage and frustration, excoriating the men with
insults until they slunk away sheepishly.

The next morning Nicole went looking for breakfast. She returned
with awful stale black bread that she threw down on the women as
they slept in the hay, saying bitterly, "Who wants breakfast? This is
what they're serving us." They had gotten used to the lovely breakfasts
they ate every morning back in Colditz, breakfasts with eggs, fresh
bread, and jam. On those mornings they would lazily chat and laugh
about the evening visits with soldiers and the previous night's dreams.

Some of their American friends from Colditz found them in their
strange new quarters. The women could see the shocked expression
on the soldiers' faces as they looked around them. This was the final straw; the women began to talk about escape again. One of the
soldiers offered, "We are on guard duty from three to eight in the
morning."

"We should try to leave then," Lon said.

"But where will we go?" Guigui asked.

"It doesn't matter! Didn't we leave before without having any idea in which direction to go?" But before they had had a goal: to find the Americans. What would they do now—just walk all the way back to Paris?

Jacky returned an hour later with another American soldier in tow. He promised to come back that night with some good food and drink, and maybe bring some of his friends.

"But we need to rest before our escape," Zaza said, exasperated. "We can't be entertaining tonight."

"Escape?" Jacky asked with a laugh. "To where?"

Jacky went on to tell them that she'd just had a checkup. Soon after arriving in Colditz, she had been sent to the military infirmary, where she was diagnosed with diphtheria. The army medics had given her the antitoxin and antibiotics, and after a week of rest she was already feeling better. She couldn't believe how close she had come to giving up. Now she told the others that the results of her checkup had been good. "I got a bunch of jabs," she said with a chuckle. "Soon I'll be as good as new."

And she had some news. The head of this Red Cross camp was a former doctor from the American Hospital in Paris, Dr. Newman. "His secretary," she added, "is a frumpy, dumb little idiot who doesn't speak a word of English. She's useless and he's overwhelmed. He needs our help."

"We could make ourselves useful," Hélène said, nodding. She and Jacky had talked about this the night before. "What do you think, Lon? Should we try to talk to the captain?"

Hélène knew Lon was leaning toward the idea of escape. She felt best on the road, where she understood her role and her importance. But Hélène also knew that escape was pointless. They would not be allowed to move freely. And more important, despite Jacky's inoculations neither she nor any of the other women were in good enough shape to walk all the way to Paris. Hélène had seen a map and now knew that they had barely covered any distance during their nine days on the road, even though they had pushed themselves to their limits. So she wanted to enlist Lon for this other option.

That afternoon Hélène and Lon left the camp, even though this was strictly forbidden; they were able, with their five languages, to negotiate their way past the guards. Two hours later they returned chauffeured in Dr. Newman's car.

They had indeed met with Captain Day, the head of the military government in the area. "A very nice man," Lon said, clearly pleased with herself and happy to bring the women gathered around her a little bit of important information. "He promises to find us a proper house in two days."

"But we will live outside the refugee camp; we will not be guarded or protected. We will be living as civilians on our own," Hélène explained. She wanted to say that they should avoid inviting men over all the time, but she held her tongue.

"That's exactly what we want!" Nicole exclaimed. "I don't want to be guarded anymore!"

"We can take care of ourselves," Zinka agreed.

"While we were meeting with the captain, Dr. Newman arrived," Hélène continued. "He said to Newman, 'Here are two escapees from your camp.'"

Lon jumped in. "And then Newman says, 'Ah, I will have to punish you, I will give you chocolates.'"

The women laughed and agreed that the Americans were always feeding them better food, always offering chocolate. It was so much nicer on the American side of things.

Hélène explained that Newman had asked what sort of work her team of nine women could do. "We told them Guigui, Lon, and myself can translate in five languages. Zinka is a trained nurse. Nicole and Zaza speak English and both are good typists."

"We also told them that several of us can drive," Lon added.

Newman had been thrilled and said he could use the help. They offered to live outside the camp and to come every day at 6:00 AM to work for him in the camp administration. Captain Day would give them a *laisser-passer* so they could move about freely. Then Hélène remarked that she had seen what his *laisser-passer* looked like: "'Please let this girl go out' with a date and his signature, all very easy to forge."

They decided they would not escape quite yet. They would wait and see.

That night they were again visited by American soldiers, six of them from the 69th Infantry Division. Jacky, Mena, and some of the others enjoyed speaking with them, but Zaza was impatient and bored with these visits. She felt that these soldiers were not nearly as gentlemanly as the ones they had met from the 2nd; it was clear that these new soldiers thought "French gals" were free with their bodies. She didn't like the reputation it seemed they were getting.

The next days were cold and gray. The same monotonous soup of rice and barley was served for all meals. And as hopeful as they had felt after Lon and Hélène's initial meeting with the captain, the days seemed to go by with little or no activity or development. Most of the time the women were just waiting for something to happen or fending off multiple visits from stray soldiers. They had been able to appropriate some chairs from another empty room and some tin bowls, which they also used to sit on.

In the evening they were visited again by a group of rowdy US soldiers. But soon one realized they had been misinformed. "They may be French, but they aren't that kind," he drunkenly told his buddies, and the men left.

Frustrated by this constant harassment, Hélène said to Lon, "Isn't there some way we can get them to understand we don't want to sleep with them? Tell them we are lesbians."

"I would," Lon said, "but I don't know the word in English for that."

On the morning of May 6, Hélène received word to go see Captain Day. The others sat around the table eating, smoking, writing, or filling out the forms they had been given as former political prisoners. Everyone was feeling anxious and in a bad mood. Hélène's meeting seemed to be taking forever.

"Hélène is never getting that damn house," Lon said. She was talking again about escape. She had met an American soldier who said he would help them. The others knew Lon resented being left out of the meeting with Captain Day. Hélène had been called early in the morning, and Lon was sleeping. Hélène knew it would take Lon forever to get ready, so she just left without her.

"But what is Hélène doing? It's been three hours since she left," Jacky said, exasperated.

"I bet she already started her work. She must be translating between a Russian, an Englishman, and a German," Mena said.

"No," Guigui said calmly, "I rather believe that she is visiting a house with the captain. They're finding a place for us."

Guigui was right. At noon Hélène returned, radiant with good news. "We have a great, huge house, the Grimma officers' mess, a stone's throw from here. Only," Hélène said, "there's a drawback: we will not be alone there. We will have to share it. But since we will be the first ones, we can take the rooms we want."

"Who are we sharing it with?" Lon asked.

"It's being turned into barracks for French female political prisoners. We will be responsible for it running smoothly. I committed myself to this. But it's a wonderful house. Pack your bags. We need to leave in the next half hour. After that, the guard will change, and it's the current guards who are instructed to let all nine of us leave."

The women rushed to gather their belongings and make their old bundles. They had already begun to acquire more things. With their new clothes, they looked like a nice group of young women going on a vacation. "All of us classically dressed, except," as Zaza described, "Mena as always ridiculous and charming, very pretty, fairly badly groomed, with her huge travel coat, a huge suitcase and, clasped to her heart, a bouquet of forget-me-nots in a vase."

They were thrilled with their new house. It had a dining room the size of an ocean liner and a huge kitchen. There were endless small corridors and staircases, arched doorways, white sliding doors with mysterious buttons, and a terrace overlooking a garden. It was light and bright, not anything like the dank room they had just left.

Captain Day needed Hélène to interpret for him that afternoon. She left the rest of them, saying that while she was away, they should organize their new apartment, which, fortunately, was separate from the rest of the house. They spent the afternoon choosing the furniture to move into their four bedrooms. Zaza picked a very small bedroom for her and Hélène; it was a former office. Mena, Jacky, and Josée had a sunny and charming bedroom that they filled with soft couches, cushions, and a large mirror. Lon, Zinka, and Nicole had a slightly colonial-style bedroom with wrought-iron beds and a heavy mahogany table. And Guigui chose a monastic cell with a very hard sofa and a basic table and wardrobe. But the room was peaceful, and Guigui was looking forward to solitude and privacy. That night, Hélène returned to find them still arranging furniture.

She had spent the afternoon with Captain Day, collecting female refugees wandering the countryside on the other side of the Mulde. She told them that a large group of women, most of whom they had known in Leipzig, had moved into their old place in the refugee camp; they were in much worse condition, dirty and infested with lice. The nine women had to arrange the house for them as soon as possible.

Quickly they decided on the arrangement of the rest of the house and listed the most urgent tasks for the next day. Having a purpose energized them. With their familiar camaraderie and humor, they distributed the responsibilities. Hélène was the boss and, naturally, was in charge of all external relations in all languages. Zaza was responsible for general stewardship, Nicole for repairs and the state of the equipment in general. These jobs evolved over time. Guigui, who on the first day took on the task of locating the keys (approximately 190 of them) and their corresponding doors, on the second day became the co-steward with Zaza.

Zinka inspected the refugees scattered around the camp and made sure the sick were taken to the infirmary. Soon she had taken over the care of the babies too. She arranged a way to bottle-feed them and procured milk. Jacky recruited a cook and two cook's assistants from the military camp to create a kitchen that made much better food.

Dr. Newman, the camp administrator who had needed help, now was angry at their initiative. He was no match for their dynamism. It didn't help that Hélène was working every day with his superior, Captain Day, whom the women now called "Jimmy."

American soldiers from Jimmy's camp brought blankets, basins, and food. The nine were able to receive fifty-five women in the space they had cleaned and arranged in just two days. Mena decorated the rooms with flowers she gathered from the house's untended garden.

By this time they had made friends with a number of officers, and they were no longer bothered by the errant visits of regular soldiers or refugees hoping to get lucky. They even had their own car, an Opel convertible with red leather seats, and a French driver assigned to them. This was a gift from a French captain named Drevon, who was apparently in charge of repatriating the political prisoners. Zaza noted that his resources were minimal, but he managed to supply them with all sorts of interesting things. He visited them whenever he could. He liked the peacefulness of the place; Mena's flower arrangements made it feel more humane and less military. And he was drawn to the nine crazy, joyful women who lived there. He had to knock on the door a long time and wait patiently because the women might be trying to figure out how to transform the fabric on an umbrella into a skirt, or three of them might be taking a bath together, scrubbing one another's backs with some newly procured soap.

But as energetic as they were, the women were also weak. Zaza had an attack of rheumatoid arthritis that kept her in bed for two days. Nicole had a gallstone attack in the middle of the night, and Zinka ran to get help, bringing back a lovely Italian doctor in his pajamas, robe, and red leather slippers to give Nicole a sedative.

Camp refugees were pouring into the Red Cross camp. Sometimes the women found old friends from Leipzig or from Ravensbrück. They peppered them with questions. Did they know where the others were, who had made it? Nicole was desperate for news of those they'd left behind in Leipzig in the *Revier*; was her friend Renée alive? Lon searched for news of her brother, Eric, among the men. Zaza and Zinka did the same, looking for their husbands. In the sea of people who seemed to have been tossed up like pebbles on a beach, the prospect of finding their loved ones felt nearly impossible. But strange reunions played out. A young Belgian man was looking without much hope for his mother. He asked Zinka if she knew the name. She wasn't sure, but she took him to look at the lists that were hung on the wall outside Dr. Newman's office. As she ran her finger down a list of names, she heard a scream of joy behind her. She turned to find mother and son collapsed in each other's arms. It was possible, she thought, that Louis Francis could be alive. She could run into him anywhere, at any time.

<hr/>

At 2:45 PM on May 7, news of the unconditional surrender of Germany was typed out and displayed on a board for all the refugees to

read. Ironically, on the same board beneath the piece of paper were the carved words NEVER AGAIN 1918, WIN. It was probably created at the start of the war as propaganda to remind the local Germans that this time around they must win.[14]

They did not gush with joy. They took in the news somberly. Mena was leaning against Guigui. Guigui was holding Lon's hand. Nicole and Josée had their arms around each other. Zaza and Zinka hugged each other; they were thinking about their husbands. All of them felt a strange emptiness, or perhaps a feeling so profound they did not know how to express it. They were thinking of all the ones who were not with them, whom they had left behind in the cattle cars, the prisons, the camps, the *Revier* beds. Now they waited for the wheels of the administration to turn, for this promised transport to France and what they would find there.

While they waited, the refugees put on a party. Once again the extraordinarily talented haute couture deportees put their skills to use, making dresses out of the curtains they found in the bombed-out office buildings next to the camp. The American soldiers came to celebrate with them, bringing bottles of champagne and distributing packets of cigarettes. Those who could danced and drank. Someone had moved the piano from their old quarters and played it with gusto. The refugees formally thanked the Americans for saving their lives. As the evening wore on, they sang the old songs: "Madelon," "Le Chant des Marais," "La Marseillaise." And then they began to recite poems from the camps. One after another stood and in feeble voices chanted the poems that they had written and passed around on tiny stolen scraps of paper, even passing poems from camp to camp clandestinely. They had repeated the poems on so many nights in the dark blocks that now they had them memorized. Some of the authors were dead, and they recollected those they had lost as they recited their poems. There was not a dry eye in the place.

CHAPTER ELEVEN

— FINDING THE WAY HOME —

Women awaiting repatriation

THE TRANSPORT TRAIN TO PARIS was ready on or around May 16. The seven women said a tearful goodbye to Jacky and Hélène. Jacky, who during the entire escape had constantly repeated the refrain "Get me back to Paris," had decided to stay in Grimma to run the convalescence home they had created. Female camp survivors who were too weak to travel could rest and recover there. When the refugees first came straggling in and Jacky saw the desperate faces of the very sick, she knew exactly how they felt. She would run this special home until it closed in late September.

Hélène stayed behind to work with the US Army. She wore an American officer's uniform and ate in the officers' canteen. She worked as an interpreter during the interrogations of German soldiers who may have been guilty of war crimes. She gathered information about the location of the deportees—Russian, Polish, and French—who were scattered all over the German countryside. To do her job she was given an enormous Chrysler, no doubt requisitioned from a wealthy German, that had been painted khaki green with a large white star on the hood. She had a *laisser-passer* for the whole US occupied zone as well as gasoline from any military unit whenever she needed it.

Hélène, who was petite and still quite thin, must have looked tiny behind the wheel of that huge American car. But she had a commanding presence. She traveled through the chaotic occupied zone, where refugees and prisoners of war wandered looking for shelter, food, water, and eventually a way home. She often ran into groups of women scattered from the camps and death marches, and she directed them to the refugee camp in Grimma.

Waving goodbye, the seven women boarded one of fifty trucks that took the refugees who could travel to a train station at Leipzig-Plagwitz, passing through the city of Leipzig. The city had been bombed into complete ruin. Germans lined up among the rubble outside the few stores that remained. They somberly watched the convoy of passing trucks, and the refugees returned their gaze.

The train was the same as the cattle cars that had brought them to Germany as prisoners, only now the floors were covered with fresh straw. The seven women, Zaza, Zinka, Guigui, Mena, Nicole, Josée, and Lon, had a whole car to themselves. They kept the doors wide open. The cars were festooned with branches and spring blossoms. The Croix de Lorraine and the *V* for victory were written in chalk on the doors. The French tricolor was draped from car to car. It was an immense convoy, carrying 1,500 refugees in a long line of wagons.

It took them six days to travel the roughly 500 kilometers to the French border. The train could only move very slowly, because the tracks in many places were destroyed and bridges had been blown up. The conductor and his crew often had to stop to repair the track ahead, and whenever they did, everyone poured out of the cars and into the surrounding fields. It was springtime, and the weather was glorious. They lit small fires in the grass by the tracks and boiled water. Some of them had a new powder they had gotten from the American soldiers: Nescafé, it was called. They prepared coffee for one another.

People from the villages came to greet those on the train with food and wine. There was music and singing at each stop. They sang old songs from before the war. And for the moment they did not think too much about what lay ahead.

The conductor learned that when the train was ready to move again, he had to blow the whistle a number of times to get everyone back on board. As the train moved off at a crawl, people ran and jumped into the cars, laughing as their friends grabbed their arms and pulled them back on board. At each station they added more cars of refugees. They found old friends and caught one another up. Mixed in with the camp survivors were POWs who knew nothing about the camps; they didn't understand how men could be in such a haggard condition, and what were women doing there? They barely knew about the Résistance. How had these survivors become so depleted and gaunt? And so the survivors told the POWs what had happened. Each person had a story. They described the different networks of the Résistance. They talked about the denunciations and their treatment by the French police and the *Milice*. They talked about waterboarding, about the gunshots and summary executions they had heard within the prison walls in France. They talked about the trains, the forced deportations to Germany, and what they discovered in the world of the concentration camps. There were some who could tell the others about the mass exterminations, whole trains of people sent directly to the crematorium. There were some from Ravensbrück who had worked in the *Revier* and could talk about the "rabbits." The POWs were astounded. They had had no idea, they said.

As they traveled through Germany they passed town after ruined town. At first it felt good to see how the country had been flattened. Then they were overwhelmed by the feeling of desolation and waste. When they saw Frankfurt, they were stunned into silence by the complete destruction of the city.

They came to Saarbrücken, the border town where they had first entered Germany as deportees, and spontaneously the whole long train broke into singing "La Marseillaise." At the end they screamed, "Vive la France!"

They crossed the border and hugged one another.

According to Lon's account, as the train stopped yet again, she finally lost her patience. She did not want to go to Paris. She wanted to go home to Holland, to find her brother, Eric. She says the seven of them had a quarrel, and she left the train to return home on foot.

The train traveled a few more hours on French soil before stopping at an immense campground near Longuyon, where a military installation had been constructed on flat open ground. It was a sea of white tents and army personnel in khaki. Everyone was told to get off the train in order to proceed with administrative formalities. The mix of concentration camp survivors, POWs, voluntary workers, and involuntary forced laborers were divided into separate groups. The six remaining women sat together on the ground and waited their turn to be processed. Luckily the weather was still gorgeous. They were registered, interviewed, and passed through a medical exam, powdered with DDT against lice, photographed, and finally given their temporary ID card, a deportee repatriation card. They were given clothes if necessary, a train ticket to the Gare de l'Est in Paris, and 1,000 old French francs, the rough equivalent of fifteen euros or twenty dollars today. They were offered a tent to sleep in that night, but the six preferred to sleep under the stars. "It may be the last night of our camping trip," Mena said, squeezing Guigui's hand. The thought of separation was terrifying. The remaining six told one another they would stick together all the way to Paris.

The next day they boarded a normal third-class passenger car with wooden bench seats and rattling windows they could slide open. They traveled through the night, and sometimes when the train stopped at a station, they heard shouts of joy as families reunited with their returnees. All the stations along the way, even the smallest, were decorated with signs welcoming them home. Railway workers saluted them. There was a kind of excitement in the corridors of the train and on the platform as people called out to each other.

"I'll write you when I'm settled."

"Good luck!"

"You have my address?"

Homecoming

As the train began to move closer to Paris, a hush descended. The six looked at one another and then turned to gaze out the window. The euphoria of return melted away. They felt a tightening in their chests. Everything, all their force of will, had been to survive for this moment of return.

At the outskirts of Paris, crowds lining the railroad tracks waved to them and threw them flowers. The train slowed down as it approached the city. They entered the grand hall of the Gare de l'Est. For most of them this was the same hall from which they had been pushed, terrified and harried, by screaming SS onto wagons. This was the same hall where mute French citizens had watched them being deported. Now it was decorated as if it were July 14, with tricolor banners and a military guard in uniform.

As they descended onto the platform, a crowd of civilians surged forward, engulfing them. They handed them flowers, but they had also brought photographs. They were looking for their family members.

"Where are you coming from?"

"Are you from Ravensbrück?"

"Have you seen her?"

"Did you know Mademoiselle . . ."

The crowd waved the photos frantically, pushing and shoving to get the returnees to look at *their* photo, a photo of their mother or sister or aunt. But the women in these photos were beautiful. They were marriage photos or photos of vibrant young girls on picnics. They were photos of mothers holding healthy, fat babies in their arms. The returnees hadn't seen anyone who looked like the women in the photographs. They wouldn't recognize any of these people. And the crowd tried to recognize in the emaciated, scared, and worn-out faces of the women someone they once knew.

It was as if the women had returned to another world, a strange world. Or as if they themselves came from a strange world. Either way, the alienation was total. The women did not know what to do. It felt as if the disappointment was their fault. They were somehow to blame for surviving. Why were they here instead of these beautiful people in the photographs? Why had they survived and not those beloved ones? Who were these strange, skeletal, disfigured, broken people, impostors in place of the ones who were so longed for?

They tried to offer some hope. "I don't know," Zaza said to the hysterical aunt shaking the photograph of her nine-year-old niece with a huge ribbon tied in a bow on her head. "There are still more returning from Germany. She may still come." But Zaza knew, as did Zinka wincing next to her, that surely a girl that young had been selected right away for extermination.

Slowly the group of deportees made their way through the crowd. They were led to a welcome room, where hostesses escorted them to special buses waiting outside the station. The buses took them through Paris—past the Opéra, past the place de la Concorde and the Louvre, and across the Seine—to the Hôtel Lutetia. Paris was beautiful. The city glowed in the morning light. After everything, it felt strangely surreal. It was as if they weren't really there but were only glimpsing a world they had once long ago belonged to.

———❨———

At first the authorities weren't prepared for the state of the survivors, even though they had heard about Auschwitz and the other camps. They imagined the returnees could simply resume their former lives. But many were in appalling health, with no homes, no families, no jobs, and no money. De Gaulle chose the Hôtel Lutetia as the center for repatriating the concentration camp survivors when he realized that their needs would not be the same as those of typical POWs.

A sumptuous luxury establishment on the Left Bank's boulevard Raspail, the hotel had been built in 1910 in a combination of Art Nouveau and the daring new Art Déco styles. The lobby featured thick velvet couches, curved windows with decorative moldings, bright colored glass chandeliers, lampshades held up by nymphs, and black and white tiled parquet. The bar displayed a large fresco of a bucolic country scene. There were seven floors and 350 rooms.

Before the war the Lutetia had been a favorite hangout for artists. James Joyce famously wrote some of *Ulysses* there; Picasso, Josephine Baker, Samuel Beckett, and Peggy Guggenheim were among the many cultural icons who spent time at the hotel. De Gaulle himself had stayed at the Lutetia on his honeymoon. At the start of the war the Lutetia housed numerous displaced refugee artists and musicians fleeing from Germany and eastern Europe. Upon occupation, the Germans requisitioned the hotel for their military intelligence service, the Abwehr. While the rest of Paris struggled to find food under the strict rationing system, decadent feasts were enjoyed here by collaborators, black marketeers, and the occupying Germans.

For many survivors, the Lutetia would be where they would begin their lives again. "Why was the Lutetia important in our story? It is because in truth our second life began here in this place. When we came in, we were only numbers; we left reborn as citizens," wrote Gisèle Guillemot.[1] It was important to provide a place of comfort. As one survivor wrote, "Nothing was too beautiful, nothing too good, nothing too clean, nothing too well-cooked, nothing too luxurious, nothing too expensive, nothing too perfect for those who had been torn from their families because they had worked for victory and they had been without for all those months, and for some for years. For the first time in my life, I saw in the public administration something that resembled love."[2]

Between mid-April and September, 20,000 returnees were processed at the Lutetia. When the six women arrived on May 21, the center was receiving on average 500 survivors a day. Of the 166,000 prisoners deported to the east, 76,000 were Jews, including 11,000 children; only 3,000 French Jews returned. Ninety thousand of the deportees were political prisoners and Résistance fighters; approximately 48,000 returned.

By May, the halls of the Lutetia had been transformed. Boards hung along the long hallway from the entrance to the restaurant where the administration put up notices and photographs of people who were missing, with details about how to contact the families who were searching for them. And they kept a running list of people known to have been found alive or dead. Booths and tables for the different networks of the Résistance lined the halls. Survivors could stop and see if anyone else in their network had returned. Next to them were tables manned by volunteers from the Red Cross, the Quakers, and the Salvation Army. The Catholic Scouts, the Protestant Éclaireurs, and the Jewish organizations provided volunteers who would accompany survivors arriving from camps throughout northern Germany. Each day new groups arrived at the train station or the airport and were brought to the hotel and then went home to their apartments or on to their next destinations. There were tables with telephones for survivors who needed to call their families; if their families had no phone, they could call the town hall in their hometowns.

Each floor of the hotel had a nurse and a doctor on call at all hours. Scouts helped the survivors navigate the corridors and sometimes carried people on stretchers or called ambulances to take them to the hospital. There were social workers helping with the paperwork. There were families who came every day for news and to greet new arrivals, hoping this time they would find the people they were looking for. There were survivors who returned each day to see who else had come back. The newly arrived, looking gaunt and vacant-eyed, wandered the photograph-lined corridor like ghosts. Some coming from other parts of Europe still wore the striped gray-and-blue garb of the camps. Their heads were shaved, and their skin was so transparent it was like a cloth tightly wrapped over their bones. Occasionally there would be a small disruption, a clamor, screams of joy, tears, and applause: a reunion. The press stalked the halls, hungry for photos of these reunions, until the staff kicked them out.

In the first days it was still chaotic. "Three or four busloads arrived at the same time. We had to do the utmost to try to avoid making them wait. I would go home at four in the morning and with a brush I tried to brush out all the lice in the bathtub. The first deportees who came back were very contagious and there were a few deaths among the staff," André Weil wrote.[3] A brilliant mathematician and Résistance fighter, Weil was put in charge of the Lutetia welcome staff by de Gaulle. Weil put out a call for volunteer nurses and got three times the required number. De Gaulle arranged for five cars to bring the nurses from their shifts at the hospital to their second shifts at the Lutetia.

The first floor of the hotel was reserved for administration. The second floor was the infirmary; the third floor was reserved for women. Even though the administration tried to be sensitive to the fragility of the survivors, the arrival procedure was difficult and often traumatic. They had to undergo a medical exam and a shower, and they were once again powdered with DDT. After they were fed, they had to endure a military interview to verify that they weren't impersonating a deportee, which happened from time to time. Former Gestapo collaborators, French militia members, torturers for the police, criminals from the black market, and volunteer French workers tried to pass as camp survivors to get the valuable deportee card that brought with it extra rations and privileges; the card could also whitewash their possible crimes. These interviews were fraught. The authorities would check that the men did not have the SS blood type tattoo near the left armpit, or that there wasn't evidence that such a mark had been removed in some way. Survivors were asked: When had they joined the Résistance? With what network? Who could speak on their behalf? What proof did they have that they hadn't worked with the Germans, since they had survived and so many hadn't? Where had they been arrested? Where had they been imprisoned? The interviewers asked for specific dates and names.

Often the fakers had been able to amass plenty of specific details from talking to returnees, while the real deportees' spatial and short-term memory was frequently confused by trauma. And the questions plunged the survivors back into the nightmare of the past months and years. "It was terrible to have to answer, as if we were the accused . . . a number of deportees revolted," wrote Odette Rosenstock, recalling her return to the Lutetia. Many remember the interview as a final insult, another trauma.

But every day the authorities caught collaborators. Sometimes it was the survivors who recognized someone trying to slip into their ranks. And at the end of every day a police car came to the hotel to gather up the four or five impostors who had been apprehended and take them to jail.

Most of the deportees weighed between sixty and seventy-five pounds. They all needed to rest and put on some weight. Sabine "Yanka" Zlatin, also known as La Dame d'Izieu, was in charge of the kitchen. A Polish Jew and a nurse, she and her husband had created a "vacation home" to hide Jewish children in Izieu. It was located in the southern zone near Switzerland and occupied by the Italians, who until the capitulation to the Germans did not actively seek out Jews. But when the Germans took over the area, anti-Semitic tensions began to rise. A number of denunciations put Sabine on alert. She thought it would be wise to disperse the children and place them in better hiding places. While she was away in Montpellier trying to secure help, she received word by telegram: "Family sick, illness contagious." The Gestapo had arrested and deported the forty-four children along with their seven adult caretakers to Auschwitz-Birkenau, where they all were murdered. She dedicated the rest of her life to the memory of those children and testified at the trial of Klaus Barbie in 1987.

Another notable Résistance hero on the staff was Dr. Toussaint Gallet. A gynecologist and obstetrician, Gallet joined the Résistance in the winter of 1942, providing essential intelligence to the British. He was arrested and tortured by the Gestapo in May 1944 and imprisoned in Fresnes. Marked as *Nacht und Nebel,* he was deported to Buchenwald on the last transport on August 15. He was known and admired by fellow prisoners for his calm, serene humanity, and for his ability to inspire them to hold on. At Buchenwald he continued as best he could to practice medicine and bring aid and comfort, though he had no medical supplies. A famous survivor, Frédéric-Henri Manhès, remembered Gallet as "le docteur aux mains nues"—the doctor with naked hands.

At liberation Gallet asked the Red Cross to get word to his parents. He wrote: "I was forced to leave my calling and I will be used finally as a doctor. Do what you can to have me repatriated fast. I will be happy to embrace you and then go to work." He was airlifted to Paris on April 18. On April 19 he presented himself to the French government as ready to work, and on April 20 he was put in charge of the medical program at the Lutetia. The survivors trusted him. He was one of them. Under his direction they would accept the government's need to weed out those who were trying to infiltrate their ranks and hide from their war crimes.

———&———

As the six women entered the lobby of the Lutetia, they were accosted from all sides by people with photographs. They searched for familiar faces. And they were almost immediately torn apart, pulled in different directions. Zaza saw the desk for the Auberge de Jeunesse and rushed to see if they had any word about René. She sat nervously, her leg jumping, as the volunteer, a young, rosy-cheeked girl, slowly scanned the list of names. Then, looking at Zaza, she shook her head.

"What? What does that mean? Is he dead?" She wanted to shake the girl.

"No, it means there is no news. His name is not on the list. He's neither confirmed dead nor alive. Do you know what camp he was in?"

"No," Zaza sobbed, "I don't know anything."

She felt dizzy, and the girl ran to get her a cup of tea. In anguish, Zaza moved over to the tables of telephones. She called her family. The voice of her mother after all this time seemed so small and distant. She wanted Zaza to come home immediately, but Zaza said she would wait here in Paris at their old apartment for news of René. In case he came, she wanted to be there.

———&———

Josée had lost her friends in the lobby while she was doing her paperwork. After she was cleared, she was assigned a room for one night in the hotel and given a train ticket for Cannes in the morning. She wasn't sure whom she would find there. She didn't want to stay with her parents; they were strangers to her. But she wanted to smell the sea. She told herself that she had good friends in the south. Surely Germaine and Alban Fort, who ran the children's home, would welcome her back. She would see if some of the families she had been supplying had survived. And yet when she thought of good friends, the only ones who came to mind were the eight women. She hadn't been able to say goodbye. Where had they all gone so suddenly? That first night she found herself alone in a hotel bedroom on the third floor of the Lutetia. She wondered where and how she would begin again. Why had she survived, if she couldn't feel joy now when she was finally here?

————⌇————

Nicole found herself alone as well, after going through the paperwork and interview. Her friends had dispersed. She felt abandoned. She had no idea where her family was. The last she knew, her mother and brother had been in Lyon; her father had been somewhere else, maybe in the Savoie. Suddenly she saw a face she knew: Claudine, with her husband, Gilles. Gilles had wired together a makeshift radio so they could listen each day to the announcement of the names of the new returnees. They were waiting to hear the name of Claudine's sister, Yvette, who had been sent to Auschwitz and then Ravensbrück, when they heard Nicole's name. They rushed to the Hôtel Lutetia, where they searched for her for a long time. At last, across the crowded lobby, they saw her. She had changed, but those sharp green eyes and dark curls were so recognizable.

For Nicole, it was a great relief to finally find a familiar face. Claudine wanted to know if Nicole had seen Yvette. Nicole wished she had news, but she didn't have any information to give her. Claudine said, "Why don't you come home to our place tonight?"

"No, I must absolutely find my family." Nicole was adamant.

"It's too late. The metros are closed. You can look for them in the morning; we can make phone calls. But come home tonight. My mother would love to see you."

Nicole wanted to search for her family immediately. She had to let them know she was alive. But Claudine convinced her to come home with her to their small three-room apartment in the Sixteenth Arrondissement. When they arrived at the apartment, Claudine's mother asked Nicole if she had seen her daughter. And she asked Nicole about the deportation; what had it been like?

Without thinking, Nicole began to describe it: the horrors of the transport, the camp, the selections. She talked and talked. It poured out of her like a river, a torrent of suffering. She wanted desperately to be understood. She wasn't thinking. She simply needed to recount what had happened there. The mother sat quietly listening, impassive, polite, but slowly blanching with the shock. And then she asked Nicole, "And Yvette, do you think she will return?"

Fifty years later, as Nicole was recounting this incident in a video interview, she began to cry, remembering her anguish.

"I said, 'Yes, she will come home.' Because I thought she would. But I realized all of a sudden what I had done. I had explained all the horrors to this mother and we still didn't know if Yvette would return. It's an intolerable memory."[4]

———≈———

Guigui and Mena had gone up for their medical exams and were separated during their interrogations. Guigui was shown to where a group of Dutch survivors was gathered around a small table in the corner of the lobby. It was a heady feeling to speak Dutch again with her countrymen. They made her laugh. She made a few phone calls, and soon her cousin James was on his way to get her. There were old friends in the gathered group. They asked about their friends who weren't there. Did Guigui ask about Timen, the man she had met briefly when they were both arrested a year earlier? Then she was out the door and walking down the city street, her arm hooked into the arm of her cousin James, before she realized that she had forgotten to say goodbye to Mena.

———≈———

During the three exhilarating months after the end of the war in Europe, there were constant celebrations in and around Paris. Everything was starting anew. Mena and Guigui went to many parties together. They were determined to have a good time, to put the ugly past behind them. A fellow Dutch resistance fighter, Albert Starink, had occasion to see Mena and Guigui together.[5] In his short account he mentions that one night they went out dancing and drinking at a nightclub. He recalls dancing with the girls until four in the morning. Hearing he was headed to Rotterdam, Mena wanted Starink to take her to a US military base in Reims, which was somewhat on his way. She had met someone; she was going to surprise him. Starink remembered the immense expanse of white tents at the army base in Reims and dropping Mena off there to find her way in the early morning fog.

According to Mena's grandson Guillaume, soon after the war Mena went to Senegal by boat to meet up with her fiancé, who was an architect working in the colony. Was he the American soldier she searched for in Reims? A Frenchman? How and when had she met this fiancé? All are unanswerable questions.

Mena, who so loved to be in love, might have exaggerated in her own feelings. She was as restless as she was generous. And though perhaps the architect's letters to her weren't nearly as ardent as she would have liked, she didn't care. She threw herself into this story. Mena was brave with her heart.

On the boat to North Africa she met a man named William Lucien Dupont. He flirted aggressively with her. I imagine her leaning against the railing and looking into the wake of the boat as she told him that she was meant for another. She told him that she was going to Senegal to marry her fiancé. Perhaps Lucien laughed at her and said she was just a silly girl, that she, who knew nothing of hardship, was just a good-time girl from Paris and could never live in Africa. She wouldn't have all the luxuries she was so used to having.

Mena said nothing. She didn't tell him that she was a survivor. She had already learned not to talk about it. The first night home when she began to tell stories, her mother had shaken her head and clicked her tongue, shushing her.

"That's all in the past," her mother had said. "Life goes on. Don't dwell there."

Mena had understood then that nobody wanted to hear about what had happened to her. Really, she didn't want to talk about it either. She wanted to dance and laugh and to feel her body in love again.

On the boat, Lucien warned her again that she had no idea what she was doing. Mena told herself that she would accept what fate brought her. But then, for whatever reason, it didn't work out. I imagine the boy in Senegal, her fiancé, was not at all how she had remembered him. She had built him up in her mind, in her dreams. Perhaps he told her he didn't love her, or perhaps he had already found someone else, and mumbled that he had wanted to tell her but hadn't found the words; she'd come to Senegal so quickly that he hadn't been able to write the letter in time. She probably wondered what Zinka would say to him, or Jacky. They would have some sharp, well-placed words. She likely wished Guigui were there with her.

When she got back on the boat to return to France, there was Lucien again. Maybe he was her fate. She was heartbroken and humiliated. She wanted to be close to someone, to feel held and safe. Mena, with her eight friends, had rescued herself, fiercely saved her own life, but maybe after all that effort, she wanted instead to be taken care of. It may have been tempting, that feeling of surrender after such a long fight. Perhaps she was completely exhausted. Perhaps she was pregnant.

In the end she married him. Mena the romantic, who lived for love, married a man who wasn't romantic. Perhaps he loved her, but he was also jealous of her past, jealous of her charm and the spell she could cast. Mena's husband, Lucien, was very controlling, and sometimes when Guigui came to see her, he would not allow her into their apartment. Guigui's daughter, Laurence, remembered Lucien: "My mother and Mena were very close, and they would go out together and have a lovely time and Lucien did not like it. He very rarely let her go out."[6]

Mena's son-in-law, Jean-Louis Leplâtre, recalled, "When she was away from her husband, she could be joyous. She had a good sense of humor, something she didn't show around him."[7] Whenever Mena came to stay with her daughter's family, she would have a glass of wine with Jean-Louis at dinner and then she'd open up. He said it was like he would discover the real Mena. It was painful to think about.

Mena with her daughter, Edith, in Brittany

Mena often went to Brittany to see her mother, who had retired and moved back there after her father's death. The family's modest house was typical of the region: a house originally built for fishermen, a *maison longère*, right on the seashore. Guillaume, Mena's grandson, reiterating what his father had said, explained that Mena and her daughter, Edith, had been extremely close, with their own world. They had a game they played: Edith and Mena would go for tea in the Galeries Lafayette department store. With fake accents, they pretended to be British. It seemed that Mena lived in her imagination, not with the harsh man she had married.

After the war, when Mena met the painter Mena Loopuyt and told her that she had used her name for her nom de guerre, the artist was not pleased. She said, "Do you realize what danger you put me in?"[8]

Mena hadn't even realized the danger she was putting herself in when she followed the boy she loved into the Résistance. But she chose that name because she admired the artist. Perhaps she also longed to have an independent artistic career. Her daughter, Edith, clearly was brimming with creativity. And her son-in-law said Mena was amazing with needle and thread. She could create any dress she had seen in a store without a pattern. She had elegance, charm, and her own style.

Mena died in 1973 at the age of fifty-one. Edith would also die young, in 2007, of cancer.

————〜————

Long after they returned to France, the survivors struggled to feel at home. There were the physical consequences of the extreme conditions they had been under. The lack of food, proper hygiene, and rest had led to illnesses like anemia, skin infections, muscular and skeletal scars; tuberculosis and the extremely widespread epidemics of typhus had long-lasting effects, including hearing loss, kidney and other organ failure, and neurological damage.

There were also psychological consequences that were much more difficult to treat and were in fact not fully recognized at first. While in the camps the deportees had struggled hard to survive. The rate of suicide was surprisingly low. They had fought with their entire being, guarding against anything that could weaken them, often blocking out the memory of the losses of their family and friends. The shock happened when they returned, when they thought they were safe and let down their guard at last.

Some deportees reported that upon returning home their families rejected them. Gisèle Guillemot wrote that her mother said, "You have made me suffer with your Résistance and all that. . . . I will have a hard time forgiving you. And look at the miserable state you are in."[9]

Marriages were called off because it would bring shame to a family to accept a woman who had been in the camps; they were no longer considered pure. Some survivors, with their shaved heads and emaciated bodies, were mistaken for *les tondues*, women who, as punishment for "horizontal collaboration"—sleeping with German soldiers—had been publicly shaved.

A woman is punished as a "horizontal collaborator"

Les tondues were paraded through the streets while people hurled insults at them. Sometimes they were halfway or fully stripped, with swastikas painted on their foreheads. A girl's alleged collaboration could have been a romantic or sexual relationship with a German soldier, but the accusations were often based on nothing more than simply providing services such as preparing food for soldiers, something a young woman could not have refused during the occupation. They were often women who had found themselves in difficulty, isolated, marginalized, single or widowed, without resources, who took in laundry for German soldiers or cooked meals for them. Roughly 20,000 women, in almost every department of France, were publicly shaved by frenzied mobs. France's humiliation, Vichy's crime of collaboration was placed on the female body, just as Pétain had placed the blame for the military's shockingly quick loss to Germany on the low morals of the female population. *Les tondues* were excommunicated from their villages and homes. And children born to a French woman with a German father bore the shame throughout their lives. By contrast, most male collaborators who had enriched themselves on the black market, or worse, were able to live with impunity.

Returning to this world, feeling misunderstood, the survivors couldn't fit in. Paris had been liberated in August, almost a year earlier. The general population had moved on. It did no good to talk about the camps. No one wanted to hear it. It might be uncomfortable for those who had stayed out of the Résistance and perhaps even out of necessity collaborated with the enemy. It was a blurry line, and the survivors were an unwelcome reminder of the past—especially the relatively few Jewish survivors. They returned often to find that they were the sole survivor in their family. An eleven-year-old survivor—one of a handful of survivors of the Vel' d'Hiv roundup, a *rafle* in which 13,000 Parisian Jews were rounded up and deported—recounted in a TV interview that when he returned, he found his family's apartment had been completely pillaged. The apartment was empty, with only one single photograph of his mother nailed on the wall, which was otherwise covered with swastikas. Surviving Jews were in a precarious economic situation. A new word, "genocide," was invented to describe the systematic extermination of an entire group of people, but few people used it or knew about it in the first years after the war.

The survivors suffered chronic depression, nightmares, insomnia, anxiety, and psychosomatic symptoms such as heart and digestive troubles. They were nervous, easily irritable, and hyperalert to potential danger, and they tended to think and expect the worst. They had obsessional recurring memories of the past that were felt as present. In 1953, for the first time, these psychological problems were recognized by the World Health Organization as war wounds and given a name: "concentration camp syndrome."

Suffering came from being closed up inside oneself. The solidarity in the camps had been a bulwark against that aloneness. At home with their families, survivors were overcome with loneliness. In response, survivors from each camp formed networks with their old camp mates. Women were the first to create these support groups, remembering how important their friendships had been to their survival. To honor those profound bonds, they created the Association des déportées et internées de la Résistance (ADIR). Geneviève de Gaulle-Anthonioz, Germaine Tillion, Denise Jacob-Vernay (the sister of Simone Veil), and Nicole were all members of ADIR. Their mission was twofold: to help and support one another and to honor the memory of those who had not survived. They obtained housing, food, clothes, and jobs for one another. They found they could talk to one another about the things no one else wanted to hear. They organized stays at convalescence centers and helped with the bureaucratic paperwork involved with getting governmental compensation and aid. They fought with the German government to keep the former prison sites as memorials and to pay compensation to the surviving "rabbits."

ADIR's newsletter, *Voix et Visages*, played a key role in bearing witness when in the late 1980s Holocaust deniers such as Robert Faurisson published articles with statements such as "they only gassed lice." This brought a collective cry of outrage. The women survivors felt an urgency to speak out. Eyewitnesses were dying, and the truth of their experience was being hijacked. *Voix et Visages* encouraged survivors to write and publish their personal accounts and correct the historical record when necessary.

Survivors found that they were better off marrying other survivors. Laurence, Guigui's daughter, recalled what her grandmother had told her: "With those people, the ones who were in the camps, they must just stick together, no one else can be married to them. They can't live like us and we can't understand them."[10] But two deeply traumatized people trying to create a family sometimes led to suffering for their children.

Six of the nine women married other survivors. It's unclear how much husbands and wives shared of their war experiences, because to the outside world, they seemed to actively want to put the past behind them.

After the Hôtel Lutetia, the group scattered; they tried to get on with their lives. A few remained close. They lost track of Josée. Most of them did not stay in contact until sixty years later, when the remaining few and their families would come back together and finally talk about their escape.

CHAPTER TWELVE

— IT'S ONLY A GOODBYE —

Hélène and Danny in Ischia

THE MILITARY FILE OF RENÉ Maudet, Zaza's husband, states that he was in Neuengamme, though he had probably spent most of his time in prison in one of Neuengamme's eighty-five *Kommando* subcamps. As British troops approached, the SS evacuated Neuengamme's 9,000 prisoners, including René, toward Lübeck, on the Baltic Sea. The prisoners were loaded onto four ships. The prisoners were in the ships' holds for several days with no food or water. Thinking that the ships contained Norway-bound fleeing Nazi officials, the British Royal Air Force attacked them during a bombing raid of the harbor on May 3. Survivors who jumped into the water were strafed by cannon fire from the RAF aircraft or shot by Nazi officials. Only about 600 prisoners survived. After almost a month of anxious waiting Zaza learned that René had survived. He arrived at the Hôtel Lutetia on June 12, 1945.

When Zaza saw him, he weighed less than seventy pounds and bore the scars of typhus. He could walk, but he was a shadow of his former self. She was overjoyed to find him alive. They moved to Nantes, and Zaza was soon pregnant with the first of their four children. In those first months after her return, she wrote down the story of the escape, giving it the title *Sans haine mais sans oubli* (Without hate but without forgetting), and indeed, her account is marked by a striking lack of animosity. The tone is optimistic and humorous. Zaza writes only about the escape. She doesn't describe the work she did in the Résistance or her arrest. Nor does she dwell on the horrific conditions and events she witnessed during her deportation and imprisonment, though she alludes to them slightly, subtly. It's there, all the horror, hovering just behind the curtain.

In 1961 she sent her manuscript to the editors at *Marie-Claire*, a women's magazine. She wrote, "I am sending you a story that might interest you: the escape of nine women who were deported and crossed the front lines . . . if this text has no literary or commercial interest, please tell me frankly."[1] Apparently the editors turned it down. Her manuscript remained known solely to an inner circle of friends and family.

Ten years after her death in 2004, her manuscript was finally published. In the preface to Zaza's book, her cousin writes that he regrets not asking her for more details about the war. Later when I interviewed Zaza's nephew Pierre Sauvanet, he explained that when he asked Zaza about the war, she responded: "If you want to know what happened, read my escape." That was all she said on the matter.[2]

I too regret my lack of curiosity. I have so many more questions now. I wish I had asked my grandfather more about his escape from Nazi Germany and what it was like to be a stateless Jew married to a French woman at the start of the war. I wish I had asked my uncle more about his time in the Résistance. I wish I had asked my grandmother more about her war years. I wish I had interviewed Hélène a few more times. And that I had started my search sooner, before all nine women had died. With my family, I can only remember a vague feeling that it would be impolite to bring up the past, to force them to talk about difficult memories. But I wonder now if they would have welcomed my questions. Maybe they thought we didn't want to hear about it.

The text Zaza wrote when she was twenty-four, soon after the events, was finally published after her death, a half a century later. Her nephew Pierre Sauvanet played a vital role in finally getting the book published. The publisher changed her title, and Pierre added dates and fixed the spelling of German words. He is sure she would be pleased.

Pierre Sauvanet, Zaza's nephew, showing his new electric
typewriter to Zaza and René Maudet, August 1985

As a young teenager, Pierre took an interest in his aunt's past, having heard from his mother that she had a manuscript. He explained, "I think it was because I had a little electric typewriter. . . . My little electric typewriter was the pretext to type out her manuscript. Then later in 1992, I retyped it into a computer. . . . Suzanne was happy to see the text, without a doubt. She wanted it published."

Zaza's book was the essential key to opening up this story for me; without it I would not have known where to start. My daughter Sophie and I drove to La Rochelle to meet Pierre and his wife, Anne-Flo. In my imagination, cheerful Zaza had been reunited with René and they had lived happily ever after.

Sitting with us in his lovely sunny apartment in La Rochelle, Pierre said that René never spoke of what he had been through. His story remained firmly shut inside him. What it had been like to work in the extremely deadly bomb-disposal squads, what had kept him alive—all those questions, and many more, would remain unanswered.

I asked Pierre about the couple's children, and he took a deep breath. "This is the sad part of the story," he said. He explained that the parents never told their children about what happened to them in the war. The four kids arrived quickly, one right after the other. After the war, Zaza and René were happy to find each other and they were still very much in love, but the return to normal life was not easy. They suffered. They became estranged. Zaza may have wanted more from life than being a homemaker. René buried himself in his work. He was often absent. She was left alone to raise four young children.

A stroke in 1963 left Zaza paralyzed on her left side, eighteen years after her liberation. Pierre only knew her in a wheelchair. When he was a young boy his family would visit her when they vacationed at their home in Saint-Gilles-Croix-de-Vie, a village on the Atlantic Coast. Zaza was always welcoming; René was too, but in a different way. Very tall and bearded, a big smoker, he was quite reserved. Zaza was more open, but after the stroke it was hard for her to talk; it was easier for her to write.

Around the time that Zaza became handicapped, the marriage improved. René took extraordinary care of her. Pierre only knows this part of their marriage, when they were happy and very much in love. But their children had a different experience. Pierre's mother, Zaza's sister, has said that the early years of their marriage were unhappy and that the children suffered. Zaza died in 1994, at age seventy-three, and René died a year later.

Three of their four children struggled with mental illness. One committed suicide, another died in a mental hospital, and the youngest tried to kill herself; the attempt left her severely handicapped, in a wheelchair like her mother, and permanently institutionalized.

Stunned by this recounting of tragedy, both Pierre and I had tears in our eyes. I asked him what sort of explanation he had for the suffering of his cousins. He felt it was two things. "On the one hand, every child asks, Why was I born? Children of survivors of the camps must know that their very existence hung by a slim thread. So much depended on chance that maybe they could think they shouldn't have been born. And second, vaguely, without being able to understand why, they must have felt that whatever they did with their life would not be as strong as what their parents did. Maybe there was even a vague guilt for existing at all."

M. Gerard Fromm studies and writes about the transmission of trauma across generations. He comments, "What human beings cannot contain of their experience—what has been traumatically overwhelming, unbearable, unthinkable—falls out of social discourse, but very often onto and into the next generation as an affective sensitivity or a chaotic urgency."[3] The field of transmission studies exploded in the 1970s when the second generation of Holocaust survivors began to show the effects of their parents' traumas in their own lives. "The children are compelled to deal with the shame, rage, helplessness, and guilt that the parents have been unable to work through themselves," Fromm notes.[4]

After years of clinical observation and treatment of children and even grandchildren of survivors, a constellation of symptoms started to emerge. Patients explained that their primary problem was navigating the unspoken, unmentionable "secret." Families of survivors felt a great sadness that could never be expressed or talked about. There was a constant sense of fear and dread, and they made attempts to avert any kind of risk. There was a generalized distrust and insecurity, especially about the state or the government. Often children would choose the medical profession and worked in life-or-death situations as emergency room doctors or cardiologists. Along with this longing to save lives, there was also the inability to really feel a connection with others. They often had a paranoid feeling of persecution and an ambivalence toward their parents or grandparents. And there was chronic depression and sadness, a sense of mourning that could not be fixed in any way but was just a pervasive feeling of loss.

Almost universally the families of the nine women whom I talked with said that the women practically never spoke of their experience during the war, and yet they also knew that those experiences had stayed with them every day. Hélène's daughter, Martine, told me that though her mother never wanted to talk about the war, the very first song her mother taught her, a song they would sing whenever they were driving in the car together, was "Le Chant des Marais." This was known as the song of the concentration camps, or "Le Chant des

Déportés." Versions of the lyrics were written down clandestinely and passed from camp to camp. The refrain contains these lines:

> *Ô terre de détresse*
> *Où nous devons sans cesse*
> *Piocher, piocher.*

> *O land of distress*
> *Where we must constantly*
> *Dig, dig.*

Through this song and in other subtle ways, Martine's mother passed to her the memory of the camps. Martine recalled a nightmare in which she was in a car being chased by the Germans. Finally the Germans caught them and put them in a room. In the middle was a deep pit. She was pushed into it, landing on a mixture of dead and live bodies. "I awoke from the nightmare, but I think I inherited her terror. For example, I always need to know where the exit is. I have a horror of being shut in. . . . Maybe if she had talked with me, I would have had children. I did not want to transmit the trauma. I think there was something in her that died in the camps. As soon as I talk about my mother I cry. We had a super-complicated relationship."[5]

In the documentary film when Lon and Hélène are reunited, Hélène asks Lon if she ever spoke about their story, and both say that they never talked about it with their families. Dori Laub, a clinician in the field of transmission studies, wrote, "Often, survivors emphasize that they indeed live in two separate worlds, that of their traumatic memories (which are self-contained, ongoing and ever-present) and that of the present. Very often they do not wish, or are completely unable, to reconcile these two different worlds."[6]

The account Zaza wrote has a surprising tone. She is happy her friends are together when the death march begins. She is full of wonder at the smell of spring grass when they shelter in a ditch as Allied bombs fall from the skies all around them. She writes joyously, euphorically. There is a sense of humor, a lightheartedness that is almost shocking when the reader recalls what they are escaping from. This dissonance between her memories and the reality of her experiences must be partly a defense mechanism, a form of resilience. After the war her grief and suffering were largely unacknowledged. She, along with the other eight and all other young women who had been in the Résistance and captured, were in the category of survivors who wound up being publicly ignored. In a sense she had no choice but to pretend everything was just fine.

Pierre and his wife, Anne-Flo, agree that although one of Zaza's daughters did read the manuscript and so knew something of her mother's story, still there was very little or no face-to-face communication about it. She may have felt the strange dislocated feeling of simultaneously knowing and not knowing. "And yet how can a parent talk about something like that?" Pierre asked. "It would have been impossible for René." As Howard Stein wrote, "What has consciously been banned from existence returns as a ghost, usually in the form of enactment. Those who must not acknowledge their grief find the loss has come to possess them."[7]

René didn't try to soften his edges. He had strange quirks. For example, Anne-Flo told us that René would watch them eat, but he never ate in front of them. He would wake up in the middle of the night, and "at four in the morning he made French fries and drank whiskey." The violence Zaza and René's children inflicted on themselves felt to me like the most haunting statement about the intergenerational trauma of war.

Pierre explained that he and Anne-Flo enjoyed being with René and Zaza. "We had some wonderful New Year's Eves with them. We were very close at the end. . . . We didn't have the burden like their children of the darker times."

Near the end Zaza was bedridden, and Pierre would go into her room and talk each afternoon. The room was full of exotic objects that they had brought back from their travels. After her stroke, when René retired, they bought an RV and traveled all over the world with their dog, including to Jordan, Syria, and other countries in the Middle East. Zaza had an appetite for life, and their travels brought the couple close together. "They found each other at the end of their lives," Pierre said. "Une belle retraite"—a beautiful retirement.

In the final years, Zaza passed her days watching the birds in her yard. Anne-Flo remembered bringing her twenty kilos of sunflower

seeds and nuts. "It was her way of traveling," Anne-Flo said. "There were clouds of birds outside her window."

———————

When Lon jumped from the train, leaving her six friends behind, she decided that all she had to do was follow the sun to find her way home to Holland. The weather was lovely; it was late spring. It was exhilarating to find herself alone at last, on the road, taking care of her own destiny. Sometimes at night in the woods she was scared, but she had been through so much that little fazed her. Everywhere she walked there was ruin and destruction and other refugees making their way home. The sides of the roads were littered with broken-down cars, discarded suitcases, and bent bicycle wheels. At night groups made campfires and roasted potatoes. Food was scarce. She was moving in a giant sea of displaced persons.

Somewhere along the way, she collapsed with exhaustion. Lon woke to find herself in an American field hospital. She wasn't sick; she simply needed rest and food. She stayed there for a week. An American nurse named Ruth gave her a new set of clothes: a khaki skirt, a khaki blouse, and good new walking shoes. The Americans had put in place a working postal system. Lon was able to write to her parents: "I don't know how long it will take, but I'm coming home."[8] The letter did arrive in Leiden; the postmarks on the envelope showed that it had traveled there via New York.

Eventually she found herself at the front door of her childhood home at three in the morning. She rang the bell and heard her beloved dog barking. She waited for a while, rang again, and then heard the sound of footsteps inside. Her heart raced. Then her mother opened the door, and after her initial scream of shock she broke down in tears. Lon embraced her.

Lon's first question was, "Where is Eric?"

Her mother started to cry all over again. She told Lon that Eric had died in the camps on January 31, 1945. For Lon, this news was an enormous blow. She had not imagined that he could be dead. She had been so sure he would be there waiting for her when she got home.

Her mother told her that her boyfriend, Jappe, had gotten engaged, and she listed their neighbors' losses too. It was all miserable news. Lon was stunned and sickened. Eventually her father came downstairs. He had visibly aged. The loss of his son had been a terrible blow to him as well. He brought out a bottle of champagne that he had miraculously saved throughout the war years.

"We shall celebrate your return," he said, trying to cheer them up.

Together, Lon recalled, they got drunk.

I had learned about Lon through her book and the documentary film *Ontsnapt*. So I was thrilled when at last I was able to contact the two filmmakers, Jetske Spanjer and Ange Wieberdink. They invited me to meet them in Amsterdam. In the morning we would discuss the film and our research, and in the afternoon Lon's daughter Patricia Wensink and her husband, Wladimir Schreiber, would come to Ange's apartment. I traveled to Amsterdam with Guigui's son, Marc Spijker. After climbing the typical and dauntingly steep Dutch stairs to Ange's apartment, we gathered in her light-filled living room for a memorable day together. In the morning, before Pat arrived, I spoke with Ange and Jetske. They generously shared their research with me. Just as their film had been a catalyst for me to travel to Germany at the start of this project, they said that my interview with Hélène had played an important role in their research. We watched their film together and stopped it at various points where I had questions. Yes, they had actually met the family of giants in Delmschütz. They thought they had met Annelise, but she was in a retirement home with dementia, so they could not be certain.

We talked about Lon's love for her brother, Eric. Lon was informed after the war that he was buried in a mass grave, and she was asked if she would identify his remains. She said she immediately recognized him by his teeth. In the 1970s it took much effort to arrange for Eric's body to be reburied at the National Field of Honor in Loenen. Any income from Lon's self-published book goes to the war grave foundation for the upkeep of Eric's gravesite.

Ange and Jetske had become close to Lon at the end of her life. They also described the moving reunion between Lon and Nicole that they witnessed. But they said that talking with her felt like talking with a bulldozer. Lon liked to be in control and stuck closely to her routines. They barely knew her daughters and had not been allowed to learn much about Lon's personal life after the war. While she was alive everything was on her terms. They were just as excited to talk with her daughter Pat as I was.

Pat and Wladimir arrived with gifts and carefully prepared notes and documents from Lon's history. Wladimir handed me a USB drive with photos. Clearly, they had organized their thoughts in advance for this meeting. They immediately began talking about Lon. Pat wanted us to know what it was like to be Lon's daughter. Twins Pamela Wensink and Patricia Elisabeth Frédérique Wensink were born in Scheveningen on April 1, 1948. Lon did not know she was pregnant with twins, and the girls were very premature.

They would never know their biological father; "our mother would not allow it." However, Pat suspects she met him later. Lon's parents insisted that she get married to save the family's honor; they paid a man named Wensink to marry her. The marriage lasted one year. "I wasn't allowed to know him either," Pat said. "I have his name and I don't even know the man."[9]

Lon was dedicated to work and was often away. The girls were raised by their grandmother and a series of nannies. Lon had difficulty with affection, showing love, and, her daughter said, "even feeling love. We were kept at a distance. It's like she wanted children but then she didn't know what to do with us." She knew her mother was proud of her and her sister, but intimacy, Pat said, was impossible for Lon.

Pat remembers her mother having terrible nightmares and her grandmother telling her to go comfort her mother, but she was only ten and had no idea what was wrong. Likewise, she was with her mother once when Lon noticed a truck from Saarbrücken parked next to the neighbor's house. Saarbrücken had been the first stop for the deportees after crossing into Germany. Lon became hysterical, screaming that they had to get that truck to leave. There were many such unexplained incidents that were terrifying for her daughters.

Writing her book in the 1990s helped calm Lon down. "A pity it took her so long to do it," Pat said. But as they read the book, both Pat and Wladimir felt it was as if Lon was frozen in time. She was stuck back there in 1945. The American soldiers had made a lasting impression. When Pat and Wladimir's son-in-law came to a dinner in his Marine uniform and pulled out a cigarette, that was all it took to completely win her over.

Pat's sister, Pam, ran away to Australia, to avoid being forced to marry a man Lon had chosen for her.

Lon never married again and had a series of affairs, always with married, unavailable men. Jetske explained to me and Pat that perhaps one reason Lon never wanted to get married was that until 1960 in Holland married women were legally forbidden to work. Jetske and Ange also told Pat the story of Lon identifying Eric's body by his teeth.

"Knowing my mother," Pat said, laughing somewhat bitterly, "she would just decide it was so, even if it wasn't Eric. Who knows? Maybe it is some stranger in that grave." Pat agreed that Lon remained heartbroken over the loss of her brother. There were photos of him everywhere in her apartment. "None of her children," Pat added. "And under the photos she had put little notes, like love letters from a teenaged girl: 'I love you, I miss you, when are you coming home?'"

Pat and Wladimir told stories about Lon's forcefulness and eccentricity. Around 1985 she started to prepare for death, but since she would live for another thirty-two years, the instructions were updated many times. A do-not-resuscitate order was taped to a door in the hall, and an envelope marked "PRIVATE to be cremated with me," containing love letters, was left in full sight on the stairs. Jetske and Ange had often seen this envelope on their visits.

Lon, like Jacky, Hélène, and Nicole, was part of the first generation of women who were able to have important professional careers. Through her work, Lon was involved in the creation of the European Union, and she held high-ranking posts supporting European industry and law. The last survivor in the group, she died at 101 on November 15, 2017.

Though she was blind and deaf in her final years, there was no question of her going to live in a retirement home. Pat, Wladimir, Jetske, and Ange all admired her strength of character, even if she could be frustrating sometimes. "Some of those character traits may have been critical for her survival," Wladimir wrote to me later.

———❧———

Guigui saw Lon often when she went to Holland to visit family. The friends stayed close. Guigui also stayed in contact with Mena, Nicole, and even Hélène from time to time. But she rarely talked

about the war directly; only later would she share anecdotes with her grandchildren.

When Timen, the man Guigui had met as they waited to be interrogated by the Gestapo, returned to Paris, he was just a shadow of himself. He had been in Dachau for two months and then was sent to Mauthausen concentration camp, where he credited the solidarity of the communists and his hope of finding Guigui with his survival. Mauthausen and the Gusen camp complex was the first large-scale concentration camp to be built by the Nazis, and the last one to be liberated, on May 5, 1945. Between 1938 and 1945, around 190,000 people from more than forty different nations were imprisoned there, and at least 90,000 of them died.[10]

Timen and Guigui both ended up working at the Dutch embassy in Paris. He helped the Dutch government search for Nazi criminals and collaborators. This was a complicated task. His own brother had been in the SS. His daughter, Laurence, explained, "While my father was in prison, his brother was on the Russian front. He too suffered terribly. He didn't talk about it for years. My father was working for the Dutch government, secret things—there were problems and it was complicated. After a while he left the secret service."

Guigui and Timen were married a year after their return to Paris, in June 1946, and Laurence was born a few months later. The young family lived in a comfortable house attached to the château owned by her cousin James outside Paris. The huge estate must have reminded Guigui of her childhood home in Hatten before the family lost its fortune. But Guigui's style was relaxed and unpretentious. She didn't care about the furniture falling apart. She cooked on a rustic wood stove. It was a bucolic place to visit, welcoming and open to nieces and grandchildren and friends. Her grandchildren remember one summer when at lunch each day she recounted another episode of the escape as if it were a TV series. She helped one grandchild write a school report about her experience. Another recalls that when Guigui asked for pajamas for her birthday, she insisted on no stripes. She didn't mind when the grandchildren wriggled in their sleep if they were sharing a bed with her, she told them, because in the camps they had slept so tightly together that if one moved, everyone had to move. She did mind, however, sharing a bathroom. The memory of the collective bathrooms had stayed with her, and she insisted on her privacy.

Guigui swore that she would never return to Germany, but she finally visited when Laurence was a student there. She saw the memorial in front of the lake at Ravensbrück—*Die Tragende*, a sculpture of one woman carrying the body of another—and that moved her. Another time Guigui took her granddaughter to Tunisia, and there were German tourists singing the old songs she remembered the SS singing; it really upset her. Laurence remembered the experience: "But then we ended up having exchange students. We had a German exchange student and I went to stay with a family in Frankfurt and my mother brought me there."

Olivier, her grandson, added, "She talked about how they stole her jewelry when she arrived at Ravensbrück, and she would say, 'Surely somewhere a German is wearing my jewelry.'"

"Yes," Laurence added, "but it was also her Dutch friends in the student house that took all her things when they heard that she and Lon had been arrested." She told Laurence that when she went back to Holland, she would see her things in their houses. "I didn't dare ask for them back and no one offered," Guigui told her daughter.

In her nonchalant way, Guigui did not care too much about these objects. But she kept the "Indian Head" sleeve insignia that must have been given to her by a US soldier in the 2nd Infantry Division in Colditz or Grimma.

Guigui died in July 2007; she was eighty-seven years old.

———❦———

Nicole retuned to Paris on the same day as another deportee from Dachau, her future husband. She had known him during the war; he was part of the circle of Résistance fighters in Lyon. They were married in 1946, and in 1947 Nicole had a baby daughter. Nicole was recruited to work for the photography agency Magnum. Though the marriage did not last, Nicole and her husband remained friends for life, calling each other weekly for the next sixty years. Their daughter feels that they married too soon. They were not ready to be a couple after all they had been through, and Nicole certainly couldn't accept not working. She often told her daughter that her war experiences

taught her how strong she was, how much she could do with her life. There was no going back.

Nicole searched for but never found her dear friend Renée Astier de Villatte, whom she had reluctantly left behind at the start of the death march. In Odette Pilpoul's archives, I discovered that Renée was put on a special emergency medical evacuation transport soon after the American troops discovered her in Leipzig. Her family later donated her camp dress to the Résistance Museum in Blois. The family explained that Renée never wanted to be recognized for her actions in the Résistance or during her deportation.

When Nicole had the opportunity to go to New York to work at Magnum's office there, she took it, leaving her thirteen-year-old daughter in Paris with her father. She made many friends and her professional career grew, but she missed her daughter and returned to France, where she was hired to work at *Elle* magazine directly under its founder, the Russian émigré journalist Hélène Lazareff.

In 1964, for the anniversary of the liberation, Nicole wrote an article about her experience in Ravensbrück and her escape for *Elle*. Another survivor from Ravensbrück wrote a scathing letter to the editor admonishing Nicole for publishing such painful memories. No one was interested in this story, the woman argued. It was unseemly. "The resistors who we were and the walking cadavers who we became upon our return in 1945, and who we are still twenty years later, who cannot forget, we do not have the right to brush against the slightest hint of pretentious boasting." She tells Nicole to be more discreet. The level of self-censorship is shocking. Nicole's account is shunned as *cabotinage*, a theatrical, overly dramatic manner of bragging about oneself. The silencing of women's experience was pervasive.

De Gaulle had created the Compagnons de la libération to acknowledge the heroes of the Résistance, but of the 1,038 whom he honored, only six were women, and four were already dead by the end of the war. He had asked women to step back and let the men take the glory. Frenchmen had suffered enough humiliation. And yet Germaine Tillion wrote, "France in 1940 was unbelievable. There were no men left. It was women who started the Résistance. Women didn't have the vote, they didn't have bank accounts, they didn't have jobs. Yet we women were capable of resisting."[11]

Zaza wrote with evident bitterness that even the French prisoners of war and the local Germans they met during their escape assumed that they were voluntary prostitutes who had gone to the camps to "service" the SS or the "free" workers there. The notion that they had in fact risked their lives in the Résistance was not considered plausible. And no one could imagine the horrors they had been subjected to. Because they were young pretty girls, in their twenties, they would not be taken seriously when they tried to tell what had happened to them.

The poet Adrienne Rich wrote, "Whatever is unnamed, unde-picted in images, whatever is omitted from biography, censored in collections of letters, whatever is mis-named as something else, made difficult-to-come-by, whatever is buried in the memory by the collapse of meaning under inadequate or lying language—this will become, not merely unspoken but unspeakable."[12]

Many of Nicole's friends from that epoch had no idea how impor-tant she had been in the Résistance. Some of her closest friends knew she had been disabled in the war and still suffered from the torture she underwent at the rue de la Pompe, but she never talked about this period of her life. Some were stunned when in 1991 she received the rosette of Officier de la Légion d'honneur next to Simone Veil.

She was a fighter, audacious and brave, which led to a brilliant thirty-year career in journalism. She was respected and liked for her lucidity, good taste, and insight. She ended her career at *Madame Figaro* before retiring to focus on her painting and gardening. She is remembered for being extremely kind and loyal. She remained quite close to the support organization for the deportees of Ravensbrück. Nicole and other survivors met for lunch on the first Monday of every month, a tradition that her daughter continues to this day with the handful of survivors who are still alive. Nicole died in August 2007, at the age of eighty-five.

———❧———

After staying behind in Grimma to run the rest home for female survi-vors for a few months, Jacky returned to Paris and the apartment where she had lived with Jean, on the boulevard de Batignolles. In late 1945 her old boss Colonel Vedel returned on a stretcher to Paris from Elrich camp. He vouched for her Résistance credentials: "Young, pretty and brave, she accomplished without fail her difficult mission as an *agent de liaison* and her deportation to Ravensbrück did not stop her smile or her desire to be useful. *Résistante parfaite*, deserving of recognition."[13] She was awarded the Croix de Guerre with a bronze star.

Eighteen days after Vedel returned, he learned from another survivor at the Hôtel Lutetia that his wife, Odette, was alive in Bergen-Belsen. But he was told, "If you want to see her alive, hurry up." She was part of the massive quarantine of survivors who were dying of typhus. The British would not release anyone, fearing the spread of the epidemic. Vedel activated his old Brutus network with its contacts in the French police. He found a group of four men with a working car and enough gas to go across Germany. They traveled to Bergen-Belsen with false papers and brought Odette back to Paris weighing fifty-seven pounds, suffering from typhus and dysentery. Vedel nursed her back to health.

Determined to have financial independence, Jacky became a film editor after the war. In 1955 she worked as an editor on the film *Les Évadés*, about a group of men escaping from a German prisoner-of-war camp. She was an assistant film editor for the 1958 version of *Les Misérables* and worked with a French leftist film couple, Emma and Jean-Paul Le Chanois.

During this period, she met and fell in love with Charles Feld, but he was married and he and his wife were expecting a child. Charles Feld had worked in the Résistance in Lyon with his young wife, Nelly. They had created an underground newspaper, *Fraternité*, which was dedicated to fighting anti-Semitism and all forms of racism. Throughout the war, Charles ran a secret printing press, no doubt providing false documents while continuing to publish the underground paper.

His younger brother, Maurice, had joined one of the first armed Résistance groups of young Jews in the early days of the occupation. The group carried out acts of sabotage and assassination, including the bombing of a cinema that was showing the anti-Semitic movie *Le Juif Süss*. Maurice was arrested and executed at age eighteen in 1942 after he threw a grenade at a hotel where the SS were staying. Charles and Maurice's parents died in Auschwitz.

Despite her feelings, Jacky continued to refuse Charles's advances. One night after she had rejected him again, he stayed outside her apartment all night long. In the morning she looked out of her window and saw that he was still standing there. Later she told her cousin Michel Lévy that it was at this moment that Charles's tenaciousness won her over. Still, Jacky didn't want Charles to divorce Nelly, and he never did. He and Jacky were married only many years later, after Nelly's death. Nelly and Maurice's daughter, Sylvie, would spend their holidays at Charles and Jacky's home. Jacky made sure that Charles stayed part of Sylvie's life. Jacky never had children; one of the lasting side effects of diphtheria is infertility. But she had a way with children. Michel Lévy, whose father and Jacky's first husband had been close cousins, knew Jacky when he was a child, and he told me that "as children we adored her, partly because she spoke with us as equals, honestly; she didn't condescend."

She worked as a film editor until the late 1970s, using a shortened version of her name, Jacqueline Aubéry—having dropped the de Boulley, which in French society often denotes nobility and could have been seen as elitist. Charles was a dedicated communist. After the war, he worked for Louis Aragon, a leading French poet and writer and longtime member of the Communist Party. But Jacky never joined the party. She was leftist in her beliefs and sympathetic to working-class struggles, but she was also very frank. She spoke her mind, and, as Michel Lévy noted, "Often political parties didn't appreciate that kind of character."[14]

Charles ran a renowned book publishing house, Cercle d'Art, which published art books with important artists such as Pablo Picasso and Marc Chagall. Philippe Monsel, who took over the business when Charles retired, said of Jacky, "She was direct, very direct. A strong character. *Bien trempé*."[15] The French expression refers to the process in which steel is tempered and dipped into acid to make it stronger; it denotes a tough, tenacious character. "She could be a little brutal; people did not take advantage of her. She did not suffer fools."

I wondered if she ever talked about the war, and he said that he had learned about that part of her story only from what I had written to him.

"Often I meet people from that period that did really heroic things and they say nothing about it. Today you do the smallest thing and it's hailed on Facebook! Never. We never talked about the past. I knew about Charles's past. He worked in a Jewish network. The drama was that he had told his little brother not to join the Résistance or get involved. He was too young. But then his brother did, and was arrested and shot. I think he carried that burden with him his whole life, that guilt about his young brother."

He told me the story of a vacation house his family had rented near Perpignan. He invited Charles and Jacky to come join them for a few days, but the house Philippe rented was invaded by cockroaches.

When Charles and Jacky arrived, she heard his wife's complaint and saw the cockroaches. Then she declared, "No, Philippe, you cannot stay here and force your wife to stay here! Fuck this place! You will finish your holiday at our house!"

There was no debate. The next morning, they packed their bags and with two cars they drove to Charles and Jacky's house.

"That was Jacky!" Philippe laughed at the memory.

Charles and Jacky were crazy about their dog, Hugo. "Really, really, crazy about him," Philippe said. "When we went on a trip in the car with them, we had the dog, who walked all over us in the back seat. We had to politely take it because the dog was the most important person."

Michel Lévy, who would remain close to Jacky and take care of her at the end of her life, recalled how they had dinner together every Sunday and played bridge. Charles, Jacky, Michel, and Flore, Jacky's mother-in-law from her first husband, got together regularly until Flore died in 1978. "Jacky could be aggravating, unbearable, and straightforward. But she was also playful and laughed easily," Michel said. "She had a deep, musical voice, with a Parisian bourgeois flair. She loved to read, to go to the theater; she knew many writers, intellectuals, artists, and painters, of course. Picasso was a friend. Charles loved to travel to Italy and Greece, so they went there often. She gave good advice and she was a good listener. She was there when you needed her. She said about surviving the camps, 'It was the appetite for life that saved people.'" Jacky passed away in 2001.

Josée virtually disappears after the war. From her military records and from the website of the Amis de la Fondation pour la Mémoire de la Déportation de l'Allier, I learned that she married Jacques Armynot du Châtelet in 1947. He came from an aristocratic family and was probably a soldier, as the family had a long military tradition. They were divorced by 1956. A year later, Jacques immigrated to the United States, and Josée moved back to the south of France, where she died in Cannes in June 2014 at the age of ninety.

France Lebon, 1946

After Zinka arrived at the Hôtel Lutetia with the others on May 21, 1945, she made inquiries in search of Louis Francis, and was informed that there was no record yet of his whereabouts. She would have telephoned her family from the hotel, if they weren't already at the hotel searching for her. That night or the next day, her sister Claude brought her baby, France, to the apartment where Zinka had lived with Louis Francis on rue Méchain, one block away from the maternity hospital where, before she was arrested, she had planned to give birth.

Above all else, Zinka had longed for two things: to see her husband and to hold her child. It's hard to say how the reunion between mother and child went. France, over a year old, had only known her mother for the first few days of her life. Zinka was a stranger to her. Lise London wrote about the difficult reunion she had with her own children. She wanted so much to hold them and kiss them, but they cried and pulled away from her arms, frightened by the intensity of her emotions and unable to really understand who she was. The searing separation of a mother from her young child had left its scars.

Zinka's brother Roger and sister Marthe returned from deportation, but there was no sign of Louis Francis. She waited for him in that apartment, believing that if she stayed there, he would find her. There were rumors about the missing deported: they were being held in Soviet camps, or they were just too weak but soon they would show up. She clung to those tales. Louis Francis was walking home, or for some reason he was delayed, but any day now he would be knocking at their door.

Months passed, and by November it was understood; everyone who was alive had been found or had returned. There were many who would never come home, whose bodies would never be found. Zinka learned from other returnees that Louis Francis had been last seen in March in Bergen-Belsen. She heard about the devastating typhus epidemic there that had killed thousands, most of whom were buried in mass graves.

In October 1946, she received an official notice from the military that Louis Francis was missing and presumed dead. She began the necessary paperwork to have him recognized as part of the Résistance. In 1948 he was awarded the status of *déporté résistant, mort pour la France*, along with a posthumous award of the rank of second lieutenant.

———◆———

From the very beginning, reading Zaza's book, I wondered about France, Zinka's baby born in Fresnes prison. Was she still alive, and could I find her? Eventually, through a series of haphazard connections and with the help of Guigui's grandson Olivier Clémentin, who has impressive detective skills with genealogical websites, we learned that in 1948 Zinka had married Michel Châtenay.

Wedding of Renée (Zinka) and
Michel Châtenay, 1948

A former Résistance fighter, Michel was eight years her junior. For a
second time, it was Zinka's father, Pierre Lebon, who served as matchmaker. There is a good chance her father and Michel's father worked
together in the Résistance. Pierre Lebon arranged for his daughter, now
a war widow, to meet the young man. Michel, who had a French father
and British mother, took after his mother. He was very British, funny,
and constantly teasing Zinka's sister Claude, who was unusually gullible.
Michel came from a highly decorated military family. His father, Victor
Châtenay, was a soldier in the First World War, and at the start of the
Second World War Victor quickly joined the first Résistance network,
Honneur et Patrie, which became closely tied to British intelligence. He
narrowly escaped capture by the Gestapo at the Gare Saint-Lazare in
Paris while delivering false identity papers to an agent in the Jade Fitzroy network, the network that Pierre Lebon led. Victor was shot in the
knee but was able to escape into the metro. His youngest son, Anthony,
was with him, however, and was caught. Even though he was a mere
teenager, Anthony was tortured and eventually sent to Buchenwald.

Michel's mother, Barbara Châtenay, was the daughter of the British
general Douglas Stirling. She had volunteered to drive ambulances
during the First World War and joined Honneur et Patrie with her
husband at the start of the Second World War. She was arrested while

trying to transport maps and architectural drawings of a German submarine base off the Atlantic coast. She was deported to Ravensbrück.

They had four sons and one daughter, all of them active in the war. A parachutist with the British Special Air Service, Michel participated in the liberation of Holland in April 1945. In 1949, Zinka and Michel had a son, Gilles, who is now a Lacanian psychoanalyst in Nantes.

I emailed Gilles Châtenay to ask if he was Zinka and Michel Châtenay's son, and if so, whether he would he talk to me about his mother. He responded that I might want to speak with his sister France. When I received that email, I sat there stunned, staring at my computer screen. I had been searching for her since the start of this project. France lived just three hours north of me, in the wild and beautiful mountains of La Drôme.

By email, she told me that she and her brother Gilles knew next to nothing about their mother's experiences in the war. I told them about Zaza's book and the documentary film, and I sent them other descriptions I had found about their mother from fellow survivors. Zinka had been well known in the camps. I told them that Lise London's book even had a drawing of her.

France, inspired by all this new information, decided to look through her mother's papers stored in her attic. She found a carbon copy of a text, nineteen single-spaced typed pages, about the escape. She and her husband, Didier, set to work typing the document into their computer. They realized it was a journal that Zaza must have written immediately after the war, and she must have sent or given a copy to Zinka and asked for her input. There were corrections in Zinka's handwriting in the margins.

Gilles sent me an essay he had written for a psychoanalytical journal in which he talks about the necessary distance and at the same time intimacy between the patient and analyst.[16] He evokes a traumatic memory he had of seeing a TV documentary of prisoners in the Nazi camps. He describes the nightmare vision of the rows of bodies in striped pajamas and the strange voiceless noise of the film.

He juxtaposes this startling imagery with the few small anecdotes his mother recounted to him as a young boy about her time in the concentration camp. "In the end, we enjoyed ourselves," Zinka had told him. She described the recipes and the poetry recitations. She portrayed to her son "a lively community in a death camp." Gilles explains that his mother and his father had a "discreet sense of humor and modesty." To him it was a kind of tact that allowed him to understand the unspoken only if he wanted to.

His parents kept themselves at a slight distance from groups and ideologies. Zinka told him that she admired the communists and the Jehovah's Witnesses for their strong sense of community and solidarity. She respected them "with a tiny step away, a certain distance, a discreet separation."

His essay made me think of one of the final pages in Lon's book:

When I visited Zinka for the last time—she was already very ill by then—she said suddenly, after a long pause: you know, *nous sommes devenues étranges* [we became strange]. And that is how it is. We even have stayed *étranges*—estranged—different from other people. This certainly applies to me, but Guigui thinks so too, even up till now.[17]

Gilles was an anxious youth and always felt like an outsider, estranged from others his age. "The slight bias of my mother and my father echoed in me as a way to hold me from the edge, to keep me from joining and suffering. I wanted to touch the reality that lives in us, but I remained separated."

He explains that the camp was not just something in the past for his mother, because it remained in her body and was in fact a sickness. Her tuberculosis progressed year after year, despite the doctors trying to surgically remove it. "To this silence and this untouchable reality answered the terrifying image of the film . . . I had some difficulty with groups and ideals, and with myself and my body."

Gilles and I met over lunch, and one of the first things he told me about himself was that he had inherited a kind of anorexia from his mother. His son Tom, Zinka's grandson, was also with us. Tom had become a chef—"perhaps," he said, "to heal the trauma of my family."[18]

Gilles explained that his mother hated to cook and always joked that she had once won "Best Cook" in a contest in the camp for her recitation of a recipe. In fact, she found eating a chore. Because of the tuberculosis, she had little appetite.

After the war, survivors were warned that their children would suffer from the past malnutrition of their parents, so they had to be extra vigilant about their diets. "It was all scientific," Gilles explained. "A calculated number of calories with so many fats. And the soundtrack of my childhood meals was 'Eat! Eat!' My mother hated to cook, and she hated to eat, so I hated to eat."

Gilles later caught tuberculosis himself, though by then there were good treatments for the disease. But he was sent to a sanatorium by his doctor, because the doctor was fearful Gilles would not eat enough. At the first sanatorium, Gilles organized a hunger strike.

He was telling me this story as we ate a lovely lunch outside in the sun on a gorgeous day. The food was delicious, roasted fish over buttery polenta. And somehow this story struck us all as hilarious. He explained that he was a child of '68. The summer of 1968 in France was a period of nationwide civil unrest led by students. A massive strike shut down the economy. The period was a moral and cultural turning point for the French. "There were too many rules in the sanatorium." What could he do? He had no choice but to revolt.

"But a hunger strike?" I was incredulous and laughing. "For people suffering with tuberculosis?"

His son Tom chimed in, "He's just like my grandmother; they are both fighters."

"I got kicked out of that sanatorium. They sent me to another one, and I got better."

Gilles said he has gradually recovered from his anorexia. But he thought it was strange that after starving, his mother would be so uninterested in food.

———❦———

My daughter Sophie drove us north through the dramatic landscape of the Drôme region to meet France. We drove alongside the running rivers that carved through a series of canyons with exposed colorful strata of rock high above us. In the town of Die, where France lives, we tasted the famous clairette de Die, a kind of sweet, bubbly wine. Die was probably popular with the back-to-the-land hippies of 1968, because it has a real alternative feel, much like parts of Vermont or Colorado. We counted five Reiki storefronts.

France Lebon Châtenay Dubroeucq, 2019

France found us in front of the Office of Tourism. When we embraced, she began to cry. She said that it was a very emotional experience to discover all this about her mother so late in life. I told her that it had been hard for me to figure out who Zinka was. And she said, "Imagine for me, at seventy-five years old, and only now to discover my mother."

France confirmed that her mother never talked about herself in the war. She did talk sometimes about Louis Francis, because he was France's father, but never about herself. France did know she was born in Fresnes prison. It was on her birth certificate. "So you couldn't hide it. And sometimes it would lead to trouble. At school when they asked where you were born, I would say, 'I was born in Fresnes prison.' Then the teacher would call my mother to find out what was going on with me."[19] France laughed as she recounted this anecdote.

It was a beautiful day, and we sat outside in the courtyard and garden of their large home. France's husband, Didier, a retired geologist, joined in the conversation. Both of them were obviously active and athletic. They mentioned that they often hiked in the mountains. They were there because though they had spent most of their marriage living overseas in Africa and South America, and though they had raised their two sons overseas, Die was where they would return for vacations. When Didier retired, they settled there. Didier had a vivid memory of Zinka near the end of her life when she had come to Dakar to visit them. They had thrown a barbecue party for Zinka on the beach, with entertainment and wonderful food. The guest of honor, she had been regaled by everyone. "It was a fantastic day," he said, "a great memory."

France continued, "She talked about my father, but not what happened to him in the camps. They were that group that never talked. My uncle Tony, his daughter only recently could interview him and ask the questions. He was a young teenager in Buchenwald. We knew nothing about it."

France knew very little about her father. Already in prison when she was born, he probably never even saw her. What she knew were the little things her mother had told her: He was funny. He made Zinka laugh. Her mother was not a morning person, and he would tease her in the mornings. But she admits it's hard for her to recall, because her mother married Michel Châtenay in 1948 and they started another life.

"Michel raised me," she said. "He adopted me. A simple adoption so I could keep both names." She felt her mother had tried the best she could to raise France with her stepfather while also keeping alive the memory of her father. France adored Michel. She had a lot of respect for the way her stepfather treated her. "He would correct my English," she said with a laugh. His sense of humor was very British.

Zinka had been athletic before the war; she swam in the ocean, played tennis, and skied in the Alps. There are photos of her, smiling, tanned, and vibrant, at the family's summer house near Saint-Jean-Cap-Ferrat on the Côte d'Azur. After the war she was changed. France showed us a photo of a family who had taken care of her for a whole year while her mother was recuperating in a tuberculosis sanatorium. France looks to be around six years old. "They already had seven children, so one more didn't make a difference. It was a very happy family. I have a good memory of that time."

I asked her, "Do you have any memories of when your mother returned from the camp?"

"No, not really. My memories are really nightmares."

Because of Zinka's illness, France was shuttled from place to place, family to family. Her childhood must have been unsettling. The whole family suffered during the war. Zinka, Marthe, Roger, Michel's little brother Tony, and Michel's mother had all been in the camps. There were losses in both families.

France remembered the birth of her brother but said, "He was five years younger than me." When they were younger there was too great an age difference for them to be close; later, with maturity, they became closer. Her mother was in very poor health. France was cared for by other members of the family. "I was very attached to my mother's side of the family. My aunt Marthe took care of me. The family really supported and helped. My uncle Roger could be hard, a little difficult when he drank, but always generous."

It was less that way with the Lebon family, her father's side. Zinka clearly made efforts to keep that connection for France. France recalled a story her mother told her about how once she walked quite a distance to bring France to visit her aunt and uncle, carrying the baby in her arms all the way. And when she left, they didn't offer to drive her home or help. She had to walk the whole way back carrying France in her arms, and that was hard for her in her condition.

Her mother was very sick. "She was often in the sanatorium. It wasn't easy for anyone. She had multiple operations. They removed a lung. And then they had to operate on the heart. She had a pacemaker. I had to take care of the house and my brother. It was a dark period. When she was home, she was so tired. I had to help her. I had to make dinner. She would be so relieved when I offered to help."

Didier, as if sensing the painful memory troubling his wife, again brought up the barbecue in Dakar. "She was happy then. Remember? Everyone was taking care of her."

France said, "I think she was happy to see we were happy. That we had good friends and our life was open and generous."

I asked her if she could describe her mother's character. France said, "Very strong and courageous. She never complained even though she was very sick. With Michel, they were a happy couple. She loved to laugh. She was a joyous person. She had a short life but a happy one."

Didier explained that you couldn't say no to Zinka. He recounted an anecdote about his marriage to France. "We were going to marry, but for Renée [Zinka] and Michel it was very important; they wanted a proper marriage. France was so important to them. They wanted it done right. But I was a child of '68. I was not interested in all those ideas about a fancy bourgeois marriage. One day they said, 'Didier, you come with us.' They brought me to a store in Paris. One of those places where they have just all those . . ." Didier searched for the words and came up with "penguin tails," saying it in English.

"Tuxedos?" I offered.

"Yes. I told her that I wasn't going to put on one of those silly costumes. And she said so sweetly, 'Didier, make me happy.' And she said it in such a nice way that I could only say, 'OK.' She was like that." He repeated, "'*Didier, faites-moi plaisir.*' So I wore penguin tails."

France felt that if the people who had suffered were unable to talk about the war, we should respect that. "I am happy with my childhood and adolescence. I wasn't traumatized. Maybe my childhood—how can I say this?—there was always a feeling, a fear that people will leave, that I will be abandoned. That has stayed with me my whole life. I was raised by so many people. It was perturbing for a small child. But I do not reproach my mother. What was more complicated was afterward because she was so ill, and I had to go live with different families. It brings up many emotions to learn her story now."

Zinka died in 1978. Her heart gave way in the end.

Before Hélène drove home from the war to her family in the great big Chrysler, she filled the trunk with all kinds of food from the American mess hall. Germany was in ruins. People were starving. The cities were in tatters and the fields had not been farmed. The male population had been ravaged. The country would be divided into east and west. Some felt that Germany would cease to exist altogether, that it would just become a colony of the two world powers, the Soviet Union and the United States.

Hélène had one more mission to complete. With the car full of canned meat, soups, chocolate, cigarettes, and American chewing gum, she drove to the town whose name Fritz Stupitz had written in the dirt on the floor of the air-raid shelter.

Hélène told me, "I found the village and found Fritz was now mayor because he was a longtime communist. I gave him all the food I had brought. Once his amazement passed, we were both overcome with emotion."

They had survived. They would survive.

Hélène returned home to France several months after the others. Arriving in Asnières-sur-Seine in her Chrysler coupe, she made quite an impression on the neighbors and her family. Everyone came out to the square to greet her. She was the returning war hero, and in uniform.

After a month or so of eating well, resting, and being cared for by her mother, she had regained her strength. She also went to a dentist to have her teeth repaired. She was impatient to get back to work. She wanted to put the past behind her. She returned to her former job at the Mazda lamp company. Her boss asked her if she would be willing to travel to Germany. A German scientist claimed to have an important patent that would be interesting for the company. He wanted to sell his patent to the French, but they needed someone to go evaluate the laboratory and his claims.

Hélène was sent to Württemberg, where she worked for eight or nine months. They had requisitioned a small hotel for her; she occupied it all alone. About twenty-five kilometers away from the hotel there was a French bomber division with a team of aviators. When she was bored on the weekends, or when she wanted to speak and hear French, she would go there to play bridge, to hunt, to fish in the Danube, or to join the soldiers for parties. It was here that she met her first husband, Martine's father, Jacques Fourcaut.

Hélène was twenty-seven. Martine recounted that her father, Jacques, was handsome, but an anxious and troubled man. He was a pilot who had a fear of flying. She said, "My mother was very beautiful. They fell in love. My father was charming. But really they fell in love with the idea of love."

Hélène told me that she was warned by Jacques's superior, "You're crazy to think of marrying that boy. He is half nuts; he has serious problems." But she married him anyway.

Martine is sure it was because her mother was already pregnant. "I was born six month later. And Hélène was born six months after *her* parents had met! So it's clear why my family had this phobia about the girls seeing or getting too close to the boys."

Martine explains that Hélène and Jacques were from two very different worlds. "My mother was Trotskyist, her father was Jewish and anti-military. A pacifist. But my father's family were completely the opposite. Catholic. He came from a family of industrialists. His father had worked his way up in business and his mother was a supporter of Pétain! She thought her son was a traitor for joining the Résistance. She said that she would kill him with her own hands."

As a military man, Jacques was often absent, but when he was around, he would flirt with and chase after Hélène's girlfriends. Martine remembered that in 1957 when her grandfather died, the family sent Martine to a camp in the mountains. When she returned home, Hélène announced that she was getting divorced.

———❧———

I knew Hélène when she was married to my uncle Danny, my grandmother's brother. Danny looms large in my imagination because he was an acknowledged hero of the Résistance and because my father adored him. As a young teenager, my father would leave his strict German father on the farm in upstate New York and travel to Europe to see his French mother for the summers, if she could find the airfare or the boat passage to get him there.

One famous summer Danny and Hélène had rented a house on the island of Ischia for all the children and nieces and nephews. My father talks about this summer as if it were a visit to utopia. When I asked Hélène's daughter, Martine, she too remembered the summer of Ischia with a dreamy voice. She laughed, saying, "Oh la la, I was in love with your father! All my cousins were there; I think there were at least ten of us. We ate every day at a restaurant at a big table. I was nine years old. I remember the roses everywhere in bloom. The smell of roses. It was paradise!"[20]

She showed me a picture from that summer of Hélène and Danny on the beach. They are beautiful, in love. They have found each other. "They told me they were married, but they weren't. They got married later. Why they thought I would care!"

———❧———

For Martine, as an only child of a rather complicated mother, Danny's entrance into her life was a godsend. "When I saw him arrive, a sort of cross between Cary Grant and John Wayne . . . he played rugby. He talked to me about the war. He would tell me stories and my eyes were wide listening to him. He taught me to swim. Every time I was afraid, he helped me through my fear."

In adolescence Martine had a rough time. Her mother wanted her to be in the symphony orchestra, but Martine wanted to play the guitar and sing folk songs with her friends on the beach. It was the 1960s. Everything was topsy-turvy. She tried many different careers before settling on psychology. She ended up being a social worker. She worked with street addicts in the 1980s, during the height of the AIDS crisis. She was dedicated to the downtrodden and the suffering. Today, in her retirement, she is the director of a homeless shelter in Paris. She feels her life's work is a direct continuation of what her mother fought for. The UN's adoption of the Universal Declaration of Human Rights in 1948, she explains, is the foundational principle she is working for, and it was created after the camps, after the Holocaust. For Martine, it is her direct inheritance. Like many second-generation Holocaust survivors, she chose a profession of helping others. And she struggled with her own mental health, with paranoia and a borderline personality disorder, common symptoms of inter-generational trauma.

I got to know my Tante Hélène in the 1980s, when she was in her sixties. During this period, Hélène was hospitalized for severe depression. I asked Martine about her mother's struggle with depression. "It began in her fifties. Three things set it off: she lost her job in a nasty firing, her mother died, and I got married." Martine acknowledges that because she was not the perfect daughter—she was working with drug addicts in the streets—the family, even Danny, blamed Martine for Hélène's mental troubles. They said her mother was depressed because she was worried about her daughter. But perhaps it was also around this time, with these losses, that her mother began to grieve and examine her own past. Hélène found a good doctor. She had always refused psychoanalysis and disparaged what Martine did in psychology. Hélène had put all of her past away. But with the depression and this good doctor, Martine feels her mother was able to start talking about all those things. She wanted to talk; she needed to talk. "When you recorded her story, she was really pleased," Martine told me.

But it also stirred up things. Near the end of her life, there were a few times when it was clear she was struggling to come to terms with her past. There was a moment when she would no longer let herself be washed. Her longtime caregiver, Ratiba, tried to get her into the bathtub. Hélène became frantic and hit her. Ratiba was devoted to and admired Hélène. When Hélène hit her, instead of getting upset, she asked Hélène if it was because of the *supplice de la baignoire*, the waterboarding. Hélène responded, "We don't talk about that." But afterward, she calmed down and let herself be bathed.

After Danny died and she approached her own death, Hélène became concerned about how she would react in the end. Hélène's father had been a militant atheist, someone who would say, "If God exists, then he is a sadist or impotent." Martine told me, "My grandmother was Catholic, but her daughters and her husband were atheists. My mother's fear at the end of her life was that she would convert to believing just out of a fear of death."

At her mother's funeral in March 2012, Martine sang "Le Chant des Marais," the first song her mother taught her. Jetske Spanjer and Ange Wieberdink, the makers of the documentary film *Ontsnapt*, showed me a video. Her deep full voice, like an intoning bell, repeats the moving refrain, "Piocher! Piocher!" (Dig! Dig!).

Hélène and Lon reunited
sixty-three years later, in 2008

Ontsnapt ends with a moving reunion of Lon and Hélène sixty-three years after their escape. Jetske and Ange explained to me that they asked Hélène if she had anything she would like to say to Lon on camera. But Hélène said she would prefer to speak to Lon in person. She would be willing to travel to meet her. Hélène took the train from Paris, and Lon traveled to The Hague, where it was arranged that the two old friends would meet. They reminisced together. Hélène remarked, "We were beautiful girls then."

Just before Nicole passed away, there was a reunion of some of the women and their families. Hélène wasn't able to attend that day. But Nicole was there, along with Guigui and her family, Zaza's family, and Lon. Jacky, Zinka, and Mena had passed away. The others had lost track of Josée, though she was still alive in Cannes. Afterward, Nicole wrote a short letter about the experience of their reunion:

> Today, as old ladies . . . in this reunion we felt so many emotions. And it confirmed why we were made for each other. Something very strong between us was present still. . . . The memory of those who disappeared a long time ago was with us, and we, despite ourselves, remained a group, a group of nine. . . . Once again, I am convinced of the strength of the ties uniting us and of our shared force. This afternoon remains a milestone, a new memory that is added, as the last stone of our special friendship, born in an elsewhere that belongs only to us nine. To all of you, *ce n'est qu'un au revoir.*

A NOTE TO READERS

> Every historian of the multitude, the dispossessed, the sub-
> altern, and the enslaved is forced to grapple with the power
> and authority of the archive and the limits it sets on what can
> be known, whose perspective matters, and who is endowed
> with the gravity and authority of historical actor.
>
> —*SAIDIYA HARTMAN*, WAYWARD LIVES,
> BEAUTIFUL EXPERIMENTS

The nine women in this book were real people. This is their shared
story, and it is a part of a greater story about what happened to women
in the Résistance in World War II in Europe. But much of their lives,
their choices, or why they made those choices is unknown, unknow-
able. And I am not a historian.

I was trained as a poet. My intention was to inhabit and imagine
the women's story, to press against the limitations of what could be
quantified, dated, marked on a map, quoted, and verified. At the
outset of the war, all nine began their radical work in the French Résistance without the right to vote. Their legal status was the same as
children's. On April 21, 1944, largely because of the contribution of
women in the Résistance, General de Gaulle declared that women in
France would have the right to vote. By then, seven of the nine were
already in prison or deported.

As I tried to uncover this story, I realized that when looking at
archives sometimes what was most important was precisely what had
been left out. This was doubly true when the person was a woman,

or poor, or living in the margins. My job as a writer was to explore around the edges of what the powerful deemed important to remember and record. I had to negotiate the tension between institutional historical memory and the personal lived story of these nine women.

Immediately after the war, the French public and most of the world did not focus on the Jewish genocide. They falsely imagined that the Jews had been liberated in the same numbers as the political deportees. They wanted to celebrate the male heroes of the Résistance, and perhaps some wanted to hide their shameful collaboration with the deportations of Jews. In France the subject of female *résistantes* and their subsequent deportation was taboo.

Following the Eichmann trials in 1961, interest in the real history of genocide grew around the world. The idea that the memories of survivors needed to be preserved and taught led to the creation of memorial museums, archives, film and video interviews, with the underlying goal to educate the public so that what had happened could never happen again.

Over the course of working on this story, my thinking about the need for concentration camp memorials and museums evolved. At first I felt a moral ambiguity about visiting sites of suffering and about an industry called "dark tourism."[1] In the age of mass tourism, when Auschwitz gets an estimated 1.5 million visitors a year, complicated questions arise about the management of the crowds and the commodification of the experience. How do you deal with people taking inappropriate selfies in sites of suffering and tragedy? What does it mean to have a gift shop at a concentration camp? Does dark tourism play a role in shaping the historical consciousness, or does it just serve our more prurient urge to gaze at horror? Does dark tourism give us a free pass, a moral license, as in "I went to Auschwitz, so I cannot possibly be a bad person and thus I do not have to examine my behavior"?

Complicating this is the fact that these sites have been used at various times as propaganda. The Auschwitz memorial camp was opened in 1947 by the Soviets with the clear intention of using it as a symbol. There was no mention of the 1.1 million Jewish deaths. In fact, Jews were not mentioned at the memorial site until after 1989. The site was called the International Monument to Victims of Fascism, and the

Soviets used it to tell the story of how "the capitalist Nazis martyred the comrades of the Revolution."

In the past, often after wars were won, nations would erect celebratory monuments. But now, with a new willingness to look at our violent past, we have these spaces that serve as memory holders. Remembering has become a moral imperative. And yet as I worked on this project I was confronted with the problems of memory. Traumatic memory is persistent, traveling through generations, and it is also fragile. Often the memories are garbled or even suppressed. If memory must save us, what do we do when memory, especially traumatic memory, is so problematic? And what do we do when all who can remember are dead?

The first time I went to Germany with Sophie, I had only a vague idea about where the women had been imprisoned and the route they had traveled in their escape. I wrongly thought they had been in Buchenwald because Leipzig was a subcamp of Buchenwald, not Ravensbrück. After visiting the museum for the Nazi Forced Labor Memorial at the HASAG Leipzig site, we went to Buchenwald. This would be the first concentration camp I visited.

It was a bitterly cold day in January. The wind whipped snow across a desolate landscape. As Sophie and I trudged from marker to marker, we were absolutely miserable with the cold, but we felt we had no right to complain, nor to cut short the torturous visit. It was good to suffer. I tried to remain focused on the sickening vastness of the operation. I didn't want to go numb. But I also held back my tears, because that felt like posturing. Then I could not stop them when I saw in the glass case some of the stuffed animals Lise London had made for her children. I thought of the stuffed teddy bear Mena had made for baby France that had been lost in the torrents of the Mulde River.

During our trip, Sophie and I talked about what a citizen must do during this moment in the world. I was the polite older generation counseling patience. But she would not have it. Perhaps it is fitting for her to push harder, to question more. Perhaps the survival of our planet depends on it. The nine young women in Hélène's group were moved by the same urgency. When they joined the Résistance, they, like Sophie, were in their twenties. It seems obvious today that they were on the right side of history, but at the time, when they were arrested by the Gestapo, they were charged as "terrorists," and that's how many French citizens saw them.

On my third trip to Germany I was better prepared. I told myself I only had to do one more camp visit. I had to see Ravensbrück if I wanted to fully understand the nine's story. I traveled this time with my sister Tilly. From the Fürstenberg train station, she and I walked the roughly three kilometers to the camp, the same route the nine would have walked, or run, hounded by SS guards and their dogs.

After we spent hours in the exhibition and walking the commemorative grounds, we entered the flattened open expanse that was once the camp. The outlines of blocks are shown with raised earth indicating the perimeters. Clutching my map, I tried to locate the *Appellplatz*, where so many hours were spent standing in the cold. I looked for the *Revier* infirmary block. We found block 24, where the French political prisoners were sent, and the area by the lake where tents were set up to house the overflowing population. It was silent except for the lapping sound of waves against the edges of the lake. I now understand that it is important that these places remain to bear witness, but a part of me longs for nature to reclaim the space. Perhaps this is the same tension and ambivalence we humans have between remembering and forgetting. How do we hold on to the past's truths without letting the past hold us back from living in the present?

A few days after visiting Ravensbrück, my sister and I rented a car and set out to retrace the steps of the women's escape. We found Kleinragewitz, where they were so warmly welcomed by the Yugoslav POWs. We found Reppen, the town of the Monocle and noodles with forks. At Raitzen, I looked for the police station, but it no longer existed; there was just a small fire station, obviously built in the Soviet era. A run-down, half-abandoned administrative building was where I imagined they got the paper they would wave in front of the German authorities. Outside Raitzen, Tilly and I tried to decide which farmhouse belonged to Annelise and Ernst. We found a farm at the end of a shady lane, a nice house with a large barn, white plaster with timber Tudor-style walls. It had a shaded central courtyard with a pump. I like to imagine that this is where Josée sang Schubert.

We found Delmschütz, where the giants lived, and the house that sits at the top of the hill. Jetske and Ange, the documentary filmmakers, met the giants' descendants, who still live there.

I found Obersteina and what must have been the children's home, now a ruin. When we got to Altenhof, where the boy soldiers played with *Panzerfaust*, I searched for the bridge and the woods. They were gone. But as we approached the Mulde, we drove through a deep forest for a moment. The car wound down a tiny road encircled by tall trees with dark branches twisting through the hilly landscape. We found the rebuilt bridge with three arches spanning the Mulde. I could imagine that the nine's confrontation with that river in flood on a cold spring day was indeed harrowing.

To tell their story, I tried to follow the trail of what is known about these nine women. Whenever possible I met their family members and friends. I searched out their personal accounts and the accounts of other women who were in the same prisons and camps. I visited archives and memorials and talked with historians. And then I had to head out into the shadows to commune with ghosts. Ralph Ellison wrote, "The act of writing requires a constant plunging back into the shadow of the past where time hovers ghostlike." I wanted to create a space where the nine women could exist.

ACKNOWLEDGMENTS

This book has taken at least five years to come into being, or even longer if I think of it starting with the first spark at the lunch with my great-aunt Hélène Podliasky Bénédite in 2002. I am forever grateful to her for entrusting me with the story that she had not told to anyone, or to only a very few. I have to also thank my aunt Eva Strauss, who encouraged me and went with me in 2002 to record the interview. Eva, the indomitable family archivist, along with her husband, Michel Paillard, made the transcription that later Hélène was able to edit and contribute to the archives at Université Paris Nanterre.

To find the story I had help from so many people.

I want to thank Suzanne Maudet's family, and especially Pierre Sauvanet and his wife, Anne-Florence, for championing Suzanne's book. They were gracious hosts when I contacted them and asked for an interview. I wish to thank as well Suzanne's editor at Arlea, Anne Bourguignon. Her passion for this story was clear when I contacted her and she responded quickly, setting me on the trail. That book along with the film *Ontsnapt* were critical in opening the story for me. Without them this book could not exist. I feel deeply grateful to Jetske Spanjer and Ange Wieberdink, two wonderfully talented and generous Dutch documentary filmmakers.

I could not have gotten far without the open generosity of so many family members of these nine women. Again and again I was humbled by their willingness to open their doors, their hearts, and their photo albums. Nicole's daughter gave me unpublished papers from her mother. She invited me for several meals at La Batelière in Paris and even took me with her companion to my first live auction at Drouot. She introduced me to Jacqueline Fleury, who was one of the 57,000 and is a survivor from Ravensbrück, a true honor for me.

Guigui's family was a great help. Her grandson Olivier Clémentin became an unofficial assistant with his crack genealogy-website skills. He helped me find Zinka's family and unsnarl the knot of double last names. Along with his mother, Laurence Spijker Clémentin, he gave me my first introduction to Guigui and led me to Mena's family. Guigui's grandchildren, Catherine, Pauline, Olivier, and Etienne Clémentin and Julie and Carine Spijker, generously shared with me their memories of her. I met and became close to Marc Spijker, Guigui's son. He knows how much he is part of this story and how grateful I am to him and to the paths this story led me down.

Mena's son-in-law, Jean-Louis Leplâtre, and her grandson Guillaume Leplâtre were marvelous storytellers. They both allowed me to interview them for hours on the phone. Guillaume shared moving stories that he had inherited from his mother. And Jean-Louis sent me an envelope of photographs without hesitation.

I am grateful for Gilles and Tom Châtenay, Zinka's son and grandson, for their visit here in the south of France, when we were able to share a memorable lunch together. One of the most emotionally powerful experiences for me during this entire project was meeting the lovely France Dubroeucq, the baby Zinka had in Fresnes prison. I am forever grateful to her and her husband, Didier, for that afternoon we spent talking together and for the document they found in their attic and shared with me—another invaluable key to the whole story.

I am grateful to Philippe Monsel, Jacky's friend. Without talking to him, I would not have known very much about her. And I want to thank Jacky's heir, Michel Lévy, for speaking so movingly about her and filling in the many gaps in her story.

The contributions of Martine Fourcaut, Hélène's daughter, were invaluable. She shared a wealth of information about that part of our family. Her humor and insight into her mother were essential to my understanding.

When Jetske and Ange arranged for Marc Spijker and me to meet with them in Amsterdam, I didn't know how important that day would be. Not only was it wonderful to finally meet the two people who had so inspired my search, but they also arranged a meeting with Lon's daughter and son-in-law, Patricia Elisabeth Frédérique Wensink and Wladimir Schreiber. Pat and Wladimir came to that meeting generously prepared with documents to share with me. Pat was candid and forthright about the difficulties of being the child of a survivor. I cannot thank them enough for spending that Sunday with me.

The archivist Anne Friebel, whom I met at the Leipzig Forced Labor Memorial, may not know how important her help was, but I am deeply grateful to her and to all the anonymous archivists whose dedication to preserving the truth is truly noble. Celeste Schenck, president of the American University of Paris, graciously invited me to consult their archives at the George and Irina Schaeffer Center for the Study of Genocide, Human Rights and Conflict Prevention, which houses the USC Shoah Foundation's Visual History Archive. There, with the help of the head archivist, Constance Pâris de Bollardière, I was able to consult hours of video interviews with Nicole Clarence, another crucial moment in this project.

Another vital step in my education about the Nazi concentration camp system came from the dedicated members of the Association française Buchenwald, Dora et Kommandos. I specially wish to thank my wonderful guides, Jean-Claude Gourdin and Christophe Rabineau, on the second trip I made to Germany. And I want to thank my companions on that voyage, most of them families of the deported. This community of memorial groups initially formed by survivors and now continued by families of the deported tirelessly carry on the work of keeping a vigilant watch over the memory and history. That history is under constant threat from neo-fascists, anti-Semites, and other Holocaust deniers. I want to also thank Dominique Durand, president of the International Committee for Buchenwald, Dora and Kommandos, and historical advisor Agnès Treibel, the general secretary. I want to thank Dominique for suggesting I work with Agnès, who read a rough draft of the manuscript and made copious, careful, and insightful notes and corrections, which were invaluable to me. She has been an important source for me and is ever generous with her time and knowledge.

Over two winters when I was on break from my regular job, I was given a place to write. I want to thank Paulina Nourissier for her apartment in Paris, where I wrote the first rough draft of this book, and the Vermont Studio Center for their generous fellowship a year later. The Callicoon Center Writers Retreat generously offered me a place, though I wasn't able to go, I want to thank Laurie Fendrich and Peter Plagens for their unflagging support.

I wish to thank my agent, Andy Ross, for his tireless help and encouragement. I thank and admire Judith Karfiol for her tenacity. And I am deeply grateful to all the team at St. Martin's Press, especially my editor, Elisabeth Dyssegaard, but also the many others involved in making this book: Alex Brown, Jennifer Fernandez, Michael Storrings, and Sue Warga.

With a project this long, you end up talking about it too much and too often with friends and family. I want to thank them for listening patiently and for encouraging me to continue. Ella Hickson was an incredible ally; without her, I might never have gotten this far. Early readers and steady supporters of my writing efforts include Martha Stark, Janet Nichols, and Karine Cariou. There are many fellow writers who have been with me through our years of writing. But four stand out as tireless comrades: Dorothy Spears, Maxine Swann, Caleb Peniman, and Sylvia Peck.

As this story is partly my family's story, I am deeply grateful to them for their endless support. My father, Julian Strauss, and stepmother, Betsy Strauss, are lovers of history and writers themselves. I wish to thank my siblings, Willy, Annie, Suzannah, and Tilly, for their lively curiosity and humor. Tilly, my first friend, my first companion in life, was with me at Ravensbrück on my last trip to Germany. Annie talked me through the math. My mother, Katie Nichols, is my number-one reader. Her talent at storytelling is why I am a writer. Emmanuelle Charlier was my research assistant; she found Guigui's family, which opened a whole story. George Bauer has been my companion, who never stopped believing in me. Finally, my three children have had to put up with a mother who is often too busy writing. I'm sorry, Noah and Eliza, that you too caught the disease. Sophie accompanied me on so many journeys of discovery for this book; her brilliant insights and her help running the recorder are an integral part of this story.

LIST OF ILLUSTRATIONS

NOTES

CHAPTER ONE: HÉLÈNE

1. Much of the information about Hélène comes from the recorded interview I conducted with her in 2002.

2. I consulted several archives online about Valentin Abeille. I knew that Hélène had received an important agent in her favorite field near Tours around this time—someone who came with a suitcase of money, she said. Records show that Fantassin reentered France via a site near Tours, and Hélène was cited in her military records for having received and aided Fantassin. See "Valentin Abeille, un exemple pour les jeunes générations," *La Dépêche du Midi*, February 27, 1999, https://www.ladepeche.fr/article/1999/02/27/208084-valentin-abeille -un-exemple-pour-les-jeunes-generations.html.

3. Suzanne Maudet, *Neuf filles jeunes qui ne voulaient pas mourir* (Paris: Arléa, 2004). I am deeply indebted to Zaza's description of the nine women and to her book—it was this more detailed account of their escape that allowed me to begin my search. Many of the details of their escape come from her book, which I highly recommend to readers of French.

4. Nicole Clarence, "Le journal de Nicole vingt ans après," *Elle* no. 962, May 29, 1964; Nicole Clarence, memorial website created by her daughter and friends, http://nicoleclarence.com/-Francais-Home.

5. Jetske Spanjer and Ange Wieberdink, *Ontsnapt* (Escape), documentary film, Wieberdink Productions and Armadillo Film, 2010.

6. From my interview with Hélène's daughter Martine Fourcaut on February 3, 2018.

7. For the purpose of this book I will call her Hélène, though she was known by the others as Christine. And in the Nazi records she is listed only as Christine.

8. Alan Bessmann and Insa Eschebach, eds., *The Ravensbrück Women's Concentration Camp: History and Memory*, exhibition catalogue (Berlin: Metropol, 2013).

9. Sarah Helm, *Ravensbrück: Life and Death in Hitler's Concentration Camp for Women* (New York: Nan A. Talese/Doubleday, 2015), 651.

10. Germaine Tillion, *Ravensbrück* (Paris: Éditions du Seuil, 1988), 492.

11. Helm, *Ravensbrück*, 279.

12. Lise London, *La mégère de la rue Daguerre* (Paris: Seuil-Mémoire, 1995), 315.

13. From the transcript of Hélène's interview with me.

14. Madelon L. Verstijnen, *Mijn Oorlogskroniek* (Voorburg: Verstijnen, 1991), 10 (Lon's translation).

15. Margaret Collins-Weitz, *Sisters in the Resistance: How Women Fought to Free France 1940–1945* (New York: John Wiley & Sons, 1995), 92–93.

16. Hélène described this incident to me.

CHAPTER TWO: ZAZA

1. Madelon L. Verstijnen, *Mijn Oorlogskroniek* (Voorburg: Verstijnen, 1991), 30 (Lon's translation).

2. Sarah Helm, *Ravensbrück: Life and Death in Hitler's Concentration Camp for Women* (New York: Nan A. Talese/Doubleday, 2015), 284.

3. Helm, *Ravensbrück*, 11.

4. The Nazi concentration camp system was guided by the principles the Nazi Party stood for. As summarized by the historian Nikolaus Wachsmann, these were "the creation of a uniform national community by removing any racial, political, or social outsiders; the sacrifice of the individual to achieve racial purity; the use of slave labor to build the fatherland; mastery of Europe and enslaving foreign nations so the Aryans could colonize the living spaces; and mass extermination of unwanted races and peoples, especially the Jews." Nikolaus Wachsmann, *KL: A History of the Nazi Concentration Camp System* (London: Little, Brown, 2015), 6.

5. Germaine Tillion, *Ravensbrück* (Paris: Éditions du Seuil, 1988), 214ff. In August 1944 Tillion calculated that there were 58,000 women registered at Ravensbrück, of whom 18,000 were dying. Calculating with 40,000 workers being rented out at 2.5 marks a day net (she deducted 1.5 as the cost of food, etc.), she estimated a profit of 100,000 marks a day, or 35 million marks annually.

6. Helm, *Ravensbrück*, 285.

7. Alan Bessmann and Insa Eschebach, eds., *The Ravensbrück Women's Concentration Camp: History and Memory*, exhibition catalogue (Berlin: Metropol, 2013), 190.

8. Helm, *Ravensbrück*, 378.

9. Lise London, *La mégère de la rue Daguerre* (Paris: Seuil-Mémoire, 1995), 327–328.

10. Sangnier was a remarkable man. He was a French Roman Catholic thinker and politician who in 1894 founded a socialist Catholic movement. He also founded a newspaper, *La Démocratie*, which campaigned for equality for women and for proportional representation at elections.

11. Juliette Bes, *Une jeune fille qui a dit: non* (Perpignan: Cap Bear Éditions, 2011), 10.

12. From the website of the Leipzig Nazi Forced Labour Memorial, Gedenkstätte für Zwangsarbeit Leipzig, https://www.zwangsarbeit-in -leipzig.de/en/nazi-forced-labour-in-leipzig/ns-forced-labour-in-leipzig.

13. Wolfgang Plaul was the commandant of HASAG Leipzig Schönefeld, and Paul Budin was his superior, being the general manager. Plaul disappeared at the end of the war and was never found, nor tried for his war crimes. It is assumed that Budin committed suicide with his wife in April 1945, when he blew up the company's head office building in Leipzig. No HASAG personnel were put on trial at the International Military Tribunal in Nuremberg.

14. London, *La mégère*, 330.

15. Felicja Karay, *HASAG-Leipzig Slave Labour Camp: The Struggle for Survival Told by the Women and Their Poetry*, trans. Sara Kitai (Portland, OR: Vallentine Mitchell, 2002), 156.

16. Karay, *HASAG-Leipzig*, 157.

17. Karay, *HASAG-Leipzig*, 93.

18. Guillaume Leplâtre, email to author, December 10, 2018.

19. The description of how Hélène sabotaged the furnaces and her friendship with Fritz Stupitz came from my interview with her.

20. Verstijnen, *Mijn Oorlogskroniek*, 28.

21. Guillaume Leplâtre, email to author.

22. London, *La mégère*, 359–362.

23. Daniel Blatman, *The Nazi Death Marches, 1944–1945*, Online Encyclopedia of Mass Violence, August 28, 2015, accessed April 27, 2020, http://bo-k2s.sciences-po.fr/mass-violence-war-massacre-resistance/en/document/nazi-death-marches-1944-1945, ISSN 1961-9898.

24. Amicales et associations des camps, *Les évasions des marches de la mort, janvier–février et avril–mai 1945*, Conférence débats, Hôtel de ville de Paris, January 12, 2012, 14.

25. Jorge Semprun, *Exercices de survie* (Paris: Éditions Gallimard, 2012), 118.

26. From Zaza's unpublished journal, given to me by Zinka's daughter, France.

27. Suzanne Maudet, *Neuf filles jeunes qui ne voulaient pas mourir* (Paris: Arléa, 2004), 26.

28. Maudet, *Neuf filles*, 21.

29. Nicole Clarence, interviewed by Raphaël Enthoven, *À voix nue*, France-Culture, 2005 (author's translation).

30. Verstijnen, *Mijn Oorlogskroniek*, 60.

CHAPTER THREE: NICOLE

1. Felicja Karay, *HASAG-Leipzig Slave Labour Camp: The Struggle for Survival Told by the Women and Their Poetry*, trans. Sara Kitai (Portland, OR: Vallentine Mitchell, 2002), 220.

2. Suzanne Maudet, *Neuf filles jeunes qui ne voulaient pas mourir* (Paris: Arléa, 2004), 33.

3. Nicole Clarence, Visual History Archive, USC Shoah Foundation, 1999, interviewed by Hélène Lévy-Wand Polak on February 16, 1996, accessed at the American University in Paris on April 15, 2019.

4. Nicole Clarence, from her private, unpublished writing, shared with me by her daughter.

5. I am deeply indebted to Nicole's daughter for showing me her mother's unpublished writing about her childhood and her time in the Résistance. The following section is largely based on those documents written by Nicole, as well as her video interview at the George and Irina Schaeffer Center for the Study of Genocide, Human Rights and Conflict Prevention, USC Shoah Foundation's Visual History Archive, American University of Paris, France, and the memorial website her daughter created after Nicole's death, http://nicoleclarence.com/Francais-Home, last accessed January 2020.

6. After the war, Marie-Madeleine Fourcade took on the duty of ensuring that the 431 agents who died under her command were not forgotten. She spent years caring for the survivors and their families. She published a memoir titled *L'arche de Noé, réseau Alliance 1940–1945* (Paris: Plon, 1989).

7. The Sicherheitsdienst's first director was Reinhard Heydrich, the man whose assassination would lead to the experimentation on the women in Ravensbrück, the *lapins*. Sarah Helm, *Ravensbrück: Life and Death in Hitler's Concentration Camp for Women* (New York: Nan A. Talese/Doubleday, 2015), 210.

8. Denise was working in the Résistance while her parents and younger sisters were living in Nice. They were rounded up and her parents were murdered in Auschwitz. Her sisters, also rounded up, would survive. Denise was later captured, tortured by the Gestapo, and imprisoned in Ravensbrück and Mauthausen.

9. From private papers written by Nicole, shared with the author by her daughter.

10. Helm, *Ravensbrück*, 403.

11. Clarence, Visual History Archive.

12. Maudet, *Neuf filles*, 56.

CHAPTER FOUR: LON AND GUIGUI

1. From Zaza's unpublished journal.

2. Nicole Clarence, from her unpublished journal, "Le journal de Nicole version complète," given to me by Marc Spijker, 7 (author's translation).

3. Madelon L. Verstijnen, *Mijn Oorlogskroniek* (Voorburg: Verstijnen, 1991), 65 (Lon's translation).

4. Verstijnen, *Mijn Oorlogskroniek*, 66.

5. Some of the information about Joanna Szumańska comes from Lon's book, but also from Felicja Karay, *HASAG-Leipzig Slave Labour Camp: The Struggle for Survival Told by the Women and Their Poetry*, trans. Sara Kitai (Portland, OR: Vallentine Mitchell, 2002), 50–51, 112–113.

6. Verstijnen, *Mijn Oorlogskroniek*, 66–68.

7. Amicale de Ravensbrück, *Les françaises à Ravensbrück* (Paris: Éditions Gallimard, 1965), 158.

8. Sarah Helm, *Ravensbrück: Life and Death in Hitler's Concentration Camp for Women* (New York: Nan A. Talese/Doubleday, 2015), 90.

9. Juliette Bes, *Une jeune fille qui a dit: non* (Perpignan: Cap Bear Éditions, 2011), 14.

10. Amicale de Ravensbrück, *Les françaises à Ravensbrück*, 217.

11. Amicale de Ravensbrück, *Les françaises à Ravensbrück*, 185.

12. Margarete Buber-Neumann, *Milena*, trans. Ralph Manheim (London: Collins Harvill, 1989), 3.

13. Verstijnen, *Mijn Oorlogskroniek*, 96.

14. Verstijnen, *Mijn Oorlogskroniek*, 54.

15. I am indebted to Guigui's family for detailed information about her character and childhood. I had conversations with Olivier Clémentin and his mother, Laurence Spijker Clémentin, on November 18, 2018, and further email exchanges and letters. I also had many conversations and emails with Marc Spijker, and correspondence with Guigui's grandchildren.

16. Bes, *Une jeune fille*, 13.

17. Helm, *Ravensbrück*, 367.

18. Verstijnen, *Mijn Oorlogskroniek*, 20.

19. Verstijnen, *Mijn Oorlogskroniek*, 24.

20. Verstijnen, *Mijn Oorlogskroniek*, 24.

21. Bes, *Une jeune fille*, 61.

CHAPTER FIVE: ZINKA

1. Lise London, *La mégère de la rue Daguerre* (Paris: Seuil-Mémoire, 1995), 361. London talks about "Zimka" making a cigarette case for her husband using a strip from her mattress.

2. Madelon L. Verstijnen, *Mijn Oorlogskroniek* (Voorburg: Verstijnen, 1991), 79 (Lon's translation).

3. Verstijnen, *Mijn Oorlogskroniek*, 78.

4. Verstijnen, *Mijn Oorlogskroniek*, 80.

5. Most of my information about Odette Pilpoul comes from the Archives Nationales, Pierrefitte-sur-Seine, dossier 72AJ/2172.

6. London, *La mégère*, 159.

7. London, *La mégère*, 293.

8. London, *La mégère*, 307.

9. London, *La mégère*, 308.

10. Musée de le Résistance et de la deportation du Cher, Archives départementales du Cher, témoignages audiovisuels portant sur la Seconde Guerre mondiale, Cote: 8NUM, Guette, Renée, 8NUM/53, 2004, 2 CDs.

11. Verstijnen, *Mijn Oorlogskroniek*, 95.

12. This story was told to me by Gilles Châtenay during an interview, July 21, 2019.

13. I have imagined this scene. With the dates, I think there is a good chance that Zinka was on this transport that was bombed near Château-Thierry, but I can't be certain.

14. Sarah Helm, *Ravensbrück: Life and Death in Hitler's Concentration Camp for Women* (New York: Nan A. Talese/Doubleday, 2015), 210–235.

CHAPTER SIX: JOSÉE

1. Information about this event comes from several sources but mostly the website https://www.zwangsarbeit-in-leipzig.de/en/nazi-forced -labour-in-leipzig.

2. Suzanne Maudet, *Neuf filles jeunes qui ne voulaient pas mourir* (Paris: Arléa, 2004), 77.

3. Maudet, *Neuf filles*, 78.

4. Amis de la Fondation pour la Mémoire de la Déportation de l'Allier, web page about Joséphine Bordanava, http://www.afmd-allier.com /PBCPPlayer.asp?ID=1532755.

5. Most of the information about Moussa Abadi and Odette Rosenstock comes from Fred Coleman, *The Marcel Network* (Dulles, VA: Potomac Books, 2013).

6. Coleman, *The Marcel Network*, 11.

7. Coleman, *The Marcel Network*, 12.

8. The Forts' work with the Marcel network was honored after the war when they received the designation "Righteous Among Nations" from the State of Israel at the Yad Vashem memorial in Jerusalem.

9. Amis de la Fondation pour la Mémoire de la Déportation de l'Allier, web page about Joséphine Bordanava.

10. 425 rue de Paradis was the infamous site used by the terrible Ernst Dunker, a low-level thug who rose to prominence in the Gestapo for his efficient use of brutal torture to decimate the Résistance in Marseille. He took part in the arrest of Jean Moulin and the execution or deportation of hundreds of Resistance fighters. Known as the "Black Legend of Marseilles," he was condemned to death and executed in 1950.

CHAPTER SEVEN: JACKY

1. Information about recipe books comes from Anne Georget, a journalist and documentary filmmaker. Her film *Festins*

imaginaires (Planète+, 2015) covers the subject of recipe books made in all kinds of prison camps and extreme conditions. She also wrote a book with Elsie Herberstein, *Les carnets de Minna* (Paris: Seuil, 2008).

2. Suzanne Maudet, *Neuf filles jeunes qui ne voulaient pas mourir* (Paris: Arléa, 2004), 91.

CHAPTER EIGHT: MENA

1. Jean-Pierre Leplâtre, phone interview on December 8, 2018.

2. Guillaume Leplâtre, email to author, December 11, 2018.

3. Albert Starink, "Mémoires pour ses enfants Casper, Dorin et Reiner," written in Dutch in April 1995 and sent to Guigui in June 1995, translated into French in October 2019 by Marc Spijker.

4. Marceline Loridan-Ivens, *Et tu n'es pas revenue* (Paris: Éditions Grasset, 2015), 63.

5. Lise London, *La mégère de la rue Daguerre* (Paris: Seuil-Mémoire, 1995), 349.

6. London, *La mégère*, 350.

7. Amicale de Ravensbrück, *Les françaises à Ravensbrück* (Paris: Éditions Gallimard, 1965), 203.

8. Sarah Helm, *Ravensbrück: Life and Death in Hitler's Concentration Camp for Women* (New York: Nan A. Talese/Doubleday, 2015), 418.

9. Helm, *Ravensbrück*, 420. This was reported to Sarah Helm by Marie-Jo Chombart de Lauwe in an interview. In Valentine Goby's, *Kinderzimmer* (Arles: Actes Sud, 2015), she confirms that of the thirty-one babies who survived until liberation, three were French: Sylvie Aymler (born March 1945), Jean-Claude Passerat (born November 1944), and Guy Poirot (born March 1945).

10. "Children at the Bergen-Belsen Concentration Camp," traveling exhibition with the Bergen-Belsen Memorial, Diana Gring, curator. Seen at the Ravensbrück Memorial in February 2019, http://kinder-in -bergen-belsen.de/en/home#stations.

CHAPTER TEN: RETURN TO LIFE

1. William W. Quinn, *Dachau* (San Francisco: Normandy Press, 2015).

2. Suzanne Maudet, *Neuf filles jeunes qui ne voulaient pas mourir* (Paris: Arléa, 2004), 136.

3. The exact numbers vary widely—some accounts say as many as 30,000 were saved, but 15,000 is the Swedish Red Cross's own estimate from a report published in 2000, https://www.redcross.se/contentassets/4b0c5a08761c417498ddb988be6dd262/the-white-buses.pdf.

4. Sarah Helm, *Ravensbrück: Life and Death in Hitler's Concentration Camp for Women* (New York: Nan A. Talese/Doubleday, 2015), 594.

5. Helm, *Ravensbrück*, 622.

6. Helm, *Ravensbrück*, 625.

7. Helm, *Ravensbrück*, 611.

8. Anonymous, *A Woman in Berlin: Diary 20 April 1945 to 22 June 1945*, trans. Philip Boehm (London: Virago, 2006). The memoir was originally published anonymously, but after her death, it was revealed that the author was Marta Hillers. She had been cooperating with the Nazis and this may have been the reason she chose to remain anonymous.

9. Joe Weston, "The GIs in Le Havre," *Life*, December 10, 1945.

10. Mary Louise Roberts, *What Soldiers Do* (Chicago: University of Chicago Press, 2013), 210.

11. Marceline Loridan-Ivens, *Et tu n'es pas revenue* (Paris: Éditions Grasset, 2015), 35.

12. Anonymous, *A Woman in Berlin*, 176.

13. Most of the information about these few weeks after they found the US soldiers comes from Suzanne Maudet's unpublished journal, shared with me by France Dubroeucq.

14. Amicale de Ravensbrück, *Les françaises à Ravensbrück*, 285.

CHAPTER ELEVEN: FINDING THE WAY HOME

1. Amis de la Fondation pour la Mémoire de la Déportation (AFMD), *Lutetia, 1945, Le retour des déportés*, exhibition catalogue, 2015, 17.

2. AFMD, *Lutetia, 1945, Le retour des déportés*, 17.

3. AFMD, *Lutetia, 1945, Le retour des déportés*, 19.

4. Nicole Clarence, Visual History Archive, USC Shoah Foundation, 1999, interviewed by Hélène Lévy-Wand Polak on February 16, 1996, accessed at the American University in Paris, April 15, 2019.

5. Albert Starink, "Mémoires pour ses enfants Casper, Dorin et Reiner," written in Dutch in April 1995 and sent to Guigui in June 1995, translated into French in October 2019 by Marc Spijker.

6. From interview with Guigui's daughter, Laurence Spijker Clémentin, on November 18, 2018, in Paris.

7. From phone interview with Mena's son-in-law, Jean-Louis Leplâtre, on December 7, 2018.

8. From phone interview with Mena's grandson, Guillaume Leplâtre, on December 19, 2018.

9. AFMD, *Lutetia, 1945, Le retour des déportés*, 47.

10. From interview with Laurence Spijker Clémentin, November 18, 2018, in Paris.

CHAPTER TWELVE: IT'S ONLY A GOODBYE

1. Suzanne Maudet, *Neuf filles jeunes qui ne voulaient pas mourir* (Paris: Arléa, 2004), 10.

2. From interview with Zaza's nephew, Pierre Sauvanet, with Sophie Strauss Jenkins and Anne-Florence Sauvanet, on November 10, 2018, in La Rochelle.

3. M. Gerard Fromm, ed., *Lost in Transmission: Studies of Trauma Across Generations* (London: Karnac, 2012), xvi.

4. Ilany Kogan, "The Second Generation in the Shadow of Terror," in *Lost in Transmission: Studies of Trauma Across Generations*, ed. M. Gerard Fromm (London: Karnac, 2012), 7.

5. From interview with Martine Fourcaut, on February 3, 2018, in Paris.

6. Dori Laub, "Traumatic Shutdown of Narrative and Symbolization: A Death Instinct Derivative?," in *Lost in Transmission: Studies of Trauma Across Generations*, ed. M. Gerard Fromm (London: Karnac, 2012), 37.

7. Howard F. Stein, "A Mosaic of Transmissions After Trauma," in *Lost in Transmission: Studies of Trauma Across Generations*, ed. M. Gerard Fromm (London: Karnac, 2012), 175.

8. Most of the description of this journey home comes from the documentary *Ontsnapt*, the filmed interview of Lon, and Lon's book.

9. From interview with Lon's daughter, Patricia Elisabeth Frédérique Wensink, and Wladimir Schreiber, Lon's son-in-law, February 23, 2020. They shared with me private documents and photos, and we had further email exchanges.

10. "The Mauthausen Concentration Camp 1938–1945," Mauthausen Memorial, https://www.mauthausen-memorial.org/en/History/The -Mauthausen-Concentration-Camp-19381945.

11. Anne Sebba, *Les Parisiennes: Résistance, Collaboration, and the Women of Paris Under Nazi Occupation* (New York: St. Martin's Press, 2016), 387.

12. Adrienne Rich, *On Lies, Secrets and Silence: Selected Prose 1966–78* (New York: W. W. Norton, 1985), 199; first published in an essay, "It Is the Lesbian in Us" in *Sinister Wisdom* 3, Spring 1977.

13. From Jacky's military records, Service historique de la Défense, Centre historique des archives, Vincennes, dossier GR 16 P 471442.

14. From phone interview with Jacky's heir, Michel Lévy, on May 6, 2020.

15. From phone interview with Jacky's friend Philippe Monsel, on December 6, 2018.

16. Gilles Châtenay, "La Psychanalyse, étrange et singulière," paper presented at the conference "Comment on devient analyste au XXIe siècle," Journées de l'École de la Cause freudienne, November 2009.

17. Madelon L. Verstijnen, *Mijn Oorlogskroniek* (Voorburg: Verstijnen, 1991), 95 (Lon's translation).

18. From conversation with Gilles and Tom Châtenay on August 28, 2019, in Ménerbes.

19. From conversation with Zinka's daughter, France Lebon Châtenay Dubroeucq, with her husband, Didier Dubroeucq, and Sophie Strauss Jenkins on March 3, 2019, in Die.

20. From interview with Martine Fourcaut, Hélène's daughter, on February 3, 2019, in Paris.

A NOTE TO READERS

1. The term "dark tourism" was coined in 1996 by J. John Lennon and Malcolm Foley, two faculty members of the Department of Hospitality, Tourism, and Leisure Management at Glasgow Caledonian University. Dark tourism involves travel to places historically associated with death, suffering, and tragedy.

BIBLIOGRAPHY

BOOKS, ARTICLES, NEWSLETTERS, AND WEBSITES

Alexievich, Svetlana. *Last Witnesses: An Oral History of the Children of World War II*. Richard Pevear and Larissa Volokhonsky, translators. New York: Penguin Random House, 2019.

Alexievich, Svetlana. *The Unwomanly Face of War: An Oral History of Women in World War II*. Richard Pevear and Larissa Volokhonsky, translators. New York: Random House, 2017.

Amicale de Ravensbrück et Association des déportées et internés de la Résistance. *Les françaises à Ravensbrück*. Paris: Éditions Gallimard, 1965.

Amicales et associations des camps d'Auschwitz (UDA et Cercle d'étude de la déportation et de la Shoah), Bergen-Belsen, Buchenwald-Dora, Dachau, Langenstein, Mauthausen, Neuengamme, Ravensbrück, Sachsenhausen. *Les évasions des marches de la mort janvier–février et avril–mai 1945*. Conférence débats, Hôtel de ville de Paris, January 12, 2012.

Amis de la Fondation pour la Mémoire de la Déportation. *Lutetia, 1945, le retour des déportés*. Catalogue for the exhibition on the seventieth anniversary of the liberation of the camps, 2015.

Amis de la Fondation pour la Mémoire de la Déportation de l'Allier. "Bordonava, Joséphine, parfois orthographié Bordanava." http://www.afmd-allier.com/PBCPPlayer.asp?ID=1532755.

Anonymous. *A Woman in Berlin, Diary 20 April 1945 to 22 June 1945*. Philip Boehm, translator. London: Virago Press, 2006. (First published 1954.)

Assouline, Pierre. *Lutetia*. Paris: Éditions Gallimard, 2005.

Berr, Hélène. *Journal 1942–1944*. Paris: Éditions Tallandier, 2008.

Bes, Juliette. *Une jeune fille qui a dit: non*. Perpignan: Cap Bear Éditions, 2011.

Bessmann, Alan, and Insa Eschebach, editors. *The Ravensbrück Women's Concentration Camp, History and Memory*. Exhibition catalogue. Berlin: Metropol, 2013.

Boivin, Yves. *Les condamnées des Sections spéciales incarcérées à la Maison centrale de Rennes, déportées les 5 avril, 2 mai et 16 mai 1944*. Monograph, January 2004, http://www.cndp.fr/crdp-rennes/crdp/crdp _dossiers/dossiers/condamneesRennes/comdamnes.pdf.

Bouju, Marie-Cecile. *Notice FELD Charles, Léon, Salomon*. Version posted online March 8, 2009, http://maitron-en-ligne.univ-paris1 .fr/spip.php?article24892, last updated April 30, 2015.

Buber-Neumann, Margarete. *Milena*. Ralph Manheim, translator. London: Collins Karvill, 1989.

Castelloe, Molly S. "How Trauma Is Carried Across Generations." *Psychology Today*, May 2012, https://www.psychologytoday.com /us/blog/the-me-in-we/201205/how-trauma-is-carried-across -generations.

Châtenay, Gilles. "La Psychanalyse, étrange et singulière." Paper presented at the conference "Comment on devient analyste au XXIe siècle," Journées de l'École de la Cause freudienne, November 2009.

Chevrillon, Claire. *Une Résistance ordinaire*. Paris: Éditions du Félin, 1999.

Clarence, Nicole. Interview 9722, Visual History Archive, USC Shoah Foundation, 1999, accessed at the George and Irina Schaeffer Center for the Study of Genocide, Human Rights and Conflict Prevention, at the American University of Paris, France, on August 26, 2019.

Clarence, Nicole. "Le journal de Nicole vingt ans après." *Elle*, no. 962, May 29, 1964.

Clarence, Nicole. Memorial website created by her daughter and friends, accessed January 2020, currently unavailable as of September 2020, http://nicoleclarence.com/-Francais-Home.

Cognet, Christophe. *Eclats: Prises de vue clandestines des camps nazis.* Paris: Éditions du Seuil, 2019.

Coleman, Fred. *The Marcel Network: How One French Couple Saved 527 Children from the Holocaust.* Dulles, VA: Potomac Books, 2013.

Collection Résistance Liberté-Mémoire. *Femmes dans la guerre, 1940–1945.* Paris: Éditions du Félin, 2003.

Delbo, Charlotte. *Aucun de nous ne reviendra.* Paris: Les Éditions de Minuit, 1970.

Delbo, Charlotte. *Le convoi du 24 janvier.* Paris: Les Éditions de Minuit, 1965.

Desnos, Robert. *Destinée arbitraire.* Paris: Éditions Gallimard, 1975.

Durand, Pierre. *La chienne de Buchenwald.* Paris: Messidor/Temps Actuels, 1982.

Eger, Edith Eva. *The Choice.* New York: Scribner, 2017.

Fallada, Hans. *Every Man Dies Alone.* Brooklyn, NY: Melville House, 2009.

Femmes résistantes. Sénat de France. Taped interviews of survivors. Jacqueline Fleury is one of the *résistantes* interviewed at length. http://www.senat.fr/evenement/colloque/femmes_resistantes/webdoc/fleury.html.

Fleury, Jacqueline. "Témoinage de Jacqueline Fleury, née Marié." http://lesamitiesdelaresistance.fr/lien17-fleury.pdf.

Fleury-Marié, Jacqueline. *Une famille du refus mais toujours l'espérance, recueils et récits 1914–1918 et 1939–1945.* Versailles: Jacqueline Fleury-Marié, 2013.

Fromm, M. Gerard, editor. *Lost in Transmission: Studies of Trauma Across Generations*. London: Karnac, 2012.

de Gaulle-Anthonioz, Geneviève. *La traversée de la nuit*. Paris: Seuil, 1998.

de Gaulle-Anthonioz, Geneviève, and Germaine Tillion. *Dialogues*. Paris: Éditions Plon, 2015.

Gildea, Robert. *Fighters in the Shadows*. London: Faber and Faber, 2015.

Hannah, Kristin. *The Nightingale*. New York: St. Martin's Griffin, 2015.

Helm, Sarah. *Ravensbrück: Life and Death in Hitler's Concentration Camp for Women*. New York: Nan A. Talese/Doubleday, 2015.

Herberstein, Elsie, and Anne Georget. *Les carnets de Minna*. Paris: Seuil, 2008.

Humbert, Agnès. *Notre guerre, journal de Résistance 1940–1945*. Paris: Éditions Tallandier, 2004.

Hunter, Georgia. *We Were the Lucky Ones*. New York: Penguin Books, 2017.

Karay, Felicja. *HASAG-Leipzig Slave Labour Camp for Women: The Struggle for Survival Told by the Women and Their Poetry*. Sara Kitai, translator. Portland, OR: Vallentine Mitchell, 2002.

Koreman, Megan. *The Escape Line: How the Ordinary Heroes of Dutch Paris Resisted the Nazi Occupation of Western Europe*. New York: Oxford University Press, 2018.

Lasnet de Lanty, Henriette. *Sous la schlague*. Paris: Éditions du Félin, 2018.

Levi, Primo. *The Drowned and the Saved*. New York: Vintage International, 1989.

Levi, Primo. *Si c'est un homme*. Paris: Julliard, 1987.

London, Lise. *La mégère de la rue Daguerre*. Paris: Éditions du Seuil, 1995.

Loridan-Ivens, Marceline. *Et tu n'es pas revenu.* Paris: Éditions Grasset, 2015.

Mason, Bobbie Ann. *The Girl in the Blue Beret.* New York: Random House, 2012.

Maudet, Suzanne. *Neuf filles jeunes qui ne voulaient pas mourir.* Paris: Arléa, 2004.

Mémoires de la guerre. "Noël 1943, ils étaient huit enfants enfermés avec leurs mamans, courageuses patriotes, dans la sombre Centrale de Rennes." http://memoiredeguerre.free.fr/biogr/fournier /fournier-lalet.htm#deb.

Mendelsohn, Daniel. *The Lost: A Search for Six of Six Million.* New York: HarperPerennial, 2007.

Moorehead, Caroline. *A House in the Mountains: The Women Who Liberated Italy from Fascism.* New York: Penguin Random House, 2019.

Moorehead, Caroline. *A Train in Winter: An Extraordinary Story of Women, Friendship, and Resistance in Occupied France.* New York: HarperPerennial, 2012.

Morris, Heather. *The Tattooist of Auschwitz.* London: Zaffre, 2018.

Olsen, Lynne. *Madame Fourcade's Secret War: The Daring Young Woman Who Led France's Largest Spy Network.* New York: Penguin Random House, 2019.

Núñez Targa, Mercedes. *El valor de la memoria, de la cárcel de Ventas al campo de Ravensbrück.* Seville: Renacimiento, 2016.

Pagniez, Yvonne. *Évasion 44, suivi de souvenirs inédits de la Grande Guerre.* Paris: Éditions du Félin, 2010.

Pavillard, Anne-Marie. "ADIR: S'entraider et témoigner." *Varia, matériaux pour l'histoire de notre temps,* no. 127–128, 2018.

Quinn, William W. *Dachau.* San Francisco: Normandy Press, 2015.

Rayon de Soleil de Cannes. Website. http://www.rayondesoleilcannes .com.

Rich, Adrienne. *On Lies, Secrets and Silence: Selected Prose 1966–78*. New York: W. W. Norton, 1985.

Roberts, Mary Louise. *What Soldiers Do*. Chicago: University of Chicago Press, 2013.

Sands, Philippe. *East West Street: On the Origins of "Genocide" and "Crimes Against Humanity."* New York: Vintage, 2017.

Sebald, W. G. *Austerlitz*. New York: Modern Library, 2011.

Sebba, Anne. *Les Parisiennes: Résistance, Collaboration, and the Women of Paris Under Nazi Occupation*. New York: St. Martin's Press, 2016.

Semprun, Jorge. *Exercices de survie*. Paris: Éditions Gallimard, 2012.

de Silva, Cara, editor. *In Memory's Kitchen: A Legacy from the Women of Terezin*. Bianca Steiner Brown, translator. Lanham, MD: Rowman and Littlefield, 2006.

Sodaro, Amy. *Exhibiting Atrocity: Memorial Museums and the Politics of Past Violence*. New Brunswick, NJ: Rutgers University Press, 2018.

Thalmann, Rita. "L'oubli des femmes dans l'historiographie de la Résistance." *Clio: Femmes, Genre, Histoire*, January 1995, http://journals.openedition.org/clio/513;DOI:10.4000/clio.513.

Tillion, Germaine. *Ravensbrück*. Paris: Éditions du Seuil, 1988.

Tillon, Raymonde. *J'écris ton nom, Liberté*. Paris: Éditions du Félin, 2002.

Verstijnen, Madelon L. *Mijn Oorlogskroniek*. Voorburg: Verstijnen, 1991.

Virgili, Fabrice. "Les 'tondues' à la Libération: Le corps des femmes, enjeu d'une réaproppriation." *Clio: Femmes, Genre, Histoire*, January 1995, http://journals.openedition.org/clio/518;DOI:10.4000/clio.518.

Wachsmann, Nikolaus. *KL: A History of the Nazi Concentration Camps*. London: Little, Brown, 2015.

Weitz, Margaret Collins. *Sisters in the Résistance: How Women Fought to Free France 1940–1945*. New York: John Wiley & Sons, 1995.

Weston, Joe. "The GIs in Le Havre." *Life*, December 10, 1945.

FILMS AND DOCUMENTARIES

Basty, Françoise. *Résistant mort en déportation*. Françoise Basty, 2015.

Bosche, Rose. *La rafle*. Legend, 2010.

Georget, Anne. *Festins imaginaires*. October Productions, 2014.

Lanzmann, Claude. *Shoah*. Aleph/Historia Films, 1985.

Loridan-Ivens, Marceline. *La petite prairie aux bouleaux*. Studio Canal, 2004.

Resnais, Alain. *Nuit et brouillard*. Nouveaux Pictures, 1955.

Spanjer, Jetske, and Ange Wieberdink. *Ontsnapt*. Wieberdink Productions and Armadillo Film, 2010.

Wechsler, Maia. *Résistance Women*. Women Make Movies Release, 2000.

INTERVIEWS

Hélène Bénédite, with Eva Paillard, on July 8, 2002, in Paris.

Hélène's daughter, Martine Fourcaut, on February 3, 2019, in Paris.

Zaza's nephew, Pierre Sauvanet, with Sophie Strauss Jenkins and Anne-Florence Sauvanet, on November 10, 2018, in La Rochelle, and further email exchanges and letters.

Guigui's grandson, Olivier Clémentin, and his mother (Guigui's daughter), Laurence Spijker Clémentin, on November 18, 2018, and further email exchanges and letters.

Guigui's son, Marc Spijker, email and conversations beginning in September 2019. Marc shared Lon's own English translation of her book with me, as well as other Dutch texts he had translated about the Dutch-French resistance networks.

Nicole's daughter, on November 19 and 21, 2018, at La Batelière in Paris, and further phone calls and email exchanges. She also shared with me unpublished writings by her mother.

Jacky's cousin through her first marriage and heir, Michel Lévy, phone interview on May 6, 2020.

Jacky's friend Philippe Monsel, phone interview on December 6, 2018.

Mena's grandson, Guillaume Leplatre, email December 11, 2018, and phone interview on December 19, 2018.

Mena's son-in-law, Jean-Louis Leplâtre, phone interview on December 7, 2018.

Zinka's daughter, France Lebon Châtenay Dubroeucq, with her husband, Didier Dubroeucq, and Sophie Strauss Jenkins on March 3, 2019, in Die, and further emails.

Zinka's son, Gilles Châtenay, with his son, Thomas Châtenay, July 21, 2019, in Ménerbes, and further emails.

Documentary filmmakers Jetske Spanjer and Ange Wieberdink, February 23, 2020, in Amsterdam.

Lon's daughter, Patricia Elisabeth Frédérique Wensink, and her husband, Wladimir Schreiber, February 23, 2020, in Amsterdam, and further email exchanges.

ARCHIVES

Department "Collections" of the Mauthausen Memorial, KZ-Gedenkstätte Mauthausen

Service historique de la Défense, le centre historique des archives, Vincennes

Université Paris Nanterre, Archives de Denise Vernay

Archives Nationales, Pierrefitte-sur-Seine

Musée de la Résistance et de la Déportation du Cher, Archives départementales du Cher, Témoignages audiovisuels portant sur la Seconde Guerre mondiale

The George and Irina Schaeffer Center for the Study of Genocide, Human Rights and Conflict Prevention, USC Shoah Foundation's Visual History Archive, American University of Paris, France

International Tracing Service, Bad Arolsen

Archiv Mahn-und Gedenkstätte Ravensbrück

Leipzig Nazi Forced Labour Memorial, Gedenkstätte für Zwangsarbeit Leipzig

United States Holocaust Memorial Museum, Washington, DC